How Animals Help Students Learn

How Animals Help Students Learn summarizes what we know about the impact of animals in education and synthesizes the thinking of prominent leaders in research and practice. It's a much-needed resource for mental health and education professionals interested in incorporating animals in school-based environments, one that evaluates the efficacy of existing programs and helps move the field toward evidence-based practice. Experts from around the world provide concrete examples of how animals have been successfully incorporated into classroom settings to achieve the highest level of benefit while also ensuring the health and welfare of the students and animals involved.

Nancy R. Gee, PhD, is research manager for the Waltham research program in human-animal interaction. She is also a professor of psychology at the State University of New York, Fredonia.

Aubrey H. Fine, EdD, is professor of education in the College of Education and Integrative Studies at California State Polytechnic University, Pomona, and a licensed psychologist with more than 40 years of experience in animal-assisted interventions.

Peggy McCardle, PhD, MPH, is president of Peggy McCardle Consulting, LLC, and an affiliated research scientist at Haskins Laboratories.

How Animals Help Students Learn

Research and Practice for Educators and Mental-Health Professionals

Edited by Nancy R. Gee, Aubrey H. Fine, and Peggy McCardle

Routledge
Taylor & Francis Group

NEW YORK AND LONDON

First edition published 2017
by Routledge
711 Third Avenue, New York, NY 10017

and by Routledge
2 Park Square, Milton Park, Abingdon, Oxon, OX14 4RN

Routledge is an imprint of the Taylor & Francis Group, an informa business

Library of Congress Cataloging-in-Publication Data
A catalog record for this book has been requested

ISBN: 978-1-138-64864-7 (hbk)
ISBN: 978-1-138-64863-0 (pbk)
ISBN: 978-1-315-62061-9 (ebk)

Typeset in ITC Giovanni Std
by Keystroke, Neville Lodge, Tettenhall, Wolverhampton

Printed in the United Kingdom
by Henry Ling Limited

Contents

viii

Foreword

Familiar Yet Different: Human-Animal Interaction and Education Research

Gerald E. Sroufe, American Education Research Association

A favorite cartoon from *The New Yorker* magazine features a couple having a romantic dinner with the caption: "You seem familiar, yet somehow strange – are you by any chance Canadian?"

This book is largely based on the discussions generated during a May, 2015, workshop, "Research on Human-Animal Interaction in Education Settings." I was invited to talk with scholars participating in a conference on human-animal interaction (HAI) about the landscape of education research, a context that was for me "familiar yet somehow strange." The general notion behind my invitation to participate was that, while exploring HAI in education settings would be similar to conducting research primarily for therapeutic interventions, there might also be some important differences to consider. As the conference unfolded it was clear that there are indeed special considerations for conducting HAI research in education settings. But it was also clear that there are reciprocal benefits to be had for HAI researchers and traditional education researchers, and that most of the problematic aspects of HAI research were, like the problem of youth, to be outgrown with time.

In most respects, research on the application of HAI approaches to learning raises the same research consideration raised by other changes in education such as the introduction of new technology or innovative after-school programs. There is the problem of demonstrating a plausible theory of causality, the problems of specification of variables, and the difficulty of designing appropriate research methods that encourage replication. In considering HAI research, one quickly encounters problems common to much education research. However, application of HAI to education settings provides some unique problems and opportunities as well.

One confounding problem in consideration of HAI research is that all three terms essentially are variables requiring specification. "Human" certainly refers to children and adults both, but for research purposes it is necessary to specify the age and circumstances of the child as well as the unique education setting of the intervention. Similarly, while dogs have been shown to be beneficial in working with reading problems, not all dogs are suitable for this task. The nature and strength of the interaction, and the period of time over which it occurs, constitute additional variables requiring specification. Chapters in this book provide guidance for developing a matrix or categorization schema based on child variables, animal variables, and education setting variables – no small task – within which to place the growing number of research studies.

The core problem of research on HAI in education settings, as is the case with most education research, can be viewed as a problem of replication. Can the research program be designed in such a manner that it is subject to replication, or is it a unique experience from which one can only draw suggestive or provocative results? One must be impressed with the relatively long and robust history of HAI research, especially in therapeutic applications. But as the field turns to an investigation of classroom and learning phenomena, one uncovers the usual challenges to replication: heavy reliance on anecdotal reports, a dearth of third-party researchers or evaluators, ambiguous specification of variables, and failure to describe procedures in sufficient detail to permit replication. HAI researchers and education researchers often fail to provide sufficient subject controls, and one finds relatively few studies involving randomization or quasi-experimental methodologies. These methodology challenges are to be anticipated in research introducing new perspectives about learning.

It is useful to consider an example from another arena involving human interactions to see how the essential research requirements apply to HAI research. *The Washington Post* has reported on recent research under the headline, "Shakespeare acting program helps veterans deal with emotions" (Antifinger, 2015). One might wish to believe that Shakespeare acting offers a useful approach to post-traumatic stress among veterans, but the central research questions noted above should be asked of this study as well. It turns out from reading the article that the innovation is conducted in only one site, on a voluntary basis, with a small number of undifferentiated veterans. The researchers evaluating the program are also the instigators of the program, their evidence is anecdotal, and the theory of causation is vague: "using Shakespeare's words helps the actors open up." One might imagine methodologies for replication of this research, but actually doing so would require operational definitions, independent investigators, an appropriate evaluation metric for "useful approach" and a plausible causal theory. Can the positive changes be assigned to attributes unique to Shakespeare? Or might they be a consequence of the process of acting out emotional issues, camaraderie of the participants, specific traumatic experiences, or other phenomena that may better explain whatever measure of success can be shown to exist?

While exploration of HAI in classrooms encounters problems common to all education research, it currently faces two circumstances that make such research especially difficult to pursue effectively. One is the enormous influence of testing as represented by legislation such as the No Child Left Behind Act of 2001 (PL 107–110) and its successor, the Every Student Succeeds Act of 2015 (PL114–95). All will agree that this legislation and the political reality it represents have forced school systems to pay great attention to mechanisms for raising academic achievement test scores. Most will agree, also, that whatever benefits the testing accountability movement may have, it has promoted development of narrow strategies for achieving school success, such as focusing on children "on the bubble" – those targeted children whose improved test scores might improve the school's status. Similarly, the testing accountability movement is intended to require classroom teachers to pay special attention to raising achievement of students in tested subjects such as reading and mathematics. The impact of these measures on student achievement remains unclear, but its impact for advocates wishing to introduce animals into the classroom is abundantly clear: teachers may not have time to deviate from their received curriculum and systems are necessarily un-receptive to innovations not directly related to improving testing achievement of their students.

A second problem in developing sites for HAI research in education is that schools, especially public schools, have good reason to be risk averse. Actual legal risk is one dimension of being risk averse, and is discussed in several places in this book, but the perceived risk of having animals in the classroom may be just as detrimental to securing research platforms as are actual regulations. And, of course, the achievement pressure felt by teachers and administrators has the unfortunate consequence of making them reluctant to try any methods beyond those in the approved pedagogical canon. Because of the inherent political vulnerability of school systems, they will flee at the first sign of a controversy – whether generated by People for the Ethical Treatment of Animals or parents concerned about allergies – regarding having animals in the classroom. Regrettably, one anticipates that most classroom research on HAI will occur initially in non-public education settings, rendering generalization more difficult.

Many of the research problems noted, as well as the potential benefits of HAI, are addressed in the chapters of this book. However, there are several aspects of the emerging opportunities for HAI research in classrooms that should be noted. Three positive aspects that serve to make the case that this research should be continued and should come to the attention of a larger audience are these: (1) it is theory-based; (2) it addresses socio-emotional learning; and (3) it introduces new variables that are in accord with contemporary research in biological and neurological science (Freund, McCune, Esposito, Gee, & McCardle, 2016).

Much of the work reported in this book about education interventions is based on the theory that stress is a significant variable in learning and that it can be mediated through interaction with animals. The theory can be readily generalized to encompass motivation and attention, executive function, and transfer of learning, three phenomena that are regarded as important conditional variables of learning. This is an important framework, broader than that being used by many education researchers, and merits further research on both a theoretical and research basis.

The therapeutic history in the development of HAI and its success in enhancing emotional supports make it ideally situated with regard to a major theory of learning that is returning to the mainstream of education policy. Social-emotional learning, with ties to the progressive movement of the 1930s, is in part an antidote to the testing movement previously discussed. Advocates for social-emotional learning research seek to demonstrate that learning is influenced by the type of emotional support long associated with HAI in therapeutic uses.

The use of biological measures in HAI research, uncommon among contemporary education researchers, fits well with the heightened attention to neurological research. Measurement of the emotional condition of the learner in terms of stress indicators such as saliva and blood characteristics is infrequent in education research today. However, the relationships between humans and animals with regard to stress reduction is well worth exploring with current biological and neurological measures and through new technology such as represented by the FMRI (Freund et al., 2016).

In addition to the positive education policy climate for HAI approaches noted, there are also elements of education research practice and research policy that create a particularly promising environment for HAI research in education at this time. Among these are (1) the development of observational research methods; (2) the development of single subject research; and (3) a more hospitable climate for exploratory research in addition to efficacy-based or scaling-up research.

The familiar technique of classroom observation has been greatly enhanced by technology and seems especially well-suited for study of HAI. Modern observational methods provide the capability to observe actual behavior and to preserve the interactions for analysis and reanalysis at a later date through video recording (Sparks, 2013, and Databrary, n.d.). This capacity, combined with more sophisticated analytic frameworks, may lead to improved understanding of HAI just as it has potential for improving the theory and practice of teacher education and the study of child development.

While single subject design ($N = 1$) research methods were not discussed formally during the May research conference, it was noted that this approach should be especially useful in examination of HAI in both therapeutic applications and education applications. While often facilitated by designs taking advantage of modern computer capacity, the concept at its simplest is intuitive, involving establishing (a) base-line behavior, (b) intervention, (a) new base-line, and (b) withdrawing the intervention to determine the effect on the new base-line (i.e., ABAB design).

Randomized-controlled trials designed to establish efficacy of interventions have been highly valued by US federal research agencies in recent years. They continue to be valued, of course, but recently the National Science Foundation and the Institute of Education Sciences have developed common standards for funding research that are more hospitable to HAI early stage research (Common Guidelines for Education Research and Development, 2013). The new standards commence with "foundational" and "early stage exploration" research – the proper location of much HAI research at the moment – and progress through a set of increasingly sophisticated and statistically rigorous stages to "efficacy" and "scale-up" research. Foundational research in the new standards is defined in terms of providing "the fundamental knowledge that may contribute to improved learning and other relevant education outcomes" (p. 9).

The chapters assembled in this book illustrate the comprehensive nature of explorations into the use of animals as an intervention in education settings, and range from practical classroom practice to sophisticated research strategies. Collectively, the chapters provide a fine status report on research in the emerging field, and signal potentially rewarding next steps in developing a robust research agenda.

Given the growing interest in inclusion of animals in education settings, it is important to continue to investigate their impact in terms of education benefits through sound evaluative research and, equally important, to continue to explore the underlying psychological and biological phenomena associated with positive learning experiences associated with HAI. This volume will help guide such efforts. The concluding chapter of the book includes an invitation for researchers currently outside the arena of HAI in education to join in furthering this work. One hopes that the book will encourage many education researchers to do so.

References

Antifinger, C. (2015). Shakespeare acting program helps veterans deal with emotions. *The Washington Post*, October 19, 2015. Retrieved from https://washingtonpost.com/national/health-science/soldier-heal-thyself-how-shakespeare-has-rescued-some-vets/2015/10/19/3c5a7cde-6dcd-11e5-9bfe-e59f5e244f92_story.html

Common guidelines for education research and development. (2013). A report from the Institute of Education Sciences, US Department of Education, and the National Science Foundation. Retrieved from http://ies.ed.gov/pdf/CommonGuidelines.pdf

Databrary. (n.d.). Databrary is a video library for developmental science. Retrieved from https://nyu.databrary.org/

Every Child Succeeds Act of 2015. P.L. 114–95. 20 (2015–2016).

Freund, L. S., McCune, S., Esposito, L., Gee, N. R., & McCardle, P. (Eds.) (2016). *Social neuroscience and human-animal interaction*. Washington, DC: American Psychological Association.

No Child Left Behind Act of 2001, P.L. 107–110, 20 U.S.C. § 6319 (2002).

Sparks, Sarah D. (2013). Gates teacher study opens video library to researchers. November 25, 2013. Retrieved from http://blogs.edweek.org/edweek/inside-school-research/2013/11/gates_teacher_study_opens_vide.html?qs=Nov.+25,+2013+classroom+observation

Acknowledgments

This volume is based largely on a foundational workshop. Research on Human-Animal Interaction in Education Settings was held in Washington, DC, on May 26–27, 2015, with support provided by Mars Incorporated, and WALTHAM, the global fundamental research center for Mars Petcare. We acknowledge Mars for making that workshop and this volume possible.

We also wish to acknowledge the following specific individuals, whose assistance and guidance were instrumental in the overall effort to focus on HAI and education.

- Anna Moore, our acquisitions editor at Routledge/Taylor Francis Group, whose guidance in the development and final preparation of the manuscript for this volume was invaluable.
- Michelle Rico, Jennifer Gomez, Madyson Kinsey and Rochelle Goodman, credential and graduate students at the California State Polytechnic University, Pomona, for the library and reference assistance in manuscript preparation.
- Karyl Hurley, Mars Inc., for her ongoing commitment to HAI and her support of the workshop and the development of this volume.
- Katherine Kruger, Mars/WALTHAM Human-Animal Interaction Research Fellow, for her invaluable assistance with indexing the volume.
- The members of the WALTHAM Internal Review Board, for their helpful and constructive comments on several of the chapters in this volume.
- The authors of the chapters in this volume, for writing without an expectation of compensation, meeting deadlines cheerfully, and working to combine their passion with scientific objectivity as the field further explores the involvement of animals in education settings.

Finally, we note that all royalties of this volume will be donated to Canine Companions for Independence and the PJ/Hart Loving Bond Award, University of Denver, Graduate School of Social Work.

The Editors
Nancy R. Gee, Aubrey H. Fine, and Peggy McCardle

About the Editors

Nancy R. Gee, PhD, is research manager, Human-Animal Interaction, WALTHAM Centre for Pet Nutrition (a part of Mars, Inc.), Leicestershire, United Kingdom, where she manages an international portfolio of HAI collaborations. She is also professor of psychology, State University of New York, Fredonia, and her research has focused primarily on the impact of dogs on aspects of cognition, including work examining the impact of animal presence/interaction on the development and learning of preschool children. Recipient of multiple grants and awards, member of journal editorial advisory boards, and reviewer of HAI research grant proposals, she has contributed chapters to HAI volumes and served as co-editor for a volume on HAI and social neuroscience.

Aubrey H. Fine, EdD, is professor of education and integrative studies, California State Polytechnic University, and a licensed psychologist with 35 years' experience specializing in treating children with ADHD, learning disabilities, and developmental disorders. Fine has been recognized by various organizations for his work with children, animals and the community, including receiving the 2016 IAHAIO William F. McCulloch Award for outstanding achievements and contributions in the field of Animal Assisted Interventions, the Wang Family Excellence Award for Distinguished Professor in California State University System (23 campuses), Educator of the Year – State for the California Learning Disabilities Association, Who's Who in America, and the 2006 Cal Poly Faculty Award for Community Engagement. Fine has published 12 books and numerous articles on animal therapy, children, and sports psychology. His books include *The Handbook on Animal Assisted Therapy 4th edition* (2015), and *The Parent Child Dance*, released June 2015.

Peggy McCardle, PhD, MPH, is associated research scientist at Haskins Laboratories, New Haven, Connecticut; and is President of Peggy McCardle Consulting, LLC, Seminole, Florida and Annapolis, Maryland. She is a consultant, science writer, and editor whose work focuses on child development, literacy, bilingualism, learning and learning disabilities, and HAI. A former branch chief at the *Eunice Kennedy Shriver* National Institute of Child Health and Human Development (NICHD), US National Institutes of Health, she oversaw research funding in child development and helped establish a partnership with the WALTHAM Centre for Pet Nutrition and Health (Mars Inc.) and a research program on HAI in child development. She has co-edited 13 volumes in the past decade, including three on various aspects of HAI.

xvii

Contributors

Andrea Beetz, Dipl-Psych, Dr Phil, Dr Phil Habil, teaches and conducts research on human-animal interactions, and animal-assisted interventions in therapy and education, with a focus on attachment theory, at the Department for Special Education, University of Rostock, Germany and the Department for Behavioral Biology, University of Vienna, Austria.

Pauleen C. Bennett, MPsych, PhD, is an anthrozoologist at the School of Psychology and Public Health, La Trobe University, Victoria, Australia. She studies relationships between humans and companion animals and has worked with government groups to develop animal care and welfare educational materials for pet owners.

Victoria Brelsford, BSc, MSc, Infant and Child Development Lab, School of Psychology, University of Lincoln, England, UK, is an academic researcher and PhD student whose work in developmental psychology focuses on visual processing in early category acquisition, teaching children stress signaling behaviors in dogs, and human-animal interaction research.

Alexa M. Carr, MA, is a doctoral student in the Prevention Science Program at Washington State University, WA. Her work focuses on examining the effects of human-animal interaction in naturalistic settings on mental, emotional and behavior health outcomes related to physiological and psychological stress reduction, emotion, social competence, and mindfulness.

Carol McDonald Connor, PhD, is Chancellor's Professor, School of Education, University of California, Irvine, CA. Her research focuses on language and literacy development, learning, and academic achievement and how individual child differences impact the effectiveness of classroom instruction. She is also an expert on conducting randomized controlled field trials in schools.

Layla Esposito, MA, PhD, is program director in the Child Development and Behavior Branch at the *Eunice Kennedy Shriver*

National Institute of Child Health and Human Development (NICHD) (US National Institutes of Health, Bethesda, MD) where her portfolio includes research on human-animal interaction, social and emotional development in children and adolescents, child and family processes, and childhood obesity.

Erika Friedmann, PhD, associate dean of research and professor, University of Maryland School of Nursing, Baltimore, MD, focuses on psychosocial research, especially human-animal interaction, contributors to human health and behavior, and is a founding member of the International Society for Anthrozoology, the scholarly society for human-animal interaction.

Robin L. Gabriels, PsyD, associate professor, University of Colorado Anschutz Medical Campus, Program Director, Neuropsychiatric Special Care Unit, Children's Hospital Colorado, is a licensed clinical psychologist and researcher, whose work focuses on interventions for children and adolescents with autism spectrum disorder and co-existing psychiatric and medical issues.

Roberta Michnick Golinkoff, PhD, is Unidel H. Rodney Sharp Professor at the University of Delaware, Newark, DE. Her work in language development, spatial learning, and play has received numerous prizes, including in 2015 the Distinguished Scientific Lecturer award from the American Psychological Association and the James McKeen Cattell Fellow Award, the highest honor conferred by the Association for Psychological Science for lifetime contributions to applied psychological science and in 2011 the Urie Bronfenbrenner Award for Lifetime Contribution to Developmental Psychology in the Service of Science and Society from the American Psychological Association. Passionate about disseminating developmental science for improving children's and families' lives, her latest book (with K. Hirsh-Pasek) is *Becoming Brilliant: What Science Tells Us about Raising Successful Children* (APA Press).

James A. Griffin, PhD, is deputy chief of the Child Development and Behavior Branch at the *Eunice Kennedy Shriver* National Institute of Child Health and Human Development (NICHD), National Institutes of Health (NIH), as well as the director of the Early Learning and School Readiness Program.

Karin Hediger, PhD, works as a psychotherapist and as a postdoc at the University of Basel, investigating effects of animal-assisted interventions. Since 2013, she is the executive director of the institute for interdisciplinary research on human-animal relationship, IEMT Switzerland, and teaches in different institutes about human-animal interaction and animal-assisted interventions.

Harold Herzog, PhD, is professor of psychology at Western Carolina University. His interests include attitudes toward animals, the evolution of pet-keeping, and the impact of pets on human health. He is the author of *Some We Love, Some We Hate, Some We Eat: Why It's So Hard To Think Straight About Animals* (2011).

Kathy Hirsh-Pasek, PhD, is Lefkowitz Faculty Fellow in Psychology at Temple University, PA, and a senior fellow at the Brookings Institution, DC. Her research examines early language and literacy, spatial development and the role of play in learning. Author of 14 books and hundreds of publications (with R. Golinkoff), she asks how science of learning can be mined for public good.

Rebecca J. Huss, JD, LLM, Valparaiso University Law School, Valparaiso, IN, is professor of law whose research focuses on legal issues relating to the relationship between humans and companion animals, including animals acting in the role of service, assistance and therapy animals.

Evan MacLean, PhD, is assistant professor at the University of Arizona, AZ. His research investigates the nature of animal minds, and cognitive evolution.

Maureen MacNamara, PhD, MSW, Appalachian State University, Boone, NC, is assistant professor of macro-practice social work, and consultant in human-animal relationships and animal-assisted interventions, whose work focuses on interprofessional relationships in organizational learning and change strategies, non-profit service development and evaluation, and factors influencing development and implementation of animal-assisted interventions.

Sandra McCune, VN, BA, PhD, The WALTHAM Centre for Pet Nutrition, is a scientific leader in human-animal interaction, partnering with the Mars Petcare business, and external organizations and individuals, to make best use of WALTHAM™ Science to make a better world for pets.

Kerstin Meints, PhD, is professor of developmental psychology and director, Lincoln Infant and Child Development Laboratory, University of Lincoln, UK. Her research includes development of language and categorization, comparative and applied research in human-animal interaction, with a focus on dog bite prevention and assessing interventions (Blue Dog bite prevention, dog body language, animal-assisted interventions in education).

Marguerite E. O'Haire, PhD, Department of Comparative Pathobiology, Center for the Human-Animal Bond, College of Veterinary Medicine, Purdue University, IN, is assistant professor of human-animal interaction with research focused on the biopsychosocial impacts of interacting with animals for various populations, including children with autism, and military veterans with Post-Traumatic Stress Disorder.

Patricia Pendry, PhD, is associate professor of human development and graduate faculty in the Prevention Science Program at Washington State University, Seattle, Washington. Her research focuses on examining causal effects of animal assisted prevention programs in education settings on human and animal participants.

Jose M. Peralta, DVM, PhD, Diplomate ACAW, Diplomate ECAWBM, Western University of Health Sciences College of Veterinary Medicine, Pomona, California, is a veterinarian and professor of animal welfare and ethics, interested on how animals respond to interactions with humans in different settings and how to improve those interactions.

Vinaya Rajan, PhD, is assistant professor of psychology at the University of the Sciences in Philadelphia, PA. Her work focuses on infant and early childhood cognitive development, memory, self-regulation, school readiness, and early mathematics learning.

John M. Rawlings, BSc, MSc, PhD, head of Welfare and Ethics, WALTHAM Centre for Pet Nutrition, UK, is a physiology graduate (Glasgow and Manchester universities). He joined WALTHAM in 1994 studying nutritional management of canine and feline health, and has a long-standing interest in animal welfare and ethics in a research environment.

Sabrina E. B. Schuck, PhD, University of California, Irvine, CA, is assistant professor of pediatrics and psychology and social behavior and the executive director of the UCI Child Development School, CA. Her research examines innovative ways to improve executive functioning skills and build resilience in children with neurodevelopmental disorders.

Alexis N. W. Schulenburg, BS, is currently pursuing her master's degree in early childhood special education at Vanderbilt University, TN. She works as a teacher for toddlers and young children who have a wide range of developmental delays. Her research interests include understanding how to best support children with special needs in school settings.

Donna Snellgrove, BSc (Hons), MSc, PhD, fish nutritionist, WALTHAM Centre for Pet Nutrition, is a researcher working with ornamental fish species to develop optimal fish nutrition, health, welfare, and behavior through internal and external research collaborations. She leads the marine ornamental fish breeding and nutrition aspect of a MARS coral reef rehabilitation program in Indonesia.

Gerald E. Sroufe, PhD, senior advisor, American Educational Research Association, Washington, DC, has been active in government relations, federal research policy, and issues in education, in particular issues related to utilization of sound research for improved education policy and practice.

Jaymie L. Vandagriff is a doctoral student in the prevention science program at Washington State University, WA, an interdisciplinary program housed in the department of human development. Her work focuses on human-animal interaction embedded within prevention programming, particularly examining human-animal interaction's effects on stress physiology and emotional functioning of college students.

The Issues

section 1

The Issues

CHAPTER 1

How Animals Help Children Learn

Introducing a Roadmap for Action

Aubrey H. Fine and Nancy R. Gee

Introduction

Albert Einstein (n.d.) once stated, "To raise new questions, new possibilities, to regard old problems from a new angle, requires creative imagination and marks real advance in science." This is a most apropos quotation as we embark on an educational journey whose destination involves the re-shaping and re-thinking of a long-standing educational practice while exploring an exciting new scientific frontier. Simply stated, the driving question is this: What is the optimal role of animals in education settings? We believe that these are exciting years for those interested in human-animal interaction (HAI) beyond the usual pet-owner relationships. Over the past half-century, there has been growing public and scientific interest in the value of HAI and animal-assisted intervention (AAI). The field is now being transformed from an exploration of mainly misunderstood relationships to an emerging field of inquiry driving toward a scientific understanding of our relationships with animals (Fine, 2015).

As the study of HAI continues to advance, there is a need to demystify its value and clarify its impact, and this is particularly true with regard to animals in education settings. Rarely do people stop to consider that they live in complex and interconnected relationships with animals that extend beyond routine feeding and care of companion animals. We need a greater understanding of how, when, where, and why animals may influence human cognition and emotion. Further, this information needs to inform best practice protocols and the methodology of involving animals in classrooms. As we witness expansion in the multi-disciplinary application of AAI in diverse settings (Fine, 2014), and as animals become more integrated into traditional therapeutic environments, it seems only logical that more attention be given to their impact in school environments. This new frontier is fertile with untapped research possibilities. This volume is intended to provide a compass and map to guide researchers, teachers, and AAI practitioners in their exploration of this new scientific frontier, and to provide young learners with a more dynamic and pedagogically sound learning experience while insuring the health and welfare of all involved.

There is a vast opportunity for a more concentrated effort bridging research and practice that effectively translates research into practice. Such a translational pipeline would drive innovation in education settings when based upon empirical evidence. Thus, we need a continuous stream of high-quality research designed to impact the quality of educational services available. As the body of knowledge regarding the efficacy of HAI in schools increases, interested educators will have stronger scaffolding on which to build their education platforms. Many who incorporate animals in schools today are doing so without formal approval of school administrators. Additionally, as best practice options are more clearly identified, these efforts should lead to improved animal welfare as teachers implement proper housing, care, and treatment of animals in their classrooms. In this introductory chapter, we provide an overview of current practices involving animals in classrooms. We address what, where, when, and why educators bring animals into their classrooms, and the challenges associated with this practice. We discuss the importance of connecting HAI in education with theories of early childhood learning and introduce the current state of research. These topics are addressed in more detail in the chapters of this book and, where possible, authors make recommendations for best practices based on the current state of research. The volume concludes with our recommendations for future research and practice that we hope will provide researchers and practitioners with a guide that they can use to explore this exciting new frontier.

Animals in Classrooms: The Current State of Affairs

There is currently no system for tracking or regulating animals in US schools today, despite the fact that more than two-thirds of the 1,400 members of the National Association for the Education of Young Children reported having animals in their classrooms (Uttley, 2013). Uttley (2013) pointed out that current educators see integrating animals into their classrooms as a way of meeting both the developmental and educational needs of their students. The most common animal found in these classrooms was fish (about 50%); the rationale for aquariums was the literature supporting their value in promoting a relaxed environment (Katcher, Segal, & Beck, 1984). Amphibians and reptiles were also reported as common in preschools, although those surveyed indicated that before early childhood educators incorporated animals in their classrooms, they should consider issues including welfare and safety (see Gee et al., Chapter 14.)

Many teachers have reported that the presence of animals lends classrooms a more "homey" atmosphere. They believe the animals may promote language, imagination, and self-reflection, especially in young children (Myers, 1998). Animals in classrooms have been incorporated as pets and mascots, and their engagement has been used by some as a platform to build character and teach children humane practices. There is also evidence (see Section II) that animals help motivate compliance and engagement in educational and therapeutic processes, which is often sustained over time (Barker & Wolen, 2008; Fine, 2015; Kale, 1992; Mallon, Ross, Klee, & Ross, 2010).

In 2015, major surveys were conducted in the US and the UK addressing the role of animals in the lives of children at school and home. Both revealed that parents and teachers believed that pets should be in classrooms because of the positive effects they can have on students. The American Humane Association's (2015) survey focused on Pet Care Trust's Pets in the Classroom program and involved 1,131 teachers, who taught preschool through 8th grade in the US or Canada, and had had a pet in their classroom for at least three months. A majority had pets at home and fish as their class pets. The second most common classroom pet was a guinea pig. About 60% of participants included their classroom pets informally without a plan, whereas 49% used formal lessons (the most common lesson

5

plans being about nature and science). Although we are pleased that current educators employ animals in various classrooms, there must be a plan for their engagement with an educational purpose, and health and safety for all must be a priority.

In contrast, the UK survey (Moorcroft, 2015) consisted of five components, including one section on pets in education; this survey revealed that small animals such as gerbils, rabbits, hamsters, and guinea pigs were the most common animals included in classrooms (60%). Additionally, respondents indicated that 28% of schools that had pets had an aquarium. Although there appeared to be great support for the value of animals in children's lives, the results indicated that most schools in the UK do not have class pets. Only 22% of parents reported that their children's schools had class pets, although many parents wanted their children to learn about pet care (73%) and have pet(s) in their classrooms (55%).

It is apparent from both of these reports that people perceive class pets as beneficial, with respondents identifying many potential psychosocial and educational benefits (e.g., increased empathy, increased responsibility, lower anxiety and stress, improved literacy skills, and improved behavior and social skills). The US survey identified some of the challenges associated with the practice: additional costs, managing the student-animal interactions, dealing with the death of a pet, ensuring student and animal welfare, and continual care of the pet (not just when school is in session.) The UK report highlighted that students and teachers need to be more prepared to care for their students and the animals, and several welfare concerns were noted: school officials need to be aware of the UK Animal Welfare Act of 2006 (Tullo, 2006), which provides penalties for activities that may be detrimental to an animal's welfare; thus educators must be responsible for the animals under their care not only while in school but on the weekends and holidays.

There are other nations that have taken a more active approach to the inclusion of animals in schools. Approximately 1,000 teachers in Germany, Austria, and Switzerland have school dogs and the list is growing exponentially (Agsten, Führing, & Windscheif, 2011; Beetz, 2013, 2015). In fact, teams of teacher-plus-dog are established and approved, allowing teachers to bring trained dogs into the schools. To be selected as a school-hound team teacher, educators must participate in a brief (four weekends) curriculum, which is one element that qualifies them to bring their dogs to school with them. To assure that the dog will be acceptable for school engagement, an assessment of the team is conducted at the beginning of the course, followed later by an observation in the classroom. All dogs must be seen annually by a veterinarian and must undergo a behavioral assessment to assure reliability of behavior. To ensure that teachers are comfortable in their roles, only experienced teachers who meet the previously noted standards and have at least four years of teaching experience may bring dogs into the classroom.

Current State of the Evidence: Theory

In any discussion of the current state of evidence in a particular area of investigation, it is critical to first provide a theory, which can support, guide, and frame research and practice on the topic. Fortunately, the practice of involving animals in education settings has a clear basis in the work of theorists of early childhood education. Mooney (2013) described a number of theoretical perspectives on which current educational practices are based. For example, Piaget posited that children construct knowledge by interacting with their environment and gaining real-world experiences. Vygotsky argued that children learn by doing, and by talking about their experiences, both of which aid in the development of language and other aspects of cognition. Montessori proposed that children take and learn responsibility by direct interaction with their environment. It is easy to see how modern educators might conceptualize animals as providing an environment for direct interaction (where children might touch, hold, or otherwise interact with the animal), an opportunity to learn by doing (e.g., feeding the animal), and opportunities for which children may take responsibility (e.g., feeding, cleaning housing, or otherwise caring for the needs of the animal).

Thus, the field of HAI has also begun to borrow, apply, develop, and test unifying theories to explain potential mechanisms by which animals may impact human responses or vice versa. Examples of such theories include attachment theory (Bowlby, 1969), originally developed to explain the human need to protect and be protected; biophillia (Wilson, 1984), which proposes that humans are drawn to and experience deep affiliations with other life forms or nature; social support (Cohen & Wills, 1985), specifically companionship support, which provides a sense of social belonging; and stress buffering as regulated by the hypothalamic-pituitary-adrenal axis, a major part of the neuroendocrine system that controls and regulates physiological reactions to stress (Friedmann, Son, & Saleem, 2015). Many of these theories are discussed in the chapters in this volume, and those discussions frame and guide HAI research in a wide variety of settings.

The Research Landscape: A Brief Snapshot

A common theme throughout this volume and the HAI literature in general is a fundamental need for more rigorous investigation in HAI to establish a scientific evidence base (Kazdin, 2011). Research at the intersection of HAI and education is no exception, but it is important to point out that a call for more rigorous investigation is not an indictment of the work conducted to date. Early stage research was needed to identify key variables and relationships that merit further investigation. It is important that a call for more rigorous research does not discount what has been accomplished thus far. The important message is that more is needed and that the standards for the quality of that work going forward must be high, to establish the evidence base and allow for stronger claims to be made with greater confidence.

The work to date on HAI in education is provocative, and serves to point researchers toward potentially fruitful avenues of future exploration. For example, in a discussion of the influence of animals on child development, Endenburg and Van Lith (2011) point out that animals can serve as powerful motivators for learning. They base this on two arguments: 1) becoming emotionally invested in a subject leads a child to greater retention of the information about it; and 2) learning is optimized for children when it occurs in the context of a meaningful relationship, which is assumed to be provided by the animal. Other reports indicate that teachers perceive a variety of benefits associated with animals in classroom settings, such as captivating students' attention and teaching humane values (Zasloff, Hart, & DeArmond, 1999), enhancing psychological well-being and providing relevant hands-on experiences (Rud & Beck, 2003), and improving socio-emotional and empathy development (Daly & Suggs, 2010).

Suggesting a Roadmap

In this volume a range of research and best practice strategies related to HAI in education are presented and discussed in a variety of contexts. Some of the work presented is in its early stages and represents outcomes, variables, contexts, or populations worthy of further exploration. Some represents findings from tightly controlled experimental investigations that can be translated into practice, including investigations of programs developed specifically for use in classrooms. We hope that the discussions of research and practice presented will provoke new questions, new investigations, and new and improved ways of safely and effectively incorporating animals into a broad range of education settings. Most of all, we hope that research and practice into HAI in education settings continues to grow and flourish. This volume is intended to guide future research and practice, to provide a map and a compass, but most importantly to install the first pieces in a critical transitional pipeline that, as it is built, will drive innovation through scientific excellence.

Carl Sagan (n.d.), a famous American astronomer, once stated "somewhere something incredible is waiting to be known." Who would have fathomed that his insightful comments would be applied to opening up a new frontier of HAI in education. Our roles as innovators, researchers, and practitioners are to forge these new frontiers. These efforts will help us to understand when and where animals may make the best contributions to learning, in a way that is mutually beneficial to the animals and the students. This increased understanding will no doubt expand the range of HAI services and opportunities while at the same time directly supporting educators in their quest to provide the most dynamic and meaningful learning experiences for their students.

9

References

Agsten, L., Führing, P., & Windscheif, M. (2011). *Praxisbuch HuPäSch. Ideen und Übungen zur Hundegestützten Pädagogik in der Schule*. Norderstedt, Germany: Books on Demand-Verlag.

American Humane Association. (2015). *Pets in the classroom study: Phase I findings report*. Retrieved from http://citationmachine.net/apa/cite-a-website/manual

Barker, S., & Wolen, A. (2008). The benefits of human-companion animal interaction: A review. *Journal of Veterinary Medical Education, 35*(4): 487–495.

Beetz, A. (2013). Social emotional correlates of a school-dog-teacher team in a classroom. *Frontiers of Psychology, 4*: 1–7.

Beetz, A. (2015). Personal communication. April 20, 2015.

Bowlby, J. (1969). *Attachment and loss. Vol. 1: Attachment* (2nd edn). New York: Basic Books.

Cohen, S., & Wills, T. A. (1985). Stress, social support, and the buffering hypothesis. *Psychological Bulletin, 98*: 310–357.

Daly, B., & Suggs, S. (2010). Teachers' experiences with humane education and animals in elementary classrooms: Implications for empathy development. *Journal of Moral Education, 39*: 101–112.

Einstein, A. (n.d.). BrainyQuote.com. Retrieved April 9, 2016, from BrainyQuote.com website: http://brainyquote.com/quotes/quotes/a/alberteins130625.html

Endenburg, N., & Van Lith, H. A. (2011). The influence of animals on the development of children. *The Veterinary Journal, 190*(2): 208–214.

Fine, A. H. (Ed.) (2014). *Handbook on animal-assisted therapy: Theoretical foundations and guidelines for practice* (3rd edn). San Diego, CA: Academic Press.

Fine, A. H. (Ed.) (2015). *Handbook on animal-assisted therapy: Foundations and guidelines for animal-assisted interventions* (4th edn). San Diego, CA: Academic Press.

Friedmann, E., Son, H., & Saleem, M. (2015). The animal-human bond: Health and wellness. In A. H. Fine (Ed.), *Handbook on animal-assisted therapy: Foundations and guidelines for animal-assisted interventions* (pp. 73–84). San Diego, CA: Academic Press.

Kale, M. (1992). How some kids gain success, self-esteem with animals. *InterActions, 10*(2): 13–17.

Katcher, A., Segal, H., & Beck, A. (1984). Comparison of contemplation of hypnosis for the reduction of anxiety and discomfort during dental surgery. *American Journal of Clinical Hypnosis, 27*: 14–21.

Kazdin, A. E. (2011). Establishing the effectiveness of animal-assisted therapies: Methodological standards, issues and strategies. In P. McCardle, S. McCune, J. A. Griffin, & V. Maholmes (Eds.), *How animals affect us: Examining the influence of human-animal interactions on child development and human health* (pp. 35–51). Washington, DC: American Psychological Association.

Mallon, G. P., Ross, S. B., Klee, S., & Ross, L. (2010). Designing and implementing animal-assisted therapy programs in health and mental health organizations: Rules and principles to guide program development. In A. Fine (Ed.), *Handbook on animal-assisted therapy: Theoretical foundations and guidelines for practice* (3rd edn, pp. 113–121). San Diego, CA: Academic Press.

Mooney, C. G. (2013). *Theories of childhood: An introduction to Dewey, Montessori, Erikson, Piaget, & Vygotsky* (2nd edn). St. Paul, MN: Redleaf Press.

Moorcroft, M. (Ed.). (2015). *The pet report 2015*. Handforth, UK: Pets at Home Press.

Myers, G. (1998). *Children and animals: Social development and our connections to other species.* Boulder, CO: Westview Press.

Rud, A. G., Jr., & Beck, A. M. (2003). Companion animals in Indiana elementary schools. *Anthrozoös, 16*: 241–251.

Sagan, C. (n.d.). BrainyQuote.com. Retrieved April 9, 2016, from BrainyQuote.com website: http://brainyquote.com/quotes/quotes/c/carlsagan101620.html

Tullo, C. (2006). UK Animal Welfare Act 2005. London: The Stationery Office.

Uttley, C. (2013). Animal attraction: Including animals in early childhood classrooms. *Young Children, 68*(4): 16.

Wilson, E. O. (1984). *Biophilia.* Cambridge, MA: Harvard University Press.

Zasloff, R. L., Hart, L. A., & DeArmond, H. (1999). Animals in elementary school education in California. *Journal of Applied Animal Welfare Science, 2*: 347–357.

11

CHAPTER 2

Animals in Education Settings

Safety for All

*Kerstin Meints, Victoria Brelsford,
Nancy R. Gee, and Aubrey H. Fine*

Animals in the Classroom

Animal-assisted interventions (AAI) are becoming increasingly popular in education settings and the application of pets in the classroom is seen as beneficial to children's learning success (e.g., Hummel & Randler, 2012), and emotional and cognitive development (Fine, 2015; Gee, Fine, & Schuck, 2015). Systematic literature reviews examining the effects of AAI have demonstrated emerging evidence on the benefits of animals in education settings (Davies et al., 2015; Hall, Gee, & Mills, 2016; Kamioka et al., 2014; Maujean, Pepping, & Kendall, 2015; O'Haire, 2013), but shortcomings across studies have also been reported. Methodological approaches and time frames used across environments and treatments vary, often making comparisons difficult. Overall, a lack in scientific rigor has been identified. However, with recent growth in research and a larger variety of measures (see Chapters 11 and 12), the field is currently seeing significant methodological improvements: steady growth of randomized controlled trials, longitudinal studies, and improved consideration for testing under (as) strictly (as possible) controlled and replicable conditions. If animals are to be integrated in classrooms in a more systematic and wide-ranging manner, it is important to continually review current practices, improve research methods, and ensure safety for all involved.

Current Practices and Research

Many infant and primary schools worldwide keep small animals within their classrooms and school grounds. These include fish, frogs, turtles, insects, "pocket pets" and even snakes (Gee et al., 2015; Uttley, 2013; Chapters 13 and 14, this volume). Animals are often taken into schools on an ad hoc basis, e.g., teachers' or children's pets. Some schools ask veterinarians or dog trainers to bring in animals, and a few countries (e.g., Austria) actively encourage teachers to bring their dogs into schools, having developed guidelines (Bundesministeruim für Bildung und Frauen, 2014). So far no single, unified international or official policies for this practice exist (see Chapter 3 on legal/policy issues).

Animals are brought into schools to enrich the school environment and enhance learning, especially with younger children, to make lessons more illustrative, and to provide commonly assumed and advertised benefits to pupils, e.g., teaching responsibility and respect, conscientiousness, care and cleanliness, empathy, sharing and altruism (Uttley, 2013; Hummel & Randler, 2012, for a meta-analysis), improved mood and motivation, and, possibly as a result, lowered stress and heightened learning ability (see overview, Gee et al., 2015). Animals are also brought into schools for targeted interventions and therapeutic use, especially for individuals with special educational needs (e.g., Schuck, Emmerson, Fine, & Lakes, 2013), and, recently, to alleviate stress in university students in the US (e.g., Bell, 2013; Crossman & Kazdin, 2015) and the UK. Finally, animals are employed in education settings for research purposes, investigating claims about beneficial effects in a growing range of studies and studying how children of various health and socio-economic backgrounds may benefit from animals within their learning environment (see reviews noted earlier and Gee et al., 2015).

13

Potential Risks of Human-Dog Interaction

All dogs have the potential to bite, including mixed and commonly owned breeds, large or small (Cornelissen & Hopster, 2010; Horisberger, Stärk, Rüfenacht, Pillonel, & Steiger 2004; Schalamon et al., 2006). In the US, dog bite costs are estimated at around \$53.9 million for hospital stays only (Holmquist & Elixhauser, 2010), with home owners liability insurance claim payments rising to \$530 million in 2014 (Insurance Information Institute, Inc. 2014). In Australia, costs to the community in 2001 were estimated to be around $7 million (Bennett & Righetti, 2001). Costs to the UK's National Health Service are estimated to be around £10 million (Responsible dog ownership, 2013). Effective prevention has been demanded repeatedly by medical and veterinary professions (e.g., Mannion, Graham, Shepherd, & Greenberg, 2015).

Annually, hospital data show about 1.5% of the general population suffers a dog bite requiring medical attention (Gilchrist, Sacks, White, & Kresnow, 2008; Gisle et al., 2001). In children, the prevalence of dog bites is twice as high (Horisberger et al., 2004; Kahn et al., 2004). Bites to the neck and head areas are suffered most frequently by young children (HSCIS, 2014; Kahn, Bauche, & Lamoureux, 2003; Reisner et al., 2011; Schalamon et al., 2006) and 43% of patients on a maxillofacial ward were children under the age of ten (Mannion et al., 2015). Post-Traumatic Stress Disorder (PTSD) has been evidenced in 55% of children who suffered severe bites wounds (Peters, Sottiaux, Appelboom, & Kahn, 2004). Dog bites are three times as high in the most deprived areas compared to the least deprived areas (HSCIS, 2014).

However, not all bites are treated in hospital or even reported. Interview data show that almost 50% of 5–12-year-old children report having been bitten (e.g., Beck & Jones, 1985; Sacks, Sattin, & Bonzo, 1989; Spiegel, 2000), most by familiar dogs. Other research has confirmed that 72–80% of bites to younger children occur with familiar dogs, often in a home environment (e.g., Kahn et al., 2003; Reisner et al., 2011; Schalamon et al., 2006). For interventions with dogs in education settings, these are vitally important findings.

Furthermore, research demonstrates that in 86% of cases, interactions initiated by children appear to trigger dog bite incidents (Kahn et al., 2003; Reisner, Schofer, & Nance, 2007; Reisner et al., 2011). About 67% of 3–4-year-olds' interactions with dogs involve touching and in young children, bites to the face are associated with the dog *lying down,* and the child's interaction prior to biting is reported to be positive or benign *from the viewpoint of the child* (Reisner et al., 2007). Again, this is vitally important for any intervention allowing or encouraging child-dog interaction.

Research has emphasized that most bites occur while there is not adequate parental supervision (Kahn et al., 2003; Reisner et al., 2007) – highlighting the importance of supervision both at home and in education settings. It is crucial to stress that enjoying the benefits of human-dog interactions in education (and other) settings and safeguarding participants and dogs requires awareness of typical behaviors and risk situations, and of dogs' signalling behaviors.

How to Keep Human-Animal Interactions Safe

A variety of student populations, settings, and methods have been employed with various species of animals. This complexity of circumstances may complicate the process of ensuring the health and safety of both students and animals; despite this complexity, risks must be recognized and targeted precautions undertaken.

To begin, a strict action plan should be developed and abided by in HAIs, be they in classrooms or university campuses. All those in education settings, including staff (teachers, lecturers, administrators) must be well-informed of interventions. Having undergone the necessary ethical or governance approval with the institution, all participants should be clearly briefed. Parental and participants' consent/assent must be obtained, questions about potential phobias, zoonosis, and allergies addressed, and insurance issues clarified. All HAIs should be closely monitored to safeguard participants' and animals' well-being and safety. Staff and students should be aware of their specific responsibilities and be taught in advance what are appropriate interactions. All should agree and adhere to a clear code of conduct, safeguarding the welfare of the animal at all times (see Chapter 14). Dogs should ideally be certified, experienced, and positive in responding to children; dog handlers should be receptive to dogs' distress signals. Gee et al. (2015, Figure 2.1) suggest an implementation framework for safety procedures focused on three key elements in animal-assisted education (AAE): student, animal, and teacher. Preparation and planning are needed for each element to ensure the safety and welfare of all.

15

Dogs in Education Settings

For safe educational interventions we must learn to "read" dogs' facial expressions and body signals and to recognize typical risk situations. In the following, we show some pitfalls of children's misinterpretations, report a successful intervention to teach the reading of dogs' body language, and provide information on the well-known Blue Dog program (www.thebluedog.org), shown to be effective in teaching children about safe behavior with familiar dogs.

Reading Dogs' Body Language – How We Can Teach It

Children and adults often miss or misunderstand dogs' signalling attempts (Bloom & Friedman, 2013; Kerswell, Bennett, Butler, &

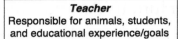

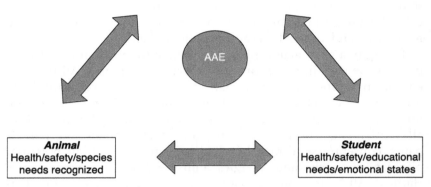

Figure 2.1 Successful AAE integrating three key elements

Gee et al., 2015, p. 202, used with permission of the publisher

Hemsworth, 2009; Mariti et al., 2012). Researchers (Dixon, Mahabee-Gittens, Hart, & Lindsell, 2012; Reisner & Shofer, 2008) have demonstrated that there is little knowledge regarding dog behavior and safety practices for child-dog interactions. Adults' interpretations can vary with experience, but dog ownership does not predict correct interpretations (e.g., Tami & Gallagher, 2009; Wan, Bolger, & Champagne, 2012). Young children often misinterpret a fearful or angry dog as friendly (Meints, Racca, & Hickey, 2010); they even comment how "happy" dogs with aggressive facial displays are (examples in Figure 2.2) and that they would approach the dogs portrayed below and "cuddle and kiss" them.

In addition, children show intrusive leaning-in behavior that could trigger a bite incident (Meints, Syrnyk, & DeKeuster, 2010; see also Reisner et al., 2007). When faced with an animate or novel object, young children lean toward the item until their face is in close proximity. Such behavior could make a dog feel crowded and restricted in its personal space, which could lead to an increased bite risk. Hence, it is vital for safe interactions that "crowding" and leaning in/over be avoided and that children, as well as supervising adults, interpret dogs' signalling correctly. To avoid injury and distress to all, we strongly advise that practitioners considering AAE receive training to enable them to supervise interactions appropriately.

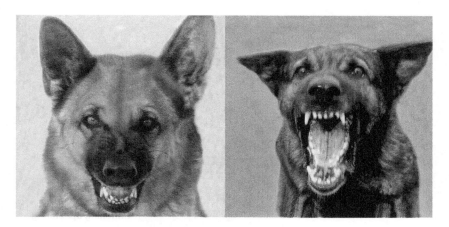

Figure 2.2 Aggressive dog facial expressions

Photos by Anais Racca, used with permission

To produce a testable tool to teach children and adults about dogs' body language, including facial expressions, Meints, Brelsford, Just, and De Keuster (2014[1]) presented participants with short video clips of distressed dogs (according to distress signals described by Shepherd, 2002) and relaxed dogs, with all videos assessed by dog-behavior specialists. Distress behaviors ranged from "lower" (e.g., nose-licking, eye-blinking) via "medium" (e.g., crouching, tail tucked under) to "higher" distress signals (e.g., growling, biting); for an overview, see Figure 2.3.

These steps show how a dog *can* react to stress or threat. It is important to be aware that these are *not* an orderly progression from one signal to the next when the animal is distressed. Distress signalling differs by the individual animal and the situation. Signals may be displayed simultaneously or follow each other closely. Importantly, dogs can switch rapidly from the "lowest" directly to the "highest" step (biting), based on their need to effect a change of situation.

Meints and colleagues investigated cross-sectionally and longitudinally how 3–5-year-olds and adults interpret dogs' signalling, having them judge on a 1–5 Likert scale whether the dogs in the videos were "very happy" (1), "happy," "neutral," "unhappy or angry," or "very unhappy/angry" (5). Given research indicating that acoustic input may help children's recognition and correct interpretation (Flom, Whipple, & Hyde, 2009; Pongrácz, Molnár, Dóka, & Miklósi, 2011), the researchers also measured whether audible distress signalling (e.g., snarling) improved judgments (Meints & Just, 2014).

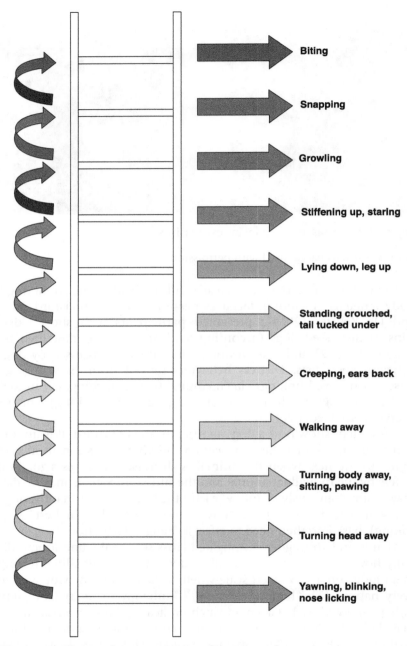

Figure 2.3 How a dog can react to distress or threat

Shepherd, 2002, used with permission of the publisher

Results before intervention showed a range of errors in all categories and age groups. Again, misinterpretations of aggressive dog faces as "happy" also occurred with videos: 50–65% of children's errors showed these dogs as being interpreted as "happy," despite their aggressive facial display and audible distress signalling. Even parents made 16% erroneous judgments, 12% being that they thought the dogs were "happy."

Children's and parents' knowledge improved significantly after training, with greater accuracy correlating with older age. Participants' results were also more improved the higher the distress category. "Lower" distress signals were overall harder to be recognized and learned.

Thus, successful teaching of dogs' distress signalling may be a promising way forward for dog bite prevention in education settings. Children from 3 years onward profit from appropriate intervention with high and medium distress signals, showing significant improvements in knowledge immediately after intervention, but also retaining this knowledge for up to a year. Increased awareness and knowledge can lead to safer behavior, lowered risk, and fewer bites, and dogs will benefit from more appropriate treatment.

Future research on dog body language should address differences in anatomy that may make interpretations more difficult as some features can obscure dogs' expressions (e.g., hair, skin folds, nose length), and signalling strategies of individual dogs may change with context.

Understanding Typical Situations With Familiar Dogs – How The Blue Dog Can Help

The Blue Dog program was created to provide an empirically evaluated dog bite prevention tool for typical situations with familiar dogs for children under the age of 7 (Meints & de Keuster, 2009). Prevention tools must be assessed for effectiveness to know whether they work or not (Zeedyk, Wallace, Carcary, Jones, & Larter, 2001), yet few have been assessed for effectiveness; these few include programs on public safety with unfamiliar dogs, targeting children over 7 years (Chapman, Cornwall, Righetti, & Sung, 2000; Spiegel, 2000) and a program targeted toward younger children, using photographs of unfamiliar dogs (Wilson, Dwyer, & Bennett, 2003).

The Blue Dog is so far the only assessed program aimed at teaching children under 7 years how to behave safely with familiar dogs in familiar settings. Because the majority of children are bitten by their own or a familiar dog in familiar surroundings, the Blue Dog program teaches children and parents about safety with *familiar dogs*.

19

The DVD contains test and story modules with integrated training; the parent booklet explains 15 typical household situations where most bite situations with children occur (Kahn et al., 2003).

Results showed children's significant improvement in knowledge about safe behavior with familiar dogs and retention of this knowledge over time. Older children performed consistently better than younger children, and parental support was especially useful for younger children (Meints & de Keuster, 2009). Thus, the Blue Dog program was shown to successfully improve children's (and parents') knowledge about safe behavior with dogs (replicated by Schwebel, Morrongiello, Davi, Stewart, & Bell, 2012; Morrongiello et al., 2013).

However, as research in other areas of child safety has shown, knowledge gain does not automatically translate into changed behavior (Zeedyk et al., 2001). Therefore, Meints, Lakestani, & de Keuster (2014) conducted additional, longitudinal, research to investigate if children use this knowledge and change their behavior with their own dog. Children again showed significantly increased knowledge over time; older children achieved higher scores than younger, and younger children with the DVD at home scored better than the group who only took the parent booklet home, suggesting that for younger children repetition with a DVD is useful. Parent compliance was very high (95% read the booklet and found the advice clear and useful, about 70% found the booklet and DVD useful to teach their children safe behavior with their dogs). To examine knowledge transfer to real life, parents were asked about their children and dogs. Almost half (48%) stated their children behaved more safely with dogs after the intervention; 38% said their children behaved more safely around their own dog, and around 30% reported changes in their own behavior and closer supervision of their children (Meints et al., 2014). This demonstrates that the Blue Dog program helps to change real-life behavior in children, with retention after 1 year.

Additional research used Blue Dog in an unfamiliar location (university psychology lab) with an unfamiliar dog and an unfamiliar dog handler. Children were instructed to "do whatever they wanted" (Morrongiello et al., 2013) or to "play with any of the items in the room, including the dog" after being shown how to play with the dog (Schwebel et al., 2012: 275). The experimenter then informed the children the dog had to get some rest and left the room with the explicit instruction to the children to "do whatever *they* (the children) preferred" (see Schwebel et al., 2012, for full instructions; see Morrongiello et al., 2013 for very similar instructions). Unsurprisingly, children chose to interact with the dog and parents did not stop them, probably because a clear authority figure had told the children explicitly to do as they preferred. The authors state "it is likely that parents assumed the dog was safe because of the context" (Morrongiello et al., 2013, p. 112).

The program was thus not used as intended, so that conclusions as to its effectiveness are called into question. To test the program's effectiveness, it would have been appropriate to test participants – all of whom had family dogs – with their own dogs in their own homes, and to use a range of the 15 Blue Dog scenarios.

However, as the above parental judgments of 48% suggest that Blue Dog does transfer to situations with unknown dogs, it would be useful if further and appropriately operationalized empirical testing were carried out with the Blue Dog scenarios to investigate the program's effectiveness as a teaching tool and the transfer of knowledge when facing unfamiliar dogs.

Conclusion

When trying to enable safe interactions between children/students and dogs, it is vital that all involved recognize risk situations that could escalate toward dog bites. To accomplish this, it is necessary to understand dogs' signals and body language and for all involved to be informed, act responsibly, and diligently safeguard the welfare of humans and animals.

The striking lack of knowledge on dogs' behavior and signalling and on safe behavior in child-dog interactions, together with common misconceptions on treatment and education of dogs (and children), does not make this an easy task, but tools like those described do make it possible. The research highlights the knowledge gaps and how empirically assessed prevention tools can contribute to improved knowledge and reduced dog bite incidents as well as promoting safe and enjoyable interactions.

Ideally, prevention tools would be used in advance of any HAI to promote understanding of dogs' behavior, signalling, and needs. Tools should be developed to further enhance learning, and made easily accessible for users. As there are clear benefits associated with HAI/AAI/AAE, it is imperative to maximize understanding and minimize risks.

However, despite all prevention efforts, we will not be able to prevent *all* dog bite incidents. While it is important that we raise awareness and educate all concerned via as many channels as possible, it is *essential* that parents and teaching staff be vigilant in supervising and educating children and giving dogs (and all classroom animals) the respect and welfare they need and deserve.

Note

1 This research project was co-funded by the *Eunice Kennedy Shriver* National Institute of Child Health and Human Development (NICHD) and the WALTHAM Centre for Pet Nutrition, a division of Mars, Incorporated; Grant Number 1R03HD071161-01.

References

Beck, A. M., & Jones, B. A. (1985). Unreported dog bites in children. *Public Health Report, 100*: 315–321.

Bell, A. (2013). Paws for a study break: Running an Animal-Assisted Therapy program at the Gerstein Science Information Centre. *The Canadian Journal of Library and Information Practice and Research, 8*(1): 1–14.

Bennett, P., & Righetti, J. (2001). The Delta Dog Safe™ Strategy. *Proceedings of the 2001 Annual Urban Animal Management Conference*, Melbourne.

Bloom, T., & Friedmann, H. (2013). Classifying dogs' (*Canis familiaris*) facial expressions from photographs. *Behavioral Processes, 96*: 1–10.

Bundesministerium für Bildung und Frauen. (2014). *Hunde in der Schule*. Retrieved from https://bmbf.gv.at/schulen/unterricht/ba/ hundeinderschule/hundeinderschule.pdf?4f7rr2

Chapman, S., Cornwall, J., Righetti, J., & Sung, L. (2000). Preventing dog bites in children: Randomized controlled trial of an educational intervention. *British Medical Journal, 320*: 1512–1513.

Cornelissen, J. M. R., & Hopster, H. (2010). Dog bites in The Netherlands: A study of victims, injuries, circumstances and aggressors to support evaluation of breed specific legislation. *The Veterinary Journal, 186*: 292–298.

Crossman, M., & Kazdin, A. (2015). Animal visitation programs in colleges and universities: An efficient model for reducing student stress. In A. H. Fine (Ed.) *Handbook of Animal-Assisted Therapy* (pp. 333–336). London: Academic Press.

Davies, T. N., Scalzo, R., Butler, E., Stauffer, M., Farah, Y. N., Perez, S., Mainor, K., Clark, C., Carter, S., Kobylecky, A., & Coviello, L. (2015). Animal-assisted interventions for children with autism spectrum disorder: A systematic review. *Education and Training in Autism and Developmental Disabilities, 50*: 316–329.

Dixon, C. A., Mahabee-Gittens, E. M., Hart, K. W., & Lindsell, C. J. (2012). Dog bite prevention: An assessment of child knowledge. *Journal of Pediatrics, 160*: 337–341.

Fine, A. H. (Ed.) (2015). *Handbook of Animal-Assisted Therapy*. London: Academic Press.

Flom, R., Whipple, H., & Hyde, D. (2009). Infants' intermodal perception of canine (*Canis familiaris*) facial expressions and vocalizations. *Developmental Psychology, 45*: 1143–1151.

Gee, N. R., Fine, A., & Schuck, S. (2015). Animals in educational settings: Research and practice. In A. H. Fine (Ed.) *Handbook of Animal-Assisted Therapy* (pp. 195–210). London: Academic Press.

Gilchrist, J., Sacks, J. J., White, D. D., & Kresnow, M.-J. (2008). Dog bites: Still a problem? *Injury Prevention, 14*: 296–330.

Gisle, L., Buziarsist, J., Van der Heyden, J., Demarest, S., Miermans, P. J., Sartor, F., Van Oyen, H, & Tafforeau, J. (2002). Health enquiry by interview, IPH/EPI Report Number 2002–2022.

Hall, S. S., Gee, N. R., & Mills, D. S. (2016). Children reading to dogs: A systematic review of the literature. *PLoS ONE, 11*: e0149759.

Holmquist, L., & Elixhauser, A. (2010). Emergency department visits and inpatient stays involving dog bites, 2008. *Healthcare Cost and Utilization Project*, pp. 1–14. Washington, DC: Agency for Healthcare Research and Quality.

Horisberger, U., Stärk, K. D. C., Rüfenacht, J., Pillonel, C., & Steiger, A. (2004). The epidemiology of dog bite injuries in Switzerland – characteristics of victims, biting dogs and circumstances. *Anthrozoös, 17*: 320–339.

HSCIS. (2014). Admissions caused by dogs and other mammals. UK: *Health and Social Care Information Centre*. Retrieved from http://hscic.gov.uk/catalogue/PUB14030/prov-mont-hes-admi-outp-ae-April%202013%20to%20January%202014-toi-rep.pdf

Hummel, E., & Randler, C. (2012). Living animals in the classroom: A meta-analysis on learning outcome and a treatment–control study focusing on knowledge and motivation. *Journal of Science Education and Technology, 21*: 95–105.

Insurance Information Institute, Inc. (2014). *Dog bite liability*. Retrieved from http://iii.org/issue-update/dog-bite-liability

Kahn, A., Bauche, P., & Lamoureux, J. (2003). Child victims of dog bites treated in emergency departments. *European Journal of Pediatrics, 162*: 254–258.

23

Kahn, A., Robert, E., Piette, D., De Keuster, T., Lamoureux, J., & Leveque, A. (2004). Prevalence of dog bites in children. A telephone survey. *European Journal of Pediatrics, 163*: 424.

Kamioka, H., Okada, S., Tsutani, K., Park, H., Okuizumi, H., Handa, S., Oshio, T., Park, S. J., Kitayuguchi, J., Abe, T., Hinda, T., & Mutoh, Y. (2014). Effectiveness of animal-assisted therapy: A systematic review of randomized controlled trials. *Complementary Therapies in Medicine, 22*: 371–390.

Kerswell, K. J., Bennett, P. J., Butler, K. L., & Hemsworth, P. H. (2009). Self-reported comprehension ratings of dog behaviour by puppy owners. *Anthrozoös, 22*: 183–193.

Mannion, C., Graham, A., Shepherd, K., & Greenberg, D. (2015). Dog bites and maxillofacial surgery: What can we do? *British Journal of Oral and Maxillofacial Surgery, 56*: 479–484.

Mariti, C., Gazzano, A., Moore, J. L., Baragli, P., Chelli, L., & Sigheri, C. (2012). Perception of dogs' stress by their owners. *Journal of Veterinary Behavior, 7*: 213–219.

Maujean, A., Pepping, C. A., & Kendall, E. (2015). A systematic review of randomized controlled trials of animal-assisted therapy on psychosocial outcomes. *Anthrozoös, 28*: 23–36.

Meints, K., & de Keuster, T. (2009). Don't kiss a sleeping dog: The first assessment of 'The Blue Dog' bite prevention program. *Journal of Pediatric Psychology, 34*(10): 1084–1090.

Meints, K., & Just, J. (2014). Growl or no growl? Differences in children's interpretation of dogs' distress signalling. *Poster presentation at the International Conference for Anthrozoology (ISAZ) in Vienna, Austria, July 2014.*

Meints, K., Brelsford, V., Just, J., & de Keuster, T. (2014). How children and parents (mis)interpret dogs' body language: A longitudinal study. *Poster presentation at the International Conference for Anthrozoology (ISAZ) in Vienna, Austria, July 2014.*

Meints, K., Lakestani, N., & De Keuster, T. (2014). Does the Blue Dog change behavior? The first longitudinal assessment of the Blue Dog Bite Prevention Program. *Poster presentation at the International Conference for Anthrozoology (ISAZ) in Vienna, Austria, July 2014.*

Meints, K., Racca, A., & Hickey, N. (2010). How to prevent dog bite injuries? Children misinterpret dog facial expressions. *Injury Prevention, 16*, supplement 1: A68.

Meints, K., Syrnyk, C., & De Keuster, T. (2010). Why do children get bitten in the face? *Injury Prevention, 16*, supplement 1: A172.

Morrongiello, B. A., Schwebel, D. C., Stewart, J., Bell, M., Davis, A. L., & Corbett, M. R. (2013). Examining parents' behaviors and supervision of their children in the presence of an unfamiliar dog: Does the Blue Dog intervention improve parent practices? *Accident Analysis and Prevention, 54*: 108–113.

O'Haire, M. E., (2013). Animal-assisted intervention for Autism Spectrum Disorder: A systematic literature review. *Journal of Autism Developmental Disorder, 43*: 1606–1622.

Peters, V., Sottiaux, M., Appelboom, J., & Kahn, A. (2004). Post-traumatic stress disorder following dog bites in children. *Journal of Pediatrics, 144*: 121–122.

Pongrácz, P., Molnár, C., Dóka, A., & Miklósi, A. (2011). Do children understand man's best friend? Classification of dog barks by pre-adolescents and adults. *Applied Animal Behavior Science, 135*: 95–102.

Reisner, I., Shofer, F., & Nance, M. (2007). Behavioral assessment of child-directed canine aggression. *Injury Prevention, 13*: 348–351.

Reisner, I. R., & Shofer, F. S. (2008). Effects of gender and parental status on knowledge and attitudes of dog owners regarding dog aggression toward children. *Journal of the American Veterinary Medical Association, 233*: 1412–1419.

Reisner, I. R., Nance, M. L., Zeller, J. S., Houseknecht, E. M., Kassam-Adams, N., & Weibe, D. J. (2011). Behavioral characteristics associated with dog bites to children presenting to an urban trauma center. *Injury Prevention, 17*: 348–353.

Responsible dog ownership. (2013). Retrieved from www.publications. parliament.uk/pa/cm201213/cmhansrd/cm130226/halltext/ 130226h0001.htm.

Sacks, J. J., Sattin, R. W., & Bonzo, S. E. (1989). Dog bite-related fatalities from 1979 through 1988. *Journal of the American Medical Association, 262*: 1489–1492.

Schalamon, J., Ainoedhofer, H., Singer, G., Petnehazy, T., Mayr, J., Kiss, K., & Höllwarth, M. E. (2006). Analysis of dog bites in children who are younger than 17 years. *Pediatrics, 117*: e374–e379.

Schuck, S. E., Emmerson, N., Fine, A. H., & Lakes, K. D. (2013). Canine-assisted therapy for children with ADHD: Preliminary findings from the positive assertive cooperative kids (PACK) study. *Journal of Attention Disorders, 19*: 125–137.

Schwebel, D. C., Morrongiello, B. A., Davis, A. L., Stewart, J., & Bell, M. (2012). The Blue Dog: Evaluation of an interactive software program to

25

teach young children how to interact safely with dogs. *Journal of Pediatric Psychology*, 37: 272–281.

Shepherd, K. (2002). Development of behavior, social behavior and communication in dogs. In D. Horwitz, D. Mills & S. Heath. (Eds.) *BSAVA manual of canine and feline behavioral medicine* (pp. 8–20). Gloucester, UK: British Small Animal Veterinary Association.

Spiegel, I. B. (2000). A pilot study to evaluate an elementary school-based dog bite prevention program. *Anthrozoös*, 13: 164–173.

Tami, G., & Gallagher, A. (2009). Description of the behavior of domestic dog (*Canis familiaris*) by experienced and inexperienced people. *Applied Animal Behavior Science*, 120: 159–169.

Uttley, C. (2013). Animal attraction: Including animals in early childhood classrooms. *Young Children*, 68: 16.

Wan, M., Bolger, N., & Champagne, F. A. (2012). Human perception of fear in dogs varies according to experience with dogs. *PLoS ONE*, 7: e51775.

Wilson, F., Dwyer, F., & Bennet, P. (2003). Prevention of dog bites: Evaluation of a brief educational intervention program for preschool children. *Journal of Community Psychology*, 31: 75–86.

Zeedyk, M. S., Wallace, L., Carcary, B., Jones, K., & Larter, K. (2001). Children and road safety: Increasing knowledge does not improve behavior. *British Journal of Educational Psychology*, 71: 573–594.

CHAPTER 3

Legal and Policy Issues for Classrooms with Animals

Rebecca J. Huss and Aubrey H. Fine

Introduction

Resistance to change is perhaps one of the greatest obstacles to legitimizing the incorporation of animals in education. It is apparent that some of the hurdles presented relate to the lack of clarity in regards to the legal and policy implications. A strong emphasis within this book pertains to the evidence demonstrating the value of animals in schools. This chapter will focus primarily on the present legal positions related to animal inclusion. Attention will also be given to some of the education policy changes that are needed to make it simpler to incorporate animals in education settings for both educational support and research purposes.

Legal Issues

Injuries Caused by Animals

In connection with animal-assisted interventions (AAI), the primary legal concern is the possibility of civil liability if a person were injured by an animal or during an AAI. "Liability" is used here to refer to the concept of tort liability for money damages. The basic legal premise is that due to an act or omission by one person, another has been harmed and should be compensated (Shapo, 2003). As discussed later, some states have guidelines and restrictions on keeping certain animals in the classroom. However, when there are no legal prohibitions restricting the keeping or use of a particular animal, if there is an incident involving that animal, general tort principles would be applied to determine liability.

State laws determine liability for injuries caused by animals. (As discussed below, federal law will be key when considering legal issues relating to the use of service animals in schools.) Each state has its own body of law to determine the circumstances under which liability could be assessed (Daller, 2014). In addition, both legislation (the state statute or code) and common law (case law establishing precedent) may apply. Even if a state has a statutory provision, case law is often used to interpret the language of the statute.

Because of this complexity, only a general overview of liability is provided in this chapter. Anyone involved in AAIs is encouraged to become familiar with the law(s) that apply to these activities in that state. In the event of an incident, an attorney who is licensed to practice in that state and is familiar with tort liability and legal issues involving animals should be consulted.

Although this chapter focuses on issues relating to animals in the classroom, practitioners involved in AAIs should be aware of special considerations involved in equine-assisted activities. Over 40 states have adopted Equine Activity Liability Acts (Sweet, 2011). Essentially, these acts codify the idea that participants in equine activities have assumed the inherent risks involved; in order to gain the protection under the Acts, persons offering the activity may be required to take certain actions such as posting signage with specified language. Most Acts contain exceptions that allow for recovery of damages if there has been gross negligence or the activity was not suitable for the participant (Sweet, 2011). Persons providing equine activities should be cautioned that these acts only provide limited protection, and providers should ensure that they have adequate liability insurance coverage and take measures to reduce risk.

Many states also have statutory provisions specifically dealing with injuries caused by animals, especially dogs (The American Law Institute, 2010, § 23). Often these statutes are applicable regardless of how the injury occurred. Strict liability statutes have been adopted in over half the states (Randolph, 2013; The American Law Institute, 2010, § 23). Strict liability statutes impose liability regardless of whether the person controlling the dog had any knowledge of the possible danger or did anything wrong. There are exceptions and affirmative defenses under these statutes, although these are unlikely to apply in situations involving AAIs. Examples of defenses would include requiring the injured individual to prove that the person did not provoke the dog or was not trespassing on the owner's property (Randolph, 2013).

Another type of state statute codifies the "one bite rule" that developed through case law in many states. This standard is that the owner knows, or should have known, that the dog was likely to cause the injury – not that the dog must have bitten someone in the past. Defenses include provocation or that the injured person voluntarily put him- or herself at risk (Randolph, 2013).

Note that in some states a person who is injured by an animal may still have the option to sue based on common law negligence standards if recovery is not possible using a statute. In order to recover under a theory of negligence, it is necessary to prove that the individual with the animal did not exercise reasonable care under the circumstances and the injury was foreseeable (The American Law Institute, 2010, § 3).

Legally, all animals are considered personal property (Huss, 2002). Regardless of whether a statute or common law applies, the legal owner is always potentially liable. Many state laws have developed to provide that persons deemed to be "possessors," "harborers," or "keepers" as well as persons who have control of an animal can be liable (Randolph, 2013).

It is common for AAI programs to require a signed waiver before a student is allowed to participate. For juveniles, a parent must sign on behalf of the student. A well-drafted waiver may shift the risk of liability – at least for certain claims. Although there is value in having waivers prepared and executed by parents, the legal status of such waivers varies substantially among the states. Courts in some states have upheld the validity of well-crafted waivers for non-essential activities, although others have ruled them unenforceable (Lintemuth, 2010). Regardless of the enforceability, programs should always have a well-drafted waiver executed in order to determine, at a minimum, whether students have allergies or other sensitivities.

In addition, if there is an incident, especially a bite, a report must be filed with local and/or state health authorities. For example, Ohio law requires "anyone who has knowledge" of a bite to a person to report the incident to the health commissioner in the local health jurisdiction (Ohio Department of Health Animal Bites, 2015, Screen 1). The information reported to the relevant authorities can

29

be extensive. For example, the State of Indiana's form contains a classification system that indicates the victim, geographic location, any history of the animal biting, and severity of the injury (Indiana State Department of Health, 2015). Depending on the circumstances surrounding the injury, the animal may be required to be quarantined for a period of time, or the animal control authorities in the jurisdiction may initiate an investigation into whether the animal should be deemed dangerous (Randolph, 2013).

This information may make people hesitant to interact with animals. Of course, persons involved in AAIs should do everything possible to decrease the risk of injuries, but it is important to put the possibility of personal liability in perspective. Accidents can happen even in the best of programs, so every program should have an adequate liability insurance policy. Especially in cases of common law negligence actions, defenses may be available (Speiser, Krause, & Gans, 1990, § 21.50).

Injuries that occur in public schools and other government-supported activities may be protected by the doctrine of governmental immunity (Lintemuth, 2010), codified through state statutes that may provide for protection from liability for certain governmental authorities unless there has been gross negligence. Gross negligence can be defined as reckless or conscious disregard for the safety of others (Lintemuth, 2010).

Service Animals in Schools

Unlike the situation of programs where schools and students voluntarily engage in activities involving animals, schools may be required to allow a student's service animal in the classroom. An increasing number of students are requesting their service animals be allowed to accompany them to school (Huss, 2016). The regulations interpreting the federal Americans with Disabilities Act (ADA) require that public entities (state and local governments) and public accommodations (including schools) shall modify "policies, practices or procedures to permit the use of a service animal by the individual with a disability" (Title II Regs, 2015; Title III Regs, 2015). This issue is complicated by the federal Individuals with Disabilities Education Act (IDEA). IDEA requires states to have policies to ensure that children with disabilities are provided a "free appropriate public education" (Individuals with Disabilities Education Act, 2012).

A school district preferring not to accommodate a student's request to be accompanied by a service animal may argue that the IDEA should be applied rather than the ADA to determine whether the animal must be allowed in the school (Huss, 2016). One requirement of the IDEA is the exhaustion of extensive administrative procedures prior to filing suit (Huss, 2016). Judges analyzing this issue have come to different conclusions (Huss, 2016). The US Supreme Court is expected to rule on a case in 2017 that should resolve this issue (*Fry v. Napoleon Cmty. Sch. Dist.*, 2016). Regardless of a school district raising the IDEA exhaustion of administrative remedies issue, eventually the ADA would be applied to determine whether a service animal must be allowed in a school (Huss, 2016).

ADA defines service animal as "any dog that is individually trained to do work or perform tasks for the benefit of an individual with a disability, including a physical, sensory, psychiatric, intellectual, or other mental disability" (Title II Regs, 2015; Title III Regs, 2015). Miniature horses may also be deemed service animals, subject to several assessment factors; however, no other animal species is covered by the definition of service animal (Title II Regs, 2015; Title III Regs, 2015). The requirement that an animal must *do work or perform tasks* means that an animal that is used solely for emotional support is not considered a service animal.

Disputes regarding service animals in school environments generally fall into a few categories. First, an educator in a school may believe the animal is inadequately trained or could pose a danger to other students. General concerns over the impact of a dog on other students, including students with allergies, are not sufficient to exclude a dog serving as a service animal (Huss, 2016). If there is another person in the school that has a conflicting need, such as having allergy issues, that rises to the level that would meet the ADA's definition of a disability, schools are expected to accommodate both individuals (Huss, 2016).

ADA regulations provide that entities may only exclude a service animal if "the animal is out of control and the animal's handler does not take effective action to control it" or the animal is not housebroken (Title II Regs, 2015; Title III Regs, 2015). The Department of Justice's (DOJ) guidance on ADA regulations and case law has established that a particular service animal's behavior and history must be considered to establish if there is a direct threat to the health or safety of others (Huss, 2015).

Another issue that has been raised in multiple school districts is that, because of the student's age and disability, the school is being asked to provide a handler for the service dog (Huss, 2016). ADA regulations provide that a service animal "shall be under control of its handler" and that entities are "not responsible for the care or supervision of a service animal" (Title II Regs, 2015; Title III Regs,

2015). This is likely to be an issue in future litigation. One court distinguished between routine animal care (e.g., feeding or washing an animal) and the tasks that the school was asked to perform (assisting the student in tethering and untethering the dog and taking the dog outside to urinate), and found that the requested accommodation that the parent not be required to provide a separate handler was reasonable (*Alboniga v. Sch. Bd. of Broward Cnty. Fla.*, 2015).

Finally, several school districts have attempted to deny access for a student accompanied by a service dog until the family provided evidence of liability insurance or records showing the dog had received vaccinations beyond those required by state law. Note that, if a service animal causes damage or injures someone, the general tort concepts discussed earlier would apply. Specifically, the parent (as the legal owner) would be responsible for damages. Concerns over whether a school district would also be sued in the event of any incident (especially if the owners of the service animal are considered judgment proof) are the logical basis for school districts requesting evidence of liability insurance. However, case law and federal administrative actions have determined that imposing these represent surcharges which are not allowed under the ADA regulations (Huss, 2016; Title II Regs, 2015; Title III Regs, 2015).

Recent administrative actions by the DOJ and Department of Education (DOE) have indicated that those agencies support the use of the ADA (regardless of the possible intersection with the IDEA) to argue that students with disabilities should be able to be accompanied by their service animals to school (Huss, 2016). DOJ and DOE administrative decisions have also supported a generous interpretation of the requirement that even students with profound disabilities be considered the handlers of their service dogs (Huss, 2016). Given the significant activity level of these federal agencies, school districts that want to deny access to students with service dogs should ensure that the law is on their side before denying such access.

In addition to the rights provided under the ADA, students utilizing service dogs may have rights of access under state law (Huss, 2016), which may allow access broader than that under the ADA. For example, the Illinois law allowing for access does not require the student be the handler of the service animal (Huss, 2016). Alabama law provides that aides assigned to assist children with disabilities be trained in basic dog commands to assist the child as a member of the team (Huss, 2016). In contrast, other state laws specifically relating to service animals in schools grant rights to a smaller class of persons, e.g., by designating protection for the use of service animals by persons with certain types of disabilities, or requiring the animal be trained by a school for service animals (Huss, 2016).

Policy Issues

"Change is the law of life and those who look only to the past or present are certain to miss the future." In many ways we need to heed these words of the late John F. Kennedy as we begin to embark on making our imprint on the future. Legitimately incorporating animals into our schools will require not only scientific support, but also a shift in public policy promoting a more positive awareness of, and a respect for, AAI. Legislators and administrators nationwide need to recognize that the value of animals in schools far surpasses any potential risks. Further, clearly drafted protocols can provide the necessary assurances to assuage any justifiable concerns that supervisors may have. But above all, the safety and welfare of all (students, staff, and all animals) must at all times be paramount. Emphasizing these concerns in the protocols will reassure educators and administrators and ensure safety and quality.

Before discussing some shifts that may occur in the future, the following section briefly identifies some common concerns that could support policy changes. Educators must be trained to learn how animals in the classroom can be integrated, including understanding appropriate husbandry and guidelines for proper hygiene (Fine, 2014). Administrators will want to make sure that the US Centers for Disease Control and Prevention (CDC) recommendations for safely interacting with specific species are adhered to, so that proper precautions are put into place (Gee, Fine, & Schuck, 2015).

Changing public policy is not insurmountable. Proper precautions must be put into place so that adminstrators' zone of tolerance is addressed (Fine, 2015). This zone of tolerance addresses the risk: benefit ratio that needs to be considered. Following this frame of reference will help administrators become more comfortable in allowing teachers to begin incorporating animals into their classroom.

Policy Issues Relating to the Inclusion of Animals in Classrooms

Surveys indicate that including animals in the classroom is commonplace (Gee et al., 2015). To avoid tort liability under a general negligence standard, an individual would need to show that he or she was *acting reasonably*, which includes following any generally accepted guidelines and relevant policies.

The US CDC has published guidelines for animals in school settings, which include basic recommendations on handling, in addition to some advice regarding specific species of animals (US Centers for Disease Control and Prevention, Appendix D Guidelines for Animals in School and Child Care Settings, 2009).

Some states have announced guidelines or have policies regarding the keeping of certain animals (such as wild animals) based on health and safety concerns. For example, Alaska's Department of Environmental Conservation, Division of Environmental Health guidelines for residential and visiting animals provides that certain animals are considered unsafe under the administrative code provision stating that a "school must be free of safety hazards." In addition, wild and poisonous animals, large birds, bats, and monkeys are not allowed in schools at all, ferrets are permitted only in grade 7–12 classrooms, and certain animals, such as chickens, reptiles, and amphibians, are only conditionally allowed with a requirement of active supervision and signage and based on the age of the students (State of Alaska, Department of Environmental Conservation, Division of Environmental Health, Animals in Schools Guidelines for Resident and Visiting Animals, n.d.).

In addition to establishing the acceptable species of animals, state guidelines may also make recommendations regarding the handling of animals. Guidelines may also include recommendations that relate to the health and proper restraint of animals (Kansas Department of Health and Environment, Offices of Epidemiologic Services and Public Information, Animals in Kansas Schools: Guidelines for Resident and Visiting Pets, n.d.).

In addition to state guidelines, school district policies may further restrict the keeping or use of animals in a classroom environment. School district policies covering this issue vary widely (Gee et al., 2015). To avoid the argument that an individual was not acting reasonably, AAIs should not occur in contravention of an individual school's or school district's policy.

Policy Issues Involving Service Animals

The policy issues involving accommodating a service animal in a school environment are impacted by the application of the ADA, which preempts any state, local guidelines, or policies that would restrict an animal's presence in a school (Huss, 2015). In fact, the state guidelines referenced above provide that service animals should not be prohibited on school grounds, and many local school districts have established policies that have a separate process in place in the event where a student requests to be accompanied by his or her service animal in school (Huss, 2016; State of Alaska, Department of Environmental Conservation, Division of Environmental Health, Animals in Schools Guidelines for Resident and Visiting Animals, n.d.; Kansas Department of Health and Environment, Offices of Epidemiologic Services and Public Information, Animals in Kansas Schools: Guidelines for Resident and Visiting Pets, n.d.).

As discussed above, some school districts have resisted allowing service dogs in the school environment due to concerns over allergies. Allergies are certainly a serious concern; however, interpretations of the ADA have not allowed schools or other public accommodations to prohibit a service animal on that basis (Huss, 2011). Even if a student's or staff member's allergies do not rise to the level of a disability, a school district can take steps to adjust the location and schedules of the affected individuals to minimize the impact (Huss, 2016).

The DOJ has established that another individual's fear of animals or general concerns over safety also are not a basis for denying access for a service animal (Huss, 2016). The fact that service animals are trained to be calm and predictable can alleviate some of these concerns (Miners, 2009). Note that case law has established that a service animal does not need to have perfect behavior at all times; however, the ADA regulations do provide that if the animal is disruptive, and the handler does not control it, the dog can be excluded from the premises (Huss, 2016; Title II Regs, 2015; Title III Regs, 2015).

Service animal etiquette can be viewed as the general issue of how others should interact (or more likely not interact) with a service dog. The general rule is that no one other than the individual with the disability, or the person assisting that individual, should interact with the service dog while the dog is "in harness." Learning not to touch or otherwise distract the dog can be challenging, not only for children but also for adults. Inappropriate interaction with a service dog can cause problems at the time, but also can negatively impact the dog's training. Many states have addressed the issue of intentional interference with a service dog by passing laws making such action a misdemeanor offense (Cruelty to a Service Animal, 1996). Though it is doubtful that a child would be charged with a criminal offense if he or she petted a service animal while the service animal was working, this illustrates the need to adequately train students and staff that the default proper behavior is to ignore the dog.

The concerns discussed above can be addressed through the use of training and a plan for integration of a service animal into the

35

school environment. Both the parents and school district have an incentive to make the transition as smooth as possible to ensure the child is benefiting to the greatest degree from partnering with a service animal. Reputable service animal placement organizations will work with the parents, and the school district, to address concerns about having a service animal in the school environment and the best way to integrate the dog into the school (Huss, 2016).

Chapters 13 and 14, in this book, address the appropriate selection and the welfare of any animals used in AAIs. This is imperative not only to protect the participants (both human and animal) in any program from injury, but also to minimize the likelihood the providers of a program will be found liable for damages. Following generally accepted guidelines and having a well-thought-through process for the introduction of animals in place also support this goal.

References

Alboniga v. School Board of Broward County, Fla., 87 F. Supp. 3d. 1319 (S.D. Fla. 2015).

Cruelty to a Service Animal, Ind. Code § 35-46-3-11.5 (West 2015).

Daller, M. F. (Ed.). (2014). *Tort law desk reference: A fifty-state compendium* (2014 edn). Frederick, MD: Wolters Kluwer.

Fine, A. (2014). *Our faithful companions.* Crawford, CO: Alpine Publications.

Fine, A. H. (Ed.). (2015). *Handbook on animal-assisted therapy: Foundations and guidelines for animal-assisted interventions* (4th edn). San Diego, CA: Academic Press.

Fry v. Napoleon Cmty. Sch. Dist., 788 F.3d 622 (6th Cir. 2015), *cert. granted,* 136 S.Ct. 2540 (June 28, 2016) (15–497).

Gee, N. R., Fine, A. H., & Schuck, S. (2015). Animals in educational settings: Research and practice. In A. H. Fine (Ed.), *Handbook on animal-assisted Therapy: Foundations and guidelines for animal-assisted interventions* (4th edn, pp. 195–210). London: Academic Press.

Huss, R. J. (2002). Valuing man's and woman's best friend: The moral and legal status of companion animals. *Marquette Law Review, 86:* 47–105.

Huss, R. J. (2011). Canines in the classroom: Service animals in primary and secondary educational institutions. *Journal of Animal Law & Ethics, 4:* 11–62.

Huss, R. J. (2015). A conundrum for animal activists: Can or should the current legal classification of certain animals be utilized to improve the lives of all animals? *Michigan State Law Review, 2015:* 1561–1598.

Huss, R. J. (2016). Canines in the classroom revisited: Recent developments relating to students' utilization of service animals at primary and secondary educational institutions. *Albany Government Law Review, 9*: 1–47.

Individuals with Disabilities Education Act, 20 U.S.C. §§ 1400–1482 (2012).

Kansas Department of Health and Environment, Offices of Epidemiologic Services and Public Information, Animals in Kansas Schools. (n.d.). *Guidelines for resident and visiting pets.* Retrieved from http://kdheks.gov/pdf/hef/ab1007.pdf

Kennedy, J. (n.d.). Change is the law of life. BrainyQuote.com. Retrieved from http://brainyquote.com/quotes/quotes/j/johnfkenn121068.html

Lintemuth, E. (2010). Parental rights v. parens patriae: Determining the correct limitation on the validity of pre-injury waivers effectuated by parents on behalf of minor children. *Michigan State Law Review, 2010*: 169–201.

Miners, Z. (2009, November 25). For student with autism, having service animal in school is 'lifesaver'. *U.S. News & World Report.* Retrieved from http://usnews.com/education/articles/2009/11/25/for-student-with-autism-having-service-animal-in-school-is-lifesaver

Ohio Department of Health Animal Bites. (2015). Retrieved from http://odh.ohio.gov/animalbites

Randolph, M. (2013). *Every dog's legal guide: A must-have book for your owner* (7th edn). Berkeley, CA: Nolo.

Shapo, M. S. (2003). *Principles of tort law.* St. Paul, MN: West Group.

Speiser, S. M., Krause, C. F., & Gans, A. W. (1990). *The American law of torts.* Rochester, NY: Lawyers Cooperative.

State of Alaska, Department of Environmental Conservation, Division of Environmental Health. (n.d.). *Animals in schools guidelines for resident and visiting animals.* Retrieved from https://kpbsd.k12.ak.us/WorkArea/DownloadAsset.aspx?id=2390

Sweet, J. (2011). Did equine liability acts save the horse industry? *Drake Journal Agricultural Law, 16*: 359–373.

The American Law Institute. (2010). *Restatement (third) of torts: Physical & emotional harm.* St. Paul, MN: Author.

US Centers for Disease Control and Prevention. (2009). *Appendix D: Guidelines for animals in school and child care settings.* Retrieved from http://cdc.gov/mmwr/preview/mmwrhtml/rr5805a5.htm

The Evidence

Does Animal Presence or Interaction Impact Social and Classroom Behaviors Conducive to Student Educational Success?

41

Patricia Pendry, Alexa M. Carr, and Jaymie L. Vandagriff

Introduction

This chapter presents research on the effects of incorporating live animals into education settings, with a focus on activities, interventions, and prevention programs designed to enhance students' social competence – the social, emotional, and behavioral skills associated with educational success, especially in the face of adversity. Our review of empirical evidence is grounded in a discussion of the key elements of social competence, its implications for educational success, and the theoretical framework guiding the design, implementation, and evaluation of school-based prevention programs promoting it. We also describe animal characteristics that may inform the mechanisms underlying program effects of equine- and canine-assisted interventions, and conclude with directions for future research.

What is Social Competence and How Does it Inform Educational Success?

Although the literature examining its predictors is expansive, the multifaceted construct of *social competence* may best encompass the essential skills and behaviors needed to attain educational success. Although the construct of social competence is intuitively understood by researchers, clinicians, and the public, there is no comprehensive, agreed-upon way to define it, nor is there one standardized way to assess it. We therefore examine the constructs that inform its conceptualization and development, which are described as a three-tiered, hierarchical model (Cavell, Meehan, & Fiala, 2003).

Cavell et al. (2003) refer to the most advanced level of social competence as *social adjustment*, where the child is developmentally on target for achieving appropriate social goals. This level reflects how well the child meets the expectations of parents, teachers, and society. The next tier is *social performance*, which incorporates the child's interactive style, the efficiency of the style, and what situations may be problematic for the child. The most basic level is *social skills*, the specific abilities the child uses within a social situation, including both how the child responds to a given situation as well as how the situation is encoded.

The multifaceted construct of social competence is considered a central domain of human development and is thought to play a critical role not only in educational success, but also in predicting future mental health outcomes and overall well-being (Luecken, Roubinov, & Tanaka, 2013). For example, lower social competence is associated with lower academic competence and performance (Sørlie & Nordhal, 1998; Wentzel, 1991), anti-social behavior (Rabiner, Coie, Miller-Johnson, Boykin, & Lochman, 2005; Rubin, Root, & Bowker, 2010; Sørlie, Hagen, & Ogden, 2008), conduct problems, depression (Rockhill, Vander Stoep, McCauley, & Katon, 2009), and substance use (Griffin, Epstein, Botvin, & Spoth, 2001). Children with lower social competence tend to have poorer social skills, and higher rates of cognitive distortions (e.g., hostile attribution bias), which may contribute to problem behavior in social situations, such as expression of anger and anxiety. They tend to have difficulty regulating negative emotions and physiological arousal (Alink, Cicchetti, Kim, & Rogosch, 2012), which can interfere with initiating and maintaining positive peer interactions (Crawford & Manassis, 2011; Crick & Dodge, 1994; Dodge & Somberg, 1987), and difficulty in other social relationships (Luecken et al., 2013). Relationship problems with peers and adults, difficulty with emotion regulation, attention, behavior, and challenges with learning and achievement contribute to the development of mental health issues and poor child well-being. Promoting behavioral, social, and emotional competence in youth is thus an effective strategy to enhance educational success and to prevent mental, emotional, and behavioral disorders in adulthood.

Theoretical Framework for Promoting Social Competence through HAI

There are several strength-based and preventive perspectives to guide the design, implementation, and evaluation of AAIs in promoting social competence. The Positive Youth Development (PYD) perspective uses both prevention and intervention strategies in an integrated way to provide opportunities for youth to develop skills and reinforce pro-social behavior (National Clearinghouse on Families and Youth, 2007). According to the Social Development Model (Catalano & Hawkins, 1996), which has guided PYD, preventive interventions need to provide opportunity for involvement in pro-social activities, demonstration of skills, and reinforcement of desired behavior. The idea underlying this model is that youth bond to the source of the reinforcement, after which they internalize the value of the person and the institution to which they are bonded. Preventive interventions guided by these perspectives have been shown to increase social competencies, prevent maladaptive behavior, violence, and delinquency, as well as improve mental health outcomes and educational success (Catalano, Hawkins, & Toumborou, 2008).

When PYD is put into place within a school setting, it is often referred to as School-Wide Positive Behavior Support (Sawka-Miller & Miller 2007), which targets social competence through the implementation of proactive behavior management strategies, pro-social skill instruction, and behavior modification techniques. The components of direct skill instruction to promote pro-social skills and competencies are also referred to as Social Emotional Learning (SEL), which

43

emphasizes the development of self-awareness, social awareness, self-management, relationship skills, and responsible decision-making (Devaney, O'Brien, Tavegia, & Resnick, 2005). Durlak, Weissberg, Dymnicki, Taylor, and Schellinger (2011) reported that SEL programs improve feelings of self-confidence and self-esteem, promote school bonding, improve school grades, reduce aggression, noncompliance, and conduct problems, and lead students to experience meaningful increases in standardized high-stakes achievement tests.

Given that AAIs provide ample rewarding and reinforcing opportunities for involvement in pro-social activities, demonstration of skills, and desired behavior, researchers and practitioners should explicitly examine the effects of incorporating HAI-focused interventions with evidence-based PYD and SEL approaches to strengthen HAI-focused program and study designs, enhance implementation, and increase the quantity and quality of evaluation efforts.

Which Elements of Social Competence are Suitable to HAI Intervention?

Whereas facility with language and the ability to interact with others within accepted cultural and social norms are important, the individual also needs to read and accurately interpret non-verbal communication cues such as facial expressions and body language. Self and social awareness are also important, informing individuals' understanding of the dynamic interplay between their own emotions, intents, and behaviors, and those with whom they are interacting. Fostering willingness and ability to evaluate someone's own behavior, assess its impact and appropriateness, and make changes if needed is a key element of enhancing elements of social competence, including goal-directed behavior, personal responsibility, optimistic thinking, and self-management. Finally, children and adolescents need experiences that require them to consider the *context* in which social interactions take place, including the quality of relationships, timing of communication, motivation, attitude, knowledge, perception (encoding) of all parties involved, and the behaviors involved in establishing and maintaining positive, productive social relationships.

How Does Participation in Equine Programming Foster Social Competence?

Participation in equine activities may enhance social competence through the following mechanisms. First, equines possess several key characteristics that influence the behavior, emotion, and cognition of humans interacting with them: e.g., horses and mules are prey animals, and have a strong fight-or-flight response and a highly-attuned awareness of their physical surroundings, characteristics which necessitate participants' self-awareness of their own behavior, cognitions, emotional intent, and verbal and non-verbal communication. By interacting with equines, participants are encouraged to reflect on the consequences of their behavior and intent, and the information non-verbal communication provides to equines (e.g., posture, emotion, physiological arousal). Since equines provide immediate, consistent, predictable, and meaningful feedback – pinning ears, swishing tail, licking lips, and blinking, human participants simultaneously gain experience in interpreting non-verbal cues. Participants also learn to manage and direct their own behavior to evoke desirable responses from the horse (e.g., licking lips, blinking, resting foot) rather than less desirable responses (e.g., swishing tail, pinning ears, tuning out). These experiences are relevant for children's social competence in the context of non-equine partners, as program facilitators can encourage children to evaluate the nature of their behavior, thoughts, and intent and their effects on a *human* partner, which improves self and social awareness, goal-directed behavior, and communication skills.

45

A second characteristic of the horse that may mediate the development of social competence is its expectation about leadership and the natural hierarchy of herd dynamics. Horses are inclined to oscillate between seeking and accepting leadership, which encourages participants to engage in behavior that elicits respect from the horse. Participants learn to assert leadership through clear non-verbal cues and redirecting their behavior when needed. Participants are reminded that self-management, fostering a give-and-take relationship, quick decision-making, and optimistic thinking are important skills that facilitate successful human-equine interaction. In sum, equine characteristics significantly influence the *nature* of interactions between participants and horses in ways that promote children's social and behavioral competencies through the practice of pro-social behavior and reflection on participants' cognition, behaviors, emotion, and intent.

Empirical Evidence of Equine Intervention Affecting Social Competence

Equine-assisted interventions are generally thought of as falling into four categories. According to PATH International (2011), *therapeutic riding* programs offer equine activities and are therapeutic in nature, as they are expected to indirectly promote physical, cognitive, emotional, and social well-being. Consultation with medical or educational professionals working with the client in other realms (e.g., school, physical therapy) may be conducted, but is not essential as the primary purpose of sessions is to teach riding skills. *Hippotherapy* refers to equine activities that utilize equine movement as a component of physical, occupational, or language therapy treatment strategies under the direction and collaboration of a riding instructor and respective medical professional to achieve functional outcomes (PATHintl.org). *Equine-facilitated psychotherapy* (EFP) is an experiential psychotherapy in a collaborative effort between a licensed mental-health professional and an appropriately credentialed horse professional to incorporate horses in working with clients to address mutually established treatment goals and objectives (Fine & Beck, 2010). Finally, *equine assisted learning* (EAL, also known as equine facilitated learning, EFL) represents a unique set of practices that combine experiential learning and equine activities to enhance life skills (e.g., mindfulness, emotion regulation, problem solving) relevant to educational, professional, and personal goals of participants. Integral to both EFP and EAL is the understanding and application of equine behavior to elicit and identify horse-human interactions that promote well-being and development in a manner that is safe for both horses and humans.

Although research exists on the effects of these programs across types (for reviews see Frewin & Gardiner, 2005; Nimer & Lundahl, 2007; Selby & Smith-Osborne, 2013), none has been conducted in education settings. While school-based, equine-assisted interventions may be less common due to the logistics of dealing with large animals, remarkably few studies have chosen to collaborate with education entities. Exceptions include correlational work by Trotter, Chandler, Goodwin-Bond, and Casey (2008), who compared traditional classroom-based counseling activities with equine-assisted intervention and found that participation in equine intervention was associated with lower levels of internalizing and externalizing behavioral problems. Recently, Fredrick, Ivey Hatz, and Lanning (2015) conducted a randomized controlled trial (RCT) examining the effects of a 5-week EFL program on academically at-risk adolescents' feelings of hope related to social relationships, academics, outside-of-school activities, and family relationships; they found that program participation significantly improved adolescents' overall feelings of hope, which has implications for social competence through its link to optimistic thinking.

46

Pendry and colleagues (Pendry & Roeter, 2013; Pendry, Carr, Smith, & Roeter, 2014; Pendry, Smith, & Roeter, 2014) collaborated closely with school administrators, counselors, and teachers to facilitate recruitment and program implementation of an 11-week after-school program for students in grades 5–8 (N_{boys} = 41; N_{girls} = 72; M_{age} = 11.35 years). Although children were classified as typically developing, children with lower levels of social competence and those deemed at risk of academic failure were especially encouraged to enroll by asking school counselors to refer children ($N_{referred}$ = 16) receiving school counseling services for academic and/or behavioral adjustment issues, or whose parents had consulted with school counseling staff about the presence of stress in the home.

Children were randomly assigned to an experimental group (N = 53) to participate in an 11-week EFL program consisting of once-weekly, 90-minute sessions of individual and team-focused equine activities, or a waitlisted control group (N = 60), which participated 16 weeks later. EFL program activities were designed with an explicit emphasis on increasing self- and social awareness, fostering optimistic thinking and responsible decision-making, self-management, goal-directed behavior, and relationship skills, as well as self-regulation skills to reduce stress and increase coping. Activities were based on a combination of structured mounted and unmounted activities and horse-human interactions, including observation of equine behavior, engagement in equine management (e.g., grooming), in-hand horse-manship, some riding, and personal and group reflection activities.

Researchers found a positive effect of program participation on participants' social competence, specifically on self-awareness, self-management, personal responsibility, goal-directed behavior, and responsible decision-making. Based on systematic observations of each participant's positive (e.g., following direction, accepting feedback, appropriately assertive) and negative (e.g., argumentative, withdrawn, hyperactive, resistant) behaviors, the trajectory of weekly change over the 11-week program revealed that participants' positive behavior significantly increased, and that greater levels of change were associated with higher levels of program attendance.

Pendry, Smith, and Roeter (2014) also demonstrated that program participation significantly reduced participants' levels of cortisol, a stress hormone, assayed from participants' saliva at pre- and post-test. They found that program participation effectively lowered participants' average daily cortisol levels, which appeared to be attributable to lower afternoon cortisol levels. Adaptive patterns of biological regulation may support children's ability to behave in a well-regulated,

47

socially appropriate manner, preventing negative peer feedback, reducing biased appraisal of the social environment, and social rejection (Alink et al., 2012). In addition, lower levels of average daily cortisol may protect individuals against the development of mental, emotional, and behavioral problems (Lupien, McEwen, Gunnar, & Heim, 2009).

How Does Interaction with Canines Affect Social Competence?

Participation in canine activities may enhance social competence through the following mechanisms. First, due to their proximity to humans throughout the period of canine domestication, dogs are thought to have developed several shared characteristics with humans (Topál et al., 2009), along with convergent behaviors (e.g., emotional synchronization, social learning, rule following, complementary cooperation, interpretation of verbal and non-verbal communication, initializing communication). These shared behaviors provide an opportunity for educators and facilitators to engage in discussion and modeling with participants. Anderson and Olsen (2006) exemplified this in their discussion about communication patterns and emotions of their classroom dog and the similarities between the dogs and students. Additionally, beyond educator-structured conversations, mere interaction with dogs may provide children the opportunity to engage in their own socially competent behaviors, with or without adult scaffolding; there is growing evidence that a dog in the classroom encourages children to engage in greater social interactions rather than remaining isolated (Kotrschal & Ortbauer, 2003; Tissen, Hergovich, & Spielg, 2007).

Second, interacting with dogs may affect human physiological arousal. A growing body of evidence has associated human-canine interaction with the release of oxytocin (Beetz, Uvnas-Moberg, Julius, & Kotrschal, 2012; Hediger & Beetz, 2015) through both physical (e.g., touching, petting, stroking; Odendaal, 2000; Odendaal & Meintjes, 2003) and non-physical interactions (e.g., mutual gazing between a dog and human; Nagasawa et al., 2015). Given that oxytocin suppresses the production of cortisol (Cardoso, Ellenbogen, Orlando, Bacon, & Joober, 2013; Quirin, Kuhl, & Düsing, 2011), reduced physiological arousal and down-regulation of the stress response system may facilitate improved self-regulation leading to more adaptive social interactions with peers and teachers (Luecken et al., 2013).

Empirical Evidence on Effects of Canine-Enhanced Social Skills Training in Elementary Schools

Explicitly targeting the promotion of an important aspect of social competence, Tissen et al. (2007) conducted an RCT of the effects of a canine-enhanced social skills training programs on elementary school children (N_{boys} = 109, N_{girls} = 121). Children were randomized to one of three conditions, each consisting of ten, 90-minute weekly training sessions: social training without dogs, social training with dogs, and dog attendance without social training. Children who completed the dog-assisted social skills training demonstrated lower levels of open and relational aggression compared to the other two conditions. However, teachers reported an increase in students' social behaviors and empathy across the three conditions, suggesting the dog's presence did not have a causal impact on enhancing children's levels of empathy and social behavior.

Effects of Dog Presence in the Elementary Classroom

Although dogs are often incorporated into education settings on a short-term basis, there is an increasing interest in including dogs as full-time classroom members. Hergovich, Monshi, Semmler, and Zieglmayer (2002) investigated the effects of a dog's daily presence in a first-grade classroom on several measures of empathy over a three-month period. In comparison to the no-dog control classroom (N = 22), children in the dog-present class (N = 24) exhibited significant improvements in field independence (a perceptual task relating to empathy), increases in empathy toward animals, and better teacher-reported integration into the classroom. Extending these findings, Kotrschal and Ortbauer (2003) recorded children's social behavior in the dog-present class (N = 24) for two hours/week from one month before the dog was introduced and through the following month. When dogs were present, children became more socially integrated (spent less time alone, more time with others), paid more attention to their teacher, and displayed fewer behavioral extremes (e.g., fewer verbal provocations and aggressive behavior, particularly among boys). Using a quasi-experimental design, Beetz (2013) examined effects of weekly school-dog presence on third-grade students' socio-emotional experiences in school, depression, and emotion regulation strategies. In the dog-present classroom, children demonstrated increases in positive attitude toward school and positive emotions related to learning. In contrast, students in the control classroom demonstrated pronounced decreases in these measures at the end of the school year.

49

Canine Visitation Programs on College Campuses

A recent review of animal visitation programs (AVP) on college campuses yielded over 925 programs within the US alone, resulting in a call to investigate their efficacy using RCTs (Crossman & Kazdin, 2015). In response, Pendry and colleagues (under review) conducted an RCT examining the effects of an AVP during finals week on students' momentary emotion. Participants (N = 182) from 30 majors were randomized into three conditions: treatment (10 minutes of direct contact with live cats and dogs), control (viewing a 10-minute slide show with photos of the same cats and dogs), and waitlist group (waiting quietly for 10 minutes while being asked to refrain from in-person or electronic social exchanges). Researchers measured the extent to which participants experienced various emotions *at that moment* in four emotional constructs: *content* (e.g., calm, joyful), *anxious* (e.g., stressed, overwhelmed), *irritable* (e.g., frustrated, annoyed), and *depressed* (e.g., sad, depressed) at two time-points, immediately before (pre-test) and after (post-test) their assigned treatment. Feelings of contentment were significantly higher for treatment students, compared to controls or those waitlisted. Students who interacted with live animals also reported feeling significantly less anxious and irritable than control and waitlisted students.

These findings provide evidence that college students' positive and negative emotions can be influenced through as little as 10 minutes of HAI. This is promising and relevant, as higher levels of positive emotion are associated with increases in school engagement and learning (Reschly, Huebner, Appleton, & Antaramian, 2008). Although literature examining the role of positive emotions on learning is limited, Fredrickson (1998, 2001) suggested that increases in students' positive emotional experiences may also be associated with greater academic competence through greater willingness to engage in academically proactive behaviors such as studying and complex synthesis of information.

Summary and Conclusion

We have reviewed literature on the impact of HAI on participants' social competence, a multifaceted construct relevant to educational success. Through a preventive and positive youth development lens, we presented potential pathways through which programs featuring equines and canines may build social competence and thereby influence education outcomes, and revealed evidence that social competence can be supported by HAI in and outside of the classroom.

To inform best practices for HAI programming in education settings, more research is needed employing rigorous study designs and thoughtful documentation of program implementation, including the degree to which animals are incorporated, as well as the nature of interactions taking place. Although theoretical and empirical work present a plausible connection between presence of, and interaction with, an animal in an education setting, we do not yet know the degree to which intentional integration of animals may provide benefits above and beyond mere presence of an animal. Furthermore, little research to date has investigated the psychobiological pathways through which HAI may influence social competence and educational success. Future research should investigate these pathways and potential implications for education programming.

References

Alink, L. R. A., Ciccheti, D., Kim, J., & Rogosch, F. A. (2012). Longitudinal associations among child maltreatment, social functioning, and cortisol regulation. *Developmental Psychology*, 48(1): 224–236. doi: 10.1037/a0024892

Anderson, J. L., & Olson, M. R. (2006). The value of a dog in a classroom of children with severe emotional disorders. *Anthrozoös*, 19: 35–49. doi: 10.2752/089279306785593919

Beetz, A. (2013). Socio-emotional correlates of a schooldog-teacher-team in the classroom. *Frontiers in Psychology*, 4: 1–7. doi: 10.3389/fpsyg.2013.00886

Beetz, A., Uvnas-Moberg, K., Julius, H., & Kotrschal, K. (2012). Psychosocial and psychophysiological effects of human-animal interactions: The possible role of oxytocin. *Frontiers in Psychology*, 3: 234. doi: 10.3389/fpsyg.2012.00234

Cardoso, C., Ellenbogen, M. A., Orlando, M. A., Bacon, S. L., & Joober, R. (2013). Intranasal oxytocin attenuates the cortisol response to physical stress: A dose-response study. *Psychoneuroendocrinology*, 38(3): 399–407. doi: 10.1016/j.psyneuen.2012.07.013

Catalano, R. F., & Hawkins, J. D. (1996). The social development model: A theory of antisocial behavior. In J. D. Hawkins (Ed.), *Delinquency and crime: Current theories* (pp. 149–197). New York: Cambridge Press.

Catalano, R. F., Hawkins, J. D., & Toumborou, J. W. (2008). Positive youth development in the United States: History, efficacy, and links to moral and character education. In L. Nucci & D. Narvaez (Eds.), *Handbook of moral and character education* (pp. 459–483). New York: Routledge.

Cavell, T. A., Meehan, S. E., & Fiala, S. E. (2003). Assessing social competence in children and adolescents. In C. R. Reynolds & R. W. Kamphaus (Eds.), *Handbook of psychological and educational assessment of children* (pp. 433–454). New York: Guilford Press.

Crawford, A. M., & Manassis, K. (2011). Anxiety, social skills, friendship quality, and peer victimization: An integrated model. *Journal of Anxiety Disorders, 25*: 924–931.

Crick, N. R., & Dodge, K. A. (1994). A review and reformulation of social information-processing mechanisms in children's social adjustment. *Psychological Bulletin, 115*: 74–101.

Crossman, M. K., & Kazdin, A. E. (2015). Animal visitation programs in colleges and universities. In A. Fine (Ed.), *Handbook on animal-assisted therapy* (pp. 333–337). London: Elsevier Academic Press.

Devaney, E., O'Brien, M. U., Tavegia, M., & Resnik, H. (2005). Promoting children's ethical development through social and emotional learning. *New Directions for Youth Development, 108*: 107–116.

Dodge, K. A., & Somberg, D. R. (1987). Hostile attributional biases among aggressive boys are exacerbated under conditions of threats to the self. *Child Development, 58*: 213–224. doi: 10.2307/1130303

Durlak, J. A., Weissberg, R. P., Dymnicki, A. B., Taylor, R. D. & Schellinger, K. (2011). The impact of enhancing students' social and emotional learning: A meta-analysis of school-based universal interventions. *Child Development, 82*(1): 405–432. doi: 10.1111/j.1467-8624.2010.01564.x

Fine, A. H., & Beck, A. (2010). Understanding our kinship with animals: Input for health care professionals interested in the human/animal bond. In A. Fine (Ed.), *Handbook on animal-assisted therapy* (pp. 3–16). New York: Academic Press.

Frederick, K. E., Ivey Hatz, J., & Lanning, B. (2015). Not just horsing around: The impact of equine-assisted learning on levels of hope and depression in at-risk adolescents. *Community Mental Health Journal, 51*(7): 809–817. doi: 10.1007/s10597-015-9836-x

Fredrickson, B. L. (1998). What good are positive emotions? *Review of General Psychology, 2*(3): 300–319. doi: 10.1037/1089-2680.2.3.300

Fredrickson, B. L. (2001). The role of positive emotions in positive psychology: The broaden-and-build theory of positive emotions. *American Psychologist, 56*(3): 218–226. doi: 10.1037/0003-066X.56.3.218

Frewin, K., & Gardiner, B. (2005). New age or old sage? A review of equine assisted psychotherapy. *The Australian Journal of Counseling Pyschology, 6*: 13–17.

Griffin, K. W., Epstein, J. A., Botvin, G. J., & Spoth, R. L. (2001). Social competence and substance use among rural youth: Mediating role of social benefit expectancies of use. *Journal of Youth and Adolescence, 30*: 485–498. doi: 0047-2891/01/0800-0485

Hediger, K., & Beetz, A. (2015). The role of human-animal interaction in education. In J. Zinsstag, E. Schelling, D. Waltner-Toews, M. Whittaker, & M. Tanner (Eds.), *One health: The theory and practice of integrated health approaches* (pp. 73–84). Wallingford, UK: CABI Publishing.

Hergovich, A., Monshi, B., Semmler, G., & Zieglmayer, V. (2002). The effects of the presence of a dog in the classroom. *Anthrozoös, 15*: 37–50. doi: 10.2752/089279302786992775

Kotrschal, K., & Ortbauer, B. (2003). Behavioral effects of the presence of a dog in a classroom. *Anthrozoös, 16*: 147–159. doi: 10.2752/089279303786992170

Luecken, L. J., Roubinov, D. S., & Tanaka, R. (2013). Childhood family environment, social competence and health across the lifespan. *Journal of Social and Personal Relationships, 30*(2): 171–178. doi: 10.1177/0265407512454272

Lupien, S. J., McEwen, B. S., Gunnar, M. G., & Heim, C. (2009). Effects of stress throughout the lifespan on the brain, behaviour and cognition. *Nature Reviews Neuroscience, 10*: 434–445. doi: 10.1038/nrn2639

Nagasawa, M., Mitsui, S., En, S., Ohtani, N., Ohta, M., … Kikusui, T. (2015). Oxytocin-gaze positive loop and the coevolution of human-dog bonds. *Science, 348*: 333–336. doi: 10.1126/science.1261022

National Clearinghouse on Families and Youth. (2007). *Putting Positive Youth Development into practice: A resource guide.* Silver Spring, MD: Family and Youth Services Bureau.

Nimer, J., & Lundahl, B. (2007). Animal-assisted therapy: A meta-analysis. *Anthrozoös, 20*(3): 225–238. doi: 10.2752/089279307X224773

Odendaal, J. S. J. (2000). Animal-assisted therapy – magic or medicine? *Journal of Psychosomatic Research, 49*(4): 275–280. doi: 10.1016/S0022-3999(00)00183-5

Odendaal, J. S., & Meintjes, R. (2003). Neurophysiological correlates of affiliative behaviour between humans and dogs. *The Veterinary Journal, 165*(3): 296–301. doi: 10.1016/S1090-0233(02)00237-X

PATH International. (2011). EAAT Fact Sheet. Retrieved from http://pathintl.org/images/pdf/about-narha/documents/2011-Fact-Sheet.pdf.

Pendry, P., & Roeter, S. M. (2013). Experimental trial demonstrates positive effects of equine facilitated learning on child social competence. *Human Animal Interaction Bulletin, 1*(1): 1–19.

Pendry, P., Carr, A. M., Roeter, S. M., & Vandagriff, J. L. (under review). Improving college student emotional health and well-being through human-animal interaction.

Pendry, P., Carr, A. M., Smith, A. N., & Roeter, S. M. (2014). Improving adolescent social competence and behavior: A randomized trial of an 11-week equine facilitated learning prevention program. *Journal of Primary Prevention*, *35*: 281–293. doi: 10.1007/s10935-014-0350-7

Pendry. P., Smith, A. N., & Roeter, S. M. (2014). Randomized trial examines effects of equine facilitated learning on adolescents' basal cortisol levels. *Human Animal Interaction Bulletin*, *2*(1): 80–95.

Quirin, M., Kuhl, J., & Düsing, R. (2011). Oxytocin buffers cortisol responses to stress in individuals with impaired emotion regulation abilities. *Psychoneuroendocrinology*, *36*(6): 898–904. doi: 10.1016/j. psyneuen.2010.12.005

Rabiner, D. L., Coie, J. D., Miller-Johnson, S., Boykin, A. M., & Lochman, J. E. (2005). Predicting the persistence of aggressive offending of African American males from adolescence into young adulthood: The importance of peer relations, aggressive behavior, and ADHD symptoms. *Journal of Emotional and Behavioral Disorders*, *13*(3): 131–140. doi: 10.1177/10634266050130030101

Reschly, A. L., Huebner, E. S., Appleton, J. J. &, Antaramian, S. (2008). Engagement as flourishing: The contribution of positive emotions and coping to adolescents' engagement at school and with learning. *Psychology in the Schools*, *45*: 419–431. doi: 10.1002/pits.20306

Rockhill, C. M., Vander Stoep, A., McCauley, E., & Katon, W. J. (2009). Social competence and social support as mediators between comorbid depressive and conduct problems and functional outcomes in middle school children. *Journal of Adolescence*, *32*: 535–553. doi: 10.1016/j. adolescence.2008.06.011

Rubin, K. H., Root, A. K., & Bowker, J. (2010). Parents, peers, and social withdrawal in childhood: A relationship perspective. *New Directions for Child and Adolescent Development*, *2010*: 79–94. doi: 10.1002/cd.264

Sawka-Miller, K. D., & Miller, D. N. (2007). The third pillar: Linking positive psychology and school-wide positive behavior support. *School Psychology Forum: Research in Practice*, *2*: 26–38.

Selby, A., & Smith-Osborne, A. (2013). A systematic review of effectiveness of complementary and adjunct therapies and interventions involving equines. *Health Psychology*, *32*(4): 418–432. doi: 10.1037/a0029188

Sørlie, M. A., & Nordahl, T. (1998). *Problematferd i skolen. Hovedfunn, forklaringer og pedagogiske implikasjoner.* Rapport 12a. Oslo: NOVA

Sørlie, M., Hagen, K. A., & Ogden, T. (2008). Social competence and antisocial behavior: Continuity and distinctiveness across early adolescence. *Journal of Research on Adolescence, 18*: 121–144. doi: 10.1111/j.1532-7795.2008.00553.x

Tissen, I., Hergovich, A., & Spielg, C. (2007). School-based social training with and without dogs: Evaluation of their effectiveness. *Anthrozoös, 20*: 365–373. doi: 10.2752/089279307X245491

Topál, J., Miklósi, Á., Gácsi, M., Dóka, A., Pongrácz, P., Kubinyi, E., ... Csanyi, V. (2009). The dog as a model for understanding human social behavior. *Advances in the Study of Behavior, 39*: 71–116. doi: 10.1016/ S0065-3454(09)39003-8

Trotter, K. S., Chandler, C. K., Goodwin-Bond, D., & Casey, J. (2008). A comparative study of the efficacy of group equine assisted counseling with at-risk children and adolescents. *Journal of Creativity in Mental Health, 3*: 254–284. doi: 10.1080/15401380802356880

Wentzel, K. R. (1991). Relations between social competence and academic achievement in early adolescence. *Child Development, 62*: 1066–1078. doi: 10.1111/j.1467-8624.1991.tb01589.x

55

Do Animals in the Classroom Improve Learning, Attention, or Other Aspects of Cognition?

Karin Hediger, Nancy R. Gee, and James A. Griffin[1]

Introduction

The primary goal of teachers is to facilitate student learning, with cognitive performance being fundamental to students' ability to learn and to long-term academic achievement. How might the presence of an animal in the classroom enhance these factors, and what might the potential mechanisms be? Because of its importance for academic success, a growing number of interventions have been developed focusing on cognition and executive function skills. Increasingly, HAI and AAI are mentioned in the context of such interventions; integrating animals into the classroom is increasing in North America and Europe (see Chapter 1). This chapter examines research evidence, demonstrating that children have shown better motivation and improved outcomes on cognitive measures such as memory, attention, and categorization in the presence of animals.

Following that, we discuss possible psychophysiological mechanisms for these effects, and conclude with implications for practice and challenges for future research.

Evidence Regarding Cognition and Learning in the Presence of Animals

Cognition can be defined as a set of processes for acquiring knowledge (i.e., learning) and comprises mental abilities like perception, thought, and recognition. These, in turn, are composed of processes such as attention, working memory (WM), problem solving, access to existing knowledge, and decision-making, all necessary for academic success. For example, for students to learn a new piece of information they need to detect it (requiring sensory memory), focus on it (pay attention), and hold in mind the new piece of information (in WM) while comparing it to information learned previously and retained (long-term memory) in order to provide a framework for understanding the problem or information. At this point, aspects of task performance such as problem solving and decision-making become important, as students focus on goals and next steps in the process, and additional cognitive processes may be required depending upon the demands of the task. In the last two decades, research on effects of interacting with animals, or AAI, on human cognition has grown. Some of these studies, presented here by categories of cognitive tasks, provide the basis for discussing the impact of dogs on children's attention and cognition.

Categorization

Object categorization is a cognitive task in which one must group objects together based on their perceptual or functional characteristics (Blanchet, Dunham, & Dunham, 2001). Objects can be classified thematically based on a relationship, or taxonomically based on hierarchies or physical similarities (e.g., a thematic classification occurs if a child puts "dog" and "ball" into the same category, because they believe that dogs like to play with balls; a taxonomic classification occurs if "car" and "truck" are categorized together based on similar physical properties). Children are assumed to shift over time from reliance on a taxonomic strategy to more frequent use of a thematic classification strategy.

Gee, Church, and Altobelli (2010) implemented a randomized-controlled trial (RCT) with cross-over design using a match-to-sample task; preschool children were asked to categorize objects in the presence of a real dog, a stuffed toy dog, or a human. The predicted developmental shift described earlier was found (younger children making more taxonomic choices and older children more thematic choices), but most relevant to this discussion, the children made fewer errors overall in the presence of the real dog, relative to the stuffed toy dog or the human. The authors conclude that the presence of the dog doesn't alter typical performance patterns, but that the presence of the dog did have a positive impact on task performance.

To further investigate whether children categorize stimuli differently in the presence of a dog, Gee, Gould, Swanson, and Wagner (2012) conducted a randomized cross-over study involving either animate (e.g., cow) or inanimate (e.g., tractor) stimuli. Preschool children were asked to classify stimuli into appropriate environments (e.g., farm, beach, or circus). In general, children tend to be better at classifying animate objects relative to inanimate ones, but in this experiment that animation effect was amplified in the presence of a dog relative to a stuffed toy dog or a human. The authors conclude that this indicates the presence of a dog may be a highly salient stimulus that encourages the children to focus more attention on animate objects in the list, or it may help them restrict their attention to the demands of the task, or possibly both. Combined with the previous study (Gee, Church et al., 2010), it does seem to indicate that the presence of a dog impacts categorization performance.

Learning and Memory

The concepts of learning and memory are so intimately interconnected that it can be challenging to discuss one without reference to the other; it appears that even the brain has trouble distinguishing between the two given that the same underlying brain structure can be responsible for both. For example, learning is commonly accepted as the acquisition or modification of knowledge or skills, whereas memory commonly refers to the processes by which information is encoded, stored, and retrieved. Evidence indicates that the frontal lobes are responsible for acquisition and encoding of information along with some aspects of retrieval (Budson & Price, 2007). Rather than attempting to disentangle this extensive conceptual overlap, we discuss learning and memory together as they intersect with HAI and education.

If retention of information is the yardstick to measure learning and memory, there are few studies that investigate this topic in an HAI context. In a small ($N = 20$) randomized cross-over study, Gee,

Belcher, Grabski, DeJesus, and Riley (2012) used an object recognition task to examine the extent to which preschool children could recognize line drawings of objects (e.g., sailboat, fork, shoe) in the presence/absence of a dog. The children were asked to indicate the drawing they had been shown earlier, when it was presented along with 1–4 similar distractor drawings. The children recognized the studied objects faster and more accurately in the presence of the dog relative to the no-dog condition.

WM can be described as a cognitive workspace for information one is currently thinking about or processing. Using a digit span task to measure WM, Hediger and Turner (2014), comparing the performance of children in the presence of a real dog versus a robotic dog, found no general effect on children's WM performance. However, there was a significant increase in performance from the first to the second testing if the real dog was present the second time but not when the children started with the dog and the robotic dog was present the second time. A similar effect was found for measures of attention described in the attention section in this chapter.

Although not a direct measure of learning and memory, instructional prompts are one tool teachers use to varying degrees. Gee, Christ, and Carr (2010) examined the number and type of instructional prompts needed to complete an object recognition task. Using a randomized cross-over design in two separate experiments, although they found no differences in object recognition across groups, Gee and colleagues found that the children required fewer general instructional prompts (e.g., "face this way") and fewer task specific prompts (e.g., "pick one of these objects") in the presence of a real dog, relative to a stuffed toy dog or a human. There are several potential explanations, but at a basic level it is possible that the children were better able to hold task goals in memory when the dog was present.

Attention

Attention is the ability to selectively concentrate on specific information while ignoring other information. Studies indirectly assessing attention indicate that the presence of a dog can have positive effects on children's ability to pay attention during class or while performing a specific task. Kotrschal and Ortbauer (2003) demonstrated that the presence of a dog in an Austrian elementary classroom reduced overt activity, withdrawal, and aggressive interactions amongst the children. The group activities and positive social interactions appeared more often. Moreover, the children paid more attention to the teacher when the dog was present. The authors concluded that having a dog present in the classroom could be a positive stimulus for social cohesion and a cost-effective way to improve teaching conditions (Kotrschal & Ortbauer, 2003). In a small study, eight children with Down Syndrome were more responsive to adults when a dog was present compared to a toy dog, and directed more attention to the real dog (Limond, Bradshaw, & Cormack, 1997). Children in a psychiatric facility rated themselves as significantly more attentive, able to concentrate, and less distractible after interacting with a dog for 30 minutes (Prothmann, Bienert, & Ettrich, 2006).

To investigate whether this effect was present in a direct measure of attention performance, Hediger and Turner (2014) designed an RCT cross-over study with a non-clinical sample of school-aged children. Besides neuropsychological attention tests, a biological correlate of attention was assessed via passive infrared hemoencephalography. In a cancellation task, a significant performance increase from the first testing was found when the dog was present during the second session compared to when the robotic dog was present during the second session and the dog in the first. Interestingly, these results were not found in continuous performance or divided attention bimodal tasks. However, heat emission (reflecting higher brain activity) in the frontal lobe was significantly higher in the presence of the dog during all three tasks. Moreover, the robotic-dog group showed a reduction in heat emission during the third (divided attention bimodal) task.

Executive Function and Motivation

Level of student engagement in cognitive processes, and ultimate performance of all learning-related tasks, are often impacted by the level of executive function (EF) skills and motivation. Although there is no single accepted definition of EF (Griffin, McCardle, Freund, DelCarmen-Wiggins, & Haydon, 2016), it is clear that students need creativity, flexibility, self-control, and discipline to success in school, skills that include mentally playing with ideas, giving a considered rather than an impulsive response, and being able to change perspective as needed, as well as remaining focused and resisting distractions (Diamond, 2016). These core EF skills, critical for cognitive, social, and psychological development, begin to emerge in infancy but continue to mature into young adulthood. So called "hot" EF is associated with learning involving motivators or feelings (e.g., rewards or punishment), whereas "cold" EF tends to be associated with rote learning and logic problems (e.g., memorization or mental puzzles) (Diamond, 2016). Although few HAI studies have explicitly examined EF as an outcome measure, there are promising results suggesting that AAI may positively impact EF skills (Borgi et al., 2015; Schuck, Emmerson, Fine, & Lakes, 2015).

Motivation is a psychological construct that represents the reasons for people's desires, needs, and actions. Recently, motivational theory has been associated with AAI. Olbrich (2009) asserted that the presence of animals may enhance implicit motives and increase the congruence between implicit and explicit motives or goals in performance and learning situations. Wohlfarth and colleagues showed that non-declarative measures can be positively influenced by AAI (Wohlfarth, Mutschler, Beetz, Kreuser, & Korsten-Reck, 2013); obese children showed more physical activity in the presence of a dog compared to the presence of a friendly person. The authors proposed that the dog triggered implicitly enhanced motivation because it served as an affectively hot stimulus. This suggests that animals could provide a way of stimulating children's implicit motivation in a classroom context.

Species-related Effects

Although classrooms may include a broad variety of species, all of the RCTs presented thus far have focused on the effects of dogs. However, O'Haire and colleagues investigated the effects of classroom-based HAIs involving guinea pigs. O'Haire, McKenzie, McCune, and Slaughter (2013) reported an eight-week program with 128 typically developing children in kindergarten through seventh grade. They found that social functioning was enhanced compared to a waitlist control but there was no effect on academic competence. In a study with children with autism spectrum disorder, the same program also led to higher social functioning (O'Haire, McKenzie, McCune, & Slaughter, 2014) – these effects are discussed in Chapter 4. Given that socio-emotional skills are a relevant prerequisite for academic functioning (Nix, Bierman, Domitrovich, & Gill, 2013), it seems clear that if animals contribute to an improved overall classroom environment they can positively affect learning. However, answering the question of how different animals might differentially affect children's cognition is not possible yet. The discussed studies with guinea pigs give promising insights, but clearly, more research is necessary to assess the impact of different animals on cognitive performance skills.

Age-related Effects

There is no systematic research on age-dependent effects of animals in children, but research on adults suggests that there may be a biological correlate of the effects of animals on children's cognitive processes. While AAIs are conducted for college students, older people in residential settings, and in dementia programs, there has been little cognition-based research in adults. Böttger and colleagues demonstrated increased cerebral activity in the visu-attentional brain network in 12 healthy volunteers aged 23–47 years while viewing moving animals compared to optokinetic computer stimuli (Böttger et al., 2010). A possible explanation is the "animate monitoring hypothesis," that animals elicit stronger spontaneous recruitment of attention than inanimate objects (New, Cosmides, & Tooby, 2007). Böttger also reported (2008) that in single-case studies of patients with severe left-sided neglect after a stroke, domestic animals had a higher effect on the perception of the neglected hemispace compared to optokinetic computer stimuli. Given all of the evidence presented, we now examine possible mechanisms underlying the effects of HAI on human cognitive processes.

Possible Psychophysiological Mechanisms

Several possible mechanisms may explain the impact of animals – and in particular dogs – on human cognition (Hediger & Turner, 2014). First, physiological changes may play an important role, including the hormones dopamine and oxytocin and the influence of dogs on the human stress-response system.

An often postulated mechanism is the stress-reducing effect of dogs. Since stress hinders learning (e.g., Wolf, Bauser, & Daum, 2011), this hypothesis could explain why learning is enhanced in the presence of a dog. Cortisol, which has dose-dependent negative effects on memory and attention (e.g., Het, Ramlow, & Wolf, 2005), may play a key role. Interacting with dogs can reduce human cortisol levels in stressful situations (Beetz et al., 2011; Odendaal & Meintjes, 2003) but also improves cardiovascular parameters such as heart rate and blood pressure (Allen, Blascovich, & Mendes, 2002; Levine et al., 2013). The resulting physical calmness might be indirectly enhancing cognition. Oxytocin is also discussed as an underlying mechanism for providing this stress-reducing effect (Beetz, Uvnäs-Moberg, Julius, & Kotrschal, 2012).

However, an accumulation of evidence suggests that interacting with an animal can also have activating rather than calming effects in different populations, potentially resulting in task performance improvement (Friedmann & Gee, Chapter 8, this volume). In their discussion of optimal arousal to achieve optimal performance, Friedmann and Gee discuss the effects of animals on the human stress-response system and the role that physical contact with an animal may play in mediating the response.

As noted, the "animate monitoring hypothesis" (New et al., 2007) presents another possible underlying biopsychological mechanism, that throughout evolution the human visual attention-system has been trained to scan the environment for animals and other humans. Moreover, animals in general seem to elicit greater interest in children than non-living objects (e.g., young children interact with animals more often than with toys and engage more with the animals; Lobue, Bloom Pickard, Sherman, Axford, & DeLoache, 2013). Borgi and colleagues, investigating the cognitive and psychological mechanisms underlying infants' attraction to animals, found that the baby schema affects both cuteness perception and gaze allocation (Borgi, Cogliati-Dezza, Brelsford, Meints, & Cirulli, 2014).

Clearly, psychological mechanisms also play an important role and may be linked with physiological changes. As discussed earlier, the presence of an animal can stimulate children's curiosity and intrinsic motivation to learn. Research supports the hypothesis that animals are perceptually interesting, especially to young children, and sustain their attention. The perceptual characteristics of living animals may stimulate children's learning, and learning is optimized in the context of meaningful relationships (Melson, 2003). In fact, children establish meaningful relationships with animals that provide relevant emotional and social support (McNicholas & Collis, 2006; Rost & Hartmann, 1994). Given the data supporting the connection between children's social relations with teachers and peers and their cognitive and academic performance, these relations have the potential to enhance the children's cognitive processes. Children's feeling supported by a present dog while solving a task (Hediger & Turner, 2014) might lead to better learning or academic performance, especially given animals are non-evaluative, which can increase the perception of helpful support and be an important stress-reducing element (Dickerson & Kemeny, 2004). Moreover, the presence of an animal such as a dog may alter perception of the environment (Wells & Perrine, 2001) and improve the atmosphere in a classroom, a central factor for children's cognitive and socio-emotional development and academic success. Also, the presence of a dog can change a therapeutic setting, so that children who under normal circumstances would refuse to join therapy may engage.

63

Implications for Practice

Integrating dogs into therapeutic settings or classrooms often leads to discussion of whether the dog will be a distractor, although there is no evidence of possible negative aspects of animals in classrooms on children's attention or cognition performance. Some research does suggest that quality of performance across a variety of tasks does not decrease when a dog is present (e.g., Allen, 2003; Gee, Christ et al., 2010; Gee, Church et al., 2010).

The existing results suggest that the presence of, and interaction with, a dog might enhance children's cognitive processes. Animals provide a perceptually captivating and often emotionally meaningful object of attention that may stimulate learning in children (O'Haire et al., 2013). Thus the presence of animals in education settings can have a preventive as well as therapeutic potential regarding children at risk for academic failure (Hediger & Beetz, 2015). We note that in the studies presented involving dogs, the animals were well-trained and often were registered therapy dogs or school-dogs. Clearly agitated and anxious animals, especially dogs, can lead to negative and distracting effects, or worse. However, different classroom pets or visiting animals will require differential levels of care and attention (see Chapter 13). We stress the importance of respecting the animal's care, housing, and general well-being, and recommend care in selecting the appropriate type of animal for any education setting or activity (see Chapters 13 and 14).

It remains unclear whether children with cognition deficits profit more from HAI than typically developing children. Several intervention studies have demonstrated promising effects related to AAIs for children with ADHD or ASD (see Chapters 6 and 7).

Conclusion and Outlook

Basic research regarding the impact of animals on children's cognition has yielded promising results. Many questions remain unanswered and represent exciting areas for additional studies. The effects on different cognitive functions should systematically be investigated. Further research should also address the extent to which effects vary in different age groups, socio-economic backgrounds, or diagnoses. Most research to date has been with dogs; there are rich opportunities for exploring the effects of other animals. Beyond these basics, translational research is also required (McCune et al., 2015). For example, what "dose" leads to effects in AAI in the classroom remains unknown.

Although some results suggest that the amount of time of interacting and attachment to a dog might influence stress-regulating effects, there is no research relating this to children's cognition. Also, the concrete circumstances that could lead to positive effects in practice need to be identified; is it simply the presence of an animal or direct contact with the animal that contributes to enhancing effects on cognition? Moreover, research is needed regarding possible differential effects on cognition and attention for HAIs with visiting dogs compared to one's own dog.

Note

1   The views expressed in this chapter are those of the authors and do not necessarily represent those of the National Institutes of Health, *Eunice Kennedy Shriver* National Institute of Child Health and Human Development, or the US Department of Health and Human Services.

References

Allen, K. (2003). Are pets a healthy pleasure? The influence of pets on blood pressure. *Current Directions in Psychological Science, 12*(6): 236–239.

Allen, K., Blascovich, J., & Mendes, W. B. (2002). Cardiovascular reactivity and the presence of pets, friends, and spouses: The truth about cats and dogs. *Psychosomatic Medicine, 64*(5): 727–739.

Beetz, A., Kotrschal, K., Turner, D. C., Hediger, K., Uvnäs-Moberg, K., & Julius, H. (2011). The effect of a real dog, toy dog and friendly person on insecurely attached children during a stressful task: An exploratory study. *Anthrozoös, 24*(4): 349–368.

Beetz, A., Uvnäs-Moberg, K., Julius, H., & Kotrschal, K. (2012). Psychosocial and psychophysiological effects of human-animal interactions: The possible role of oxytocin. *Frontiers in Psychology, 3*: 234–248.

Blanchet, N., Dunham, P. J., & Dunham, F. (2001). Differences in preschool children's conceptual strategies when thinking about animate entities and artifacts. *Developmental Psychology, 37*(6): 791–800.

Borgi, M., Cogliati-Dezza, I., Brelsford, V., Meints, K., & Cirulli, F. (2014). Baby schema in human and animal faces induces cuteness perception and gaze allocation in children. *Frontiers in Psychology, 5*: 411.

Borgi, M., Loliva, D., Cerino, S., Chiarotti, F., Venerosi, A., Bramini, M., … Circulli, F. (2015). Effectiveness of a standardized equine-assisted therapy program for children with autism spectrum disorder. *Journal of Autism and Developmental Disorders, 46*: 1–9.

Böttger, S. (2008). Neurologische Frührehabilitation von Funktion und Emotion mit Hilfe der tiergestützten Therapie. *Ergotherapie & Rehabilitation, 47*: 17–20.

Böttger, S., Haberl, R., Prosiegel, M., Audebert, H., Rumberg, B., Forsting, M., ... Gizewski, E. R. (2010). Differences in cerebral activation during perception of optokinetic computer stimuli and video clips of living animals: An fMRI study. *Brain Research, 1354*: 132–139.

Budson, A. E., & Price, B. H. (2007). Memory dysfunction in neurological practice. *Practical Neurology, 7*: 42–47.

Diamond, A. (2016). Why improving and assessing executive functions early in life is critical. In J. A. Griffin, P. McCardle, & L. S. Freund (Eds.), *Executive function in preschool-age children: Integrating measurement, neurodevelopment, and translational research* (pp. 11–43). Washington, DC: American Psychological Association.

Dickerson, S. S., & Kemeny, M. E. (2004). Acute stressors and cortisol responses: A theoretical integration and synthesis of laboratory research. *Psychological Bulletin, 130*(3): 355–391.

Gee, N. R., Belcher, J., Grabski, J., DeJesus, M., & Riley, W. (2012). The presence of a therapy dog results in improved object recognition performance in preschool children. *Anthrozoös, 25*: 289–300.

Gee, N. R., Christ, E. M., & Carr, D. N. (2010). Preschool children require fewer instructional prompts to perform a memory task in the presence of a dog. *Anthrozoös, 23*(2): 173–184.

Gee, N. R., Church, M. T., & Altobelli, C. L. (2010). Preschoolers make fewer errors on an object categorization task in the presence of a dog. *Anthrozoös, 23*(3): 223–230.

Gee, N. R., Gould, J. K., Swanson, C. C., & Wagner, A. K. (2012). Preschoolers categorize animate objects better in the presence of a dog. *Anthrozoös, 25*: 187–198.

Griffin, J. A., Freund, L. S., McCardle, P., DelCarmen-Wiggins, R., & Haydon, A. (2016). Introduction to Executive Function in Preschool-Age Children. In J. A. Griffin, P. McCardle, & L. S. Freund (Eds.), *Executive function in preschool-age children: Integrating measurement, neurodevelopment, and translational research* (pp. 3–7). Washington, DC: American Psychological Association.

Hediger, K., & Beetz, A. (2015). The role of human-animal interaction in education. In J. Zinsstag, E. Schelling, D. Waltner-Toews, M. Whittaker,

& M. Tanner (Eds.), *One health. The theory and practice of integrated health approaches* (pp. 73–84). Oxford: CABI International.

Hediger, K., & Turner, D. C. (2014). Can dogs enhance children's attention performance? A randomized controlled cross-over trial. *Human-Animal Interaction Bulletin, 2*(2): 21–39.

Het, S., Ramlow, G., & Wolf, O. T. (2005). A meta-analytic review of the effects of acute cortisol administration on human memory. *Psychoneuroendocrinology, 30*(8): 771–784.

Kotrschal, K., & Ortbauer, B. (2003). Behavioral effects of the presence of a dog in a classroom. *Anthrozoös, 16*(2): 147–159.

Levine, G. N., Allen, K., Braun, L. T., Christian, H. E., Friedmann, E., Taubert, K. A., … Lange, R. A. (2013). Pet ownership and cardiovascular risk: A scientific statement from the American heart association. *Circulation, 127*(23): 2353–2363.

Limond, J. A., Bradshaw, J. W. S., & Cormack, K. F. M. (1997). Behavior of children with learning disabilities interacting with a therapy dog. *Anthrozoös, 10*(2–3): 84–89.

Lobue, V., Bloom Pickard, M., Sherman, K., Axford, C., & DeLoache, J. S. (2013). Young children's interest in live animals. *British Journal of Developmental Psychology, 31*(Pt 1): 57–69.

McCune, S., Kruger, K. A., Griffin, J. A., Esposito, L., Freund, L. S., Bures, R., … Gee, N. R. (2015). Strengthening the foundation of human-animal interaction research: Recent developments in a rapidly-growing field. In A. H. Fine (Ed.), *Handbook on animal-assisted therapy, fourth edition: Foundations and guidelines for animal-assisted interventions* (pp. 408–413). San Diego, CA: Academic Press.

McNicholas, J., & Collis, G. M. (2006). Animal as social supports: Insights for understanding animal-assisted therapy. Theoretical foundations and guidelines for practice. In A. H. Fine (Ed.), *Handbook on animal-assisted therapy. Theoretical foundations and guidelines for practice* (2nd edn, pp. 49–71). San Diego, CA: Elsevier.

Melson, G. F. (2003). Child development and the human-companion animal bond. *American Behavioral Scientist, 47*(1): 31–39.

New, J., Cosmides, L., & Tooby, J. (2007). Category-specific attention for animals reflects ancestral priorities, not expertise. *Proceedings of the National Acaddemy of Sciences USA, 104*(42): 16598–16603.

Nix, R. L., Bierman, K. L., Domitrovich, C. E., & Gill, S. (2013). Promoting children's social-emotional skills in preschool can enhance academic and behavioral functioning in kindergarten: Findings from Head Start REDI. *Early Education and Development, 24*(7): 1000–1019.

67

Odendaal, J. S., & Meintjes, R. A. (2003). Neurophysiological correlates of affiliative behaviour between humans and dogs. *The Veterinary Journal, 165*(3): 296–301.

O'Haire, M. E., McKenzie, S. J., McCune, S., & Slaughter, V. (2013). Effects of animal-assisted activities with guinea pigs in the primary school classroom. *Anthrozoös, 26*(3): 445–458.

O'Haire, M. E., McKenzie, S. J., McCune, S., & Slaughter, V. (2014). Effects of classroom animal-assisted activities on social functioning in children with autism spectrum disorder. *Journal of Alternative and Complementary Medicine, 20*(3): 162–168.

Olbrich, E. (2009). Bausteine einer Theorie der Mensch-Tier-Beziehung. In C. Otterstedt & M. Rosenberger (Eds.), *Gefährten–Konkurrenten–Verwandte. Die Mensch-Tier-Beziehung im wissenschaftlichen Diskurs* (pp. 159–181). Göttingen, Germany: Vandenhoeck and Ruprecht.

Prothmann, A., Bienert, M., & Ettrich, C. (2006). Dogs in child psychotherapy: Effects on state of mind *Anthrozoös, 19*(3): 265–277.

Rost, D. H., & Hartmann, A. (1994). Children and their pets. *Anthrozoös, 7*(4): 242–254.

Schuck, S. E., Emmerson, N., Fine, A. H., & Lakes, K. D. (2015). Canine assisted therapy for children with ADHD: Preliminary findings from the positive assertive cooperative kids study. *Journal of Attention Disorders, 19*(2): 125–137.

Wells, M., & Perrine, R. (2001). Pets go to college: The influence of pets on students' perceptions of faculty and their offices. *Anthrozoös, 14*(3): 161–168.

Wohlfarth, R., Mutschler, B., Beetz, A., Kreuser, F., & Korsten-Reck, U. (2013). Dogs motivate obese children for physical activity: Key elements of a motivational theory of animal-assisted interventions. *Frontiers in Psychology, 4*: 796.

Wolf, O. T., Bauser, D. S., & Daum, I. (2011). Eyeblink conditional discrimination learning in healthy young men is impaired after stress exposure. *Psychophysiology, 49*(2): 164–171.

CHAPTER 6

School-based Animal-Assisted Interventions for Children with Deficits in Executive Function

Sabrina E. B. Schuck and Aubrey H. Fine

Introduction

Many neurodevelopmental disorders of childhood are characterized by impaired executive function (EF), or, more specifically, deficits in inhibition, shifting mental set, and working memory. Attention-Deficit/Hyperactivity Disorder (ADHD) is the most commonly occurring neurodevelopmental disorder, affecting approximately 5% of school-age children in the US (Farone, Sergeant, Gillberg, & Biederman, 2003). ADHD is considered to be a result of a physiological disruption of dopaminergic systems resulting in impaired EF (Godinez et al., 2015). In addition to ADHD, other disorders including oppositional defiant disorder (ODD), specific learning disorder (SLD; e.g., dyslexia, dyscalculia), and autism spectrum disorder (ASD) all present with deficits in skills requiring EF. Impaired EF is associated with lifelong adverse outcomes and therefore developing interventions that will help to mitigate this impairment is indicated.

Although many do not consider deficits in EF to be serious or life-threatening, students who manifest such difficulties in school often experience what we refer to as "collateral damage" along the course of their education and across their life. They are at greater risk for oppositional behavior, impaired social interactions, school failure, and problems with the law (Estes, Rivera, Bryan, Cali, & Dawson, 2011; Grzadzinski et al., 2011; Satterfield et al., 2007; Simonoff et al., 2011). Despite intact intellect, approximately 30% of children with ADHD fail to complete high school compared to 15% of their typically developing peers (Breslau, Miller, Chung, & Schweitzer, 2011). A longitudinal multi-modal treatment study of children with ADHD revealed that, regardless of interventions received, individuals with ADHD were at significantly greater risk for substance abuse than their typically developing peers eight years later (Molina et al., 2013).

While the prevalence of children with disorders of EF is relatively low in the general population, these children likely comprise the vast majority of the school-age children eligible for special education services under the Individuals with Disabilities Education Act (2004) in the US. Since the early 1980s, a proportionately greater number of these children has been found eligible each year (Kotkin & Fine, 2003). The impact of these conditions, as a whole, on the educational system and the classroom setting is exceptionally taxing on teachers and staff. In efforts to address this growing burden, Positive Behavioral Interventions in Schools (PBIS) programs have been widely implemented across the US (Sugai & Horner, 2002). These programs aim to improve outcomes for children with high-incidence disabilities, such as disorders of EF, by providing a tiered behavior intervention system in public schools. Key elements include primary or Tier 1 school-wide prevention programs; secondary or Tier 2 interventions with daily behavior contracts and group socials skills training; and tertiary or Tier 3 intervention strategies consisting of functional behavioral analysis and individualized intervention implemented as school-based mental health services.

Animals in Schools

Evidence for the biological basis of HAI and how that interaction may contribute to well-being has been described by numerous investigators (Freund, McCune, Esposito, Gee, & McCardle, 2016). Recent rigorous empirical studies provide evidence supporting the claim that HAI may have specific benefits for typically developing youth, especially in classrooms (Gee, Church, & Altobelli, 2010; Gee, Crist, & Carr, 2010; le Roux, Swartz, & Swart, 2014; O'Haire, Mckenzie, McCune, & Slaughter, 2013). Less is known about how AAI may impact special populations.

Over the past five years we have conducted a large-scale random-ized clinical trial examining the safety and efficacy of implementing canine-assisted interventions (CAI) with children with ADHD in an after-school setting (Schuck, Emmerson, Fine, & Lakes, 2015). We developed a standardized protocol for CAI and aimed to treat those EF deficits thought most likely to impair social relationships for these children: cognitive under-arousal and poor self-regulation. We identi-fied a number of commonly shared anecdotal reports of HAI that we posit contribute to three overarching hypotheses related to the effi-cacy of CAI with children: (1) dogs mitigate physiological stress reac-tions; (2) dogs prime cognitive arousal; and (3) interaction with dogs improves self-regulation and facilitates its generalizability.

There is extensive literature supporting the role of AAI practices in reducing physiological stress responses and emotional distress in general populations (e.g., reduced salivary cortisol, lowered heart rate) (e.g., Barker, Knisely, McCain, Schubert, & Pandurangi, 2010; Friedmann, Thomas, Son, Chapa, & McCune, 2013; Gee, Friedmann, Stendahl, Fisk, & Coglitore, 2014; Krause-Parello, & Friedmann, 2014; Melson, 2003). These findings suggest the presence of an animal may reduce stress and allow anxious or over-stimulated children to better focus, perhaps as a byproduct of a euthymic state. There are fewer studies examining how animals may elicit cognitive arousal in chil-dren, especially children with ADHD – a condition commonly asso-ciated with sluggish cognitive tempo (Lahey, Schaughency, Hynd, Carlson, & Nieves, 1987; Neeper & Lahey, 1986) – and there are even fewer studies examining the use of dog-training programs aimed at generalizing improved self-regulation acquired from social skills training programs.

In this chapter, we describe theoretical constructs we believe con-tribute to the efficacy of these less studied ideas: (1) dogs prime or optimize cognitive arousal, and (2) enhance access to traditional therapies for children with disorders of EF, thereby (3) making them ideal for promoting generalization of social and behavioral treatment gains. Additionally, we discuss how dogs can feasibly and safely accompany and assist educators and other school personnel (e.g., counselors, speech-language pathologists, occupational therapists) in real-world school-based settings with special populations.

Practical Applications for Children with Deficits of EF

Animals: A Catalyst for Optimal Arousal

Traditional theories of learning indicate that cognitive or mental arousal must be optimal (i.e., not over- or under-aroused) in order for learning to take place (Yerkes & Dodson, 1908). Teachers and parents anecdotally note that animals seem to motivate children to perform otherwise avoided tasks, acting as a catalyst for improving engagement and sustained attention in difficult and/or non-preferred tasks. As noted earlier, many children with ADHD present with a sluggish cognitive tempo and a lack of motivation thought to be caused by dysregulation of the sub-cortical neurological pathways, particularly the dopaminergic systems, resulting in poor EF or dysregulated mental arousal more than primary distractibility (Diamond, 2006; Leopold et al., 2016; Luman, Oosterlaan, & Sergeant, 2005; Tomasi & Volkow, 2012). For these children, distractibility may be simply a reflection of inability to keep task-relevant information in the forefront of consciousness and/or the inability to screen out irrelevancies – both EF skills that are dependent on optimal arousal levels. Arousal, then, is the energic element of the executive control processes. We theorize that arousal stimulated by the presence of the dog makes the child (a) more aware of the salient features of her or his surroundings; (b) more energetic in screening out irrelevancies; and (c) more likely to preserve task-relevant information in the forefront of consciousness, which facilitates learning.

The relative effectiveness of EF is dependent on the physiological capacity to achieve and maintain optimal arousal levels, thereby providing the necessary energetic substrate for sustaining attention, completing tasks, and monitoring outcomes as one adapts to myriad environmental challenges. Each specific EF, whether working memory, shifting and/or maintaining a mental set, inhibiting erroneous responses, or emotional self-regulation, will be constrained by the degree to which arousal is optimized. We posit that the sensory stimulation associated with HAI contributes to eliciting arousal of sub-cortical systems thought to be necessary for capturing and sustaining attention, the metaphorical "hook" for pulling a child into a learning experience. We theorize, interaction with a dog acts as a proxy for a neural exercise in ways similar to the strategies implemented in mindfulness training, thereby optimizing cognitive stamina.

The relations among emotion, motivation, and attention/learning processes have been well described (e.g., Kilpatrick & Cahill, 2003; Phelps, 2006). Dodge and Rabiner's (2004) article, "Returning to roots: On social information processing and moral development", captures the essence of why we believe animals are likely to help special populations of children:

Borrowing from Piaget (1962, 1973) and Cowan (1978, 1982), I propose that all information processing is emotional, in that emotion is the energy level that drives, organizes, amplifies, and attenuates cognitive activity and in turn is the experience and expression of this activity. There is no such act that is nonemotional.

Dodge (1991, p. 159)

As noted, there is thought to be a unique regulation of cognitive and emotional arousal in the presence of a dog that seems to be capable of enhancing learning and cognitive performance. Theoretically, as novel stimuli, AAIs may "prime" children for learning by optimizing arousal, leading to improved attention and engagement. Given the important role of emotion in learning, it may well be that integrating animals into academic environments, especially for those individuals with EF deficits, could generate the acquisition of attentional skills sufficient to support improved academic performance. This may be true for all individuals but may be especially applicable for children with atypical neurodevelopment, whose attention challenges may pose special limitations on academic performance.

HAI during instruction may in fact be perceived as a reward or "hook" that elicits engagement via heightened arousal. For typically developing children, when dogs were integrated into classrooms, the children demonstrated fewer behavior difficulties and stayed on task for longer periods (Kotrschal & Ortbauer, 2003). Just the presence of an animal in instructional settings seems to contribute to a shift in autonomic arousal toward a more euthymic state, optimizing arousal necessary to support EF. For typically developing children, when dogs were integrated into classrooms, the children demonstrated fewer behavior difficulties and stayed on task for longer periods (Kotrschal & Ortbauer, 2003). Benefits of AAI relevant to school success for special populations range from improved attention and cognitive performance to improved social skills and decreased problem behavior (Gabriels et al., 2015; O'Haire, McKenzie, McCune, & Slaughter, 2014;

Schuck et al., 2015). These phenomena are also discussed in greater detail in Chapters 5 and 8.

Specifically, the acts of reading and writing to a registered therapy dog as a captive audience are thought to elicit engagement and allow a child to more easily access instructional tasks that they may consider boring or too hard – both hallmarks of EF deficits. Based on elements of the Reading Education Assistance Dogs program of the Intermountain Therapy Animals organization (Intermountain Therapy Animals, n.d.), in which children read aloud to dogs in small groups, we implemented a semi-structured reading and writing time in Project P.A.C.K. Small groups of 2–3 children were paired with a live dog (or the comparison group) and handler (or counselor) to read animal-themed books aloud to the dog/toy; children also kept a journal in which they wrote to the dog as the intended audience. We found children with ADHD who read with live animals showed improved attention earlier in treatment relative to those not exposed to live dogs, with significant differences between groups eight weeks into treatment (Schuck et al., under review).

Animal Interaction: A Mechanism for Generalizing Social and Behavioral Treatment Gains

74

Social skills training and behavioral parent training programs are the most empirically supported non-pharmacological interventions for children with ADHD (Pelham & Fabiano, 2008). Perhaps one of the greatest problems with these programs, however, is the poor real-world generalizability of therapeutic gains in self-regulation made in the treatment setting. Humane education "not only instills the desire and capacity to live with compassion, integrity, and wisdom, but as a process, it also provides the knowledge and tools to put our values into action in meaningful and far reaching ways" (Institute for Humane Education, n.d.). Humane education also encourages the practice of valuing all living things (National Humane Education Society, n.d.). To maximize AAI, interventions should not occur in isolation of children's natural settings (e.g., school). Similar to best practice guidelines for other psychosocial interventions, AAI is most effective when implemented across environments (Eber, Sugai, Smith, & Scott, 2002). For treatment to optimally generalize, the more similar the training setting is to the child's every day environment, the more likely that behavior will be elicited across settings. Proponents of humane education programs argue that the social/character skills learned (e.g., respect, kindness, compassion) are easily generalized across settings and support the use of these programs in primary education (Ascione, 1997; George, 1999). Research supports that animal-based humane education activities could be specifically helpful in generalizing human-directed empathy in children and sustaining treatment gains (Paul, 2000).

Several specific strategies for enhancing perspective-taking skills and social competence and reducing problem behaviors are implemented in schools and communities today where AAI can easily blend. Specifically, peer mentoring has been found to support social skills in elementary school students with ADHD (DuPaul, Ervin, Hook, & McGoey, 1998). Teaching humane practices with animals can very naturally be incorporated with traditional social skills training and even the Tier 3 behavior interventions of PBIS described earlier. Animals present children with immediate and consistent non-verbal feedback. Caring for an animal in an instructional setting may teach self-regulation by means of non-verbal communication that occurs with HAI; the dog observes the child's behavior and communicates approval/disapproval through sensory cues.

Dog-training programs appear to support social development and demonstrate improved perspective-taking skills (Arluke, 2007). Helping others in an instructional format can be a viable therapeutic treatment for social skill development in itself (Ascher, 1988; Musick & Wilson, 2008), and students acting as mentors often communicate better and achieve a clearer sense of identity and introspective skills (Ginsburg-Block, Rohrbeck, Fantuzzo, & Lavigne, 2006). Similarly, children with ADHD who participate in peer mentoring programs show significant improvement in numerous academic and pro-social behaviors (Plumer & Stoner, 2005). Furthermore, feedback by instructors and parents promotes skills generalization and encourages maintenance of mastered skills, as with Reciprocal Peer Tutoring.

Having adolescents act as trainers/mentors to dogs seems to have promise in this regard for all children, but may be especially effective for children with ADHD. The Project P.A.C.K. training model was built on the assumption that children could benefit from mentoring as an activity by teaching an animal, that providing a 1:1 (child:dog) training experience with direct instructor feedback, and parental support, would enhance social skills and generalization across settings. There are numerous dog-training programs for US youth; for most, the major instructional goal is enhancing psychosocial development, which can then transfer to other life activities. Usually, sessions focus on positive dog-training techniques and animal care; some go beyond this and address issues such as anger management, frustration

75

tolerance, conflict resolution, and reflection with journal writing. In select residential treatment programs, boys presenting with mild behavior problems were engaged in raising puppies in training to be service dogs; many of the boys demonstrated numerous pro-social skills as a consequence (Fine, Dennis, & Bowers, 2011). Arluke (2007) evaluated dog-training programs in five settings treating teens at risk for incarceration, all of whose major goals were to provide the opportunity to act as mentors and teachers for the animals to build character and responsibility.

Similar to the theories underpinning *peer mentoring* strategies and programs for special populations in schools, we posit that by providing one-to-one semi-structured opportunities to interact with a registered therapy dog in the instructional setting will allow for a natural child-animal bond to develop that will foster social competence in that setting. Similarly, we suggest that teaching *humane education* in the context of these HAIs offers children opportunities to implement related humane practices *in vivo*, thereby supporting the generalization of learned social skills and reduced problem behaviors at school. Influenced by constructs integral to *peer mentoring* and *humane education*, Project P.A.C.K.'s *How to be a Good Teacher* dog training program was developed specifically to improve social skills, reduce problematic behaviors, and support their generalization through school-based one-to-one canine-child bonding opportunities. For Project P.A.C.K., the children had to follow a specific format in their dog-training activities and were given organized feedback from staff to supplement the feedback naturally obtained from the child-dog interaction. Additionally, humane education activities were integrated to teach children about dog behavior and care. Preliminary data indicate more enhanced pro-social skills and reduced problem behaviors in the live-dog groups, and greater gains relative to the comparison group (Schuck et al., 2015).

Summary

In examining the relationship of anecdotal observations, hypothesized actions, related intervention aims, and respective practical applications about AAIs thought to be safe and effective for use in schools for children with ADHD and related challenges, we conclude that the literature supports three very specific AAIs found to benefit children with deficits of EF (see Table 6.1).

Specifically, 1) the simple presence of a well-screened registered therapy animal can reduce stress in the learning environment – especially for children impaired by hyper-sensory stimulation. 2) For

Table 6.1 Proposed mechanisms of AAI in school settings

Anecdotal reports	Theoretical action	Aim of intervention	School-based AAI application
"Children are less worried when animals are around"	Animals mitigate stress	Reduce fears and anxiety	Animal present in classroom/intervention setting
"Children seem less stressed out when animals are around"	Animals mediate stress	Increase relaxation and improve mood	Animal present in classroom/intervention setting
"Kids seem less active in the presence of an animal"	Animals prime mental arousal; animals elicit engagement and motivation	Self-regulation; reduce hyperactivity/impulsivity	Animal incorporated in instructional lesson
"Kids seem to do better at academic tasks in the presence of an animal"	Animals prime mental arousal, improve cognitive skills, especially EF	Optimize learning; improve attention	Child reads to animal, writes journal/letters to animal
"Animals improve the social milieu of group activities like peer to peer mentoring"	Animals act as non-verbal feedback	Improve generalization of social skills: social competence, relationships, empathy	Humane education
"Taking care of animals makes kids more responsible"	Animals act as non-verbal feedback	Improve generalization of self-efficacy, patience, self-empowerment, and reduce problem behaviors	Child: animal training with humane education

children impaired by sluggish cognitive tempo, when the dog is incorporated directly in instruction, cognitive arousal is primed for optimal learning. 3) The non-verbal feedback provided by dogs can enhance traditional social skills training programs and better support generalization when coupled with AAIs and one-to-one dog/puppy training. Including dogs in educational settings can potentially improve outcomes for children with ADHD, a population historically very difficult to engage in the classroom.

References

Arluke, A. (2007). Mechanisms of change: An introductory ethnography of five programs. Paper presented at The National Technology Assessment Workshop on Animal Assisted Programs for Youth At Risk and Incarcerated Children and Young Adults. December 6–7, 2007, Baltimore, Maryland.

Ascher, C. (1988). The mentoring of disadvantaged youth. *ERIC Clearinghouse on Urban Education (47)*. New York: ERIC Digests.

Ascione, F. R. (1997). Humane education research: Evaluating efforts to encourage children's kindness and caring toward animals. *Genetic, Social, and General Psychology Monographs, 123*: 59–77.

Barker, S. B., Knisely, J. S., McCain, N. L., Schubert, C. M., & Pandurangi, A. K. (2010). Exploratory study of stress-buffering response patterns from interaction with a therapy dog. *Anthrozoös, 23*(1): 79–91. doi: http://dx.doi.org/10.2752/175303710X12627079939341

Breslau, J., Miller, E., Chung, W.-J., & Schweitzer, J. B. (2011). Childhood and adolescent onset psychiatric disorders, substance use, and failure to graduate high school on time. *Journal of Psychiatric Research, 45*(3): 295–301. doi: http://dx.doi.org/10.1016/j.jpsychires.2010.06.014

Diamond, A. (2006). The early development of executive functions. In E. Bialystok & F. I. M. Craik (Eds.), *Lifespan cognition: Mechanisms of change* (pp. 70–95). New York: Oxford University Press.

Dodge, K. A. (1991). Emotion and social information processing. In J. Garber & K. A. Dodge (Eds.), *The development of emotion regulation and dysregulation* (pp. 159–181). New York: Cambridge University Press. doi: http://dx.doi.org/10.1017/CBO9780511663963.009

Dodge, K. A., & Rabiner, D. L. (2004). Returning to roots: On social information processing and moral development. *Child Development, 75*(4): 1003–1008. Retrieved from http://search.proquest.com/docview/37965878?accountid=14509

DuPaul, G. J., Ervin, R. A., Hook, C. L., & McGoey, K. E. (1998). Peer tutoring for children with attention deficit hyperactivity disorder: Effects on classroom behavior and academic performance. *Journal of Applied Behavior Analysis*, *31*(4): 579–592.

Eber, L., Sugai, G., Smith, C. R., & Scott, T. M. (2002). Wraparound and positive behavioral interventions and supports in the schools. *Journal of Emotional and Behavioral Disorders*, *10*: 171–180.

Estes, A., Rivera, V., Bryan, M., Cali, P., & Dawson, G. (2011). Discrepancies between academic achievement and intellectual ability in higher-functioning school-aged children with autism spectrum disorder. *Journal of Autism and Developmental Disorders*, *41*(8): 1044–1052. doi: http://dx.doi.org/10.1007/s10803-010-1127-3

Farone, S. V., Sergeant, J., Gillberg, C., Biederman (2003). The worldwide prevalence of ADHD: Is it an American condition? *World Psychiatry*, *2*(2): 104–113.

Fine, A. H., Dennis, A. L., & Bowers, C. (2011). Incorporating animal-assisted interventions in therapy with boys at risk. In C. Haen (Ed.), *Engaging boys in treatment: Creative approaches to the therapy process* (pp. 115–133). New York: Routledge/Taylor & Francis Group.

Freund, L. S., McCune, S., Esposito, L., Gee, N. R., & McCardle, P. (2016). *The social neuroscience of human-animal interaction*. Washington, DC: American Psychological Association.

Friedmann, E., Thomas, S. A., Son, H., Chapa, D., & McCune, S. (2013). Pet's presence and owner's blood pressures during the daily lives of pet owners with pre- to mild hypertension. *Anthrozoös*, *26*(4): 535–550. doi: http://dx.doi.org/10.2752/175303713X13795775536138

Gabriels, R. L., Pan, Z., Dechant, B., Agnew, J. A., Brim, N., & Mesibov, G. (2015). Randomized controlled trial of therapeutic horseback riding in children and adolescents with autism spectrum disorder. *Journal of the American Academy of Child & Adolescent Psychiatry*, *54*(7): 541–549. doi: http://dx.doi.org/10.1016/j.jaac.2015.04.007

Gee, N. R., Church, M. T., & Altobelli, C. L. (2010). Preschoolers make fewer errors on an object categorization task in the presence of a dog. *Anthrozoös*, *23*(3): 223–230. doi: http://dx.doi.org/10.2752/175303710X12750451258896

Gee, N. R., Crist, E. N., & Carr, D. N. (2010). Preschool children require fewer instructional prompts to perform memory task in the presence of a dog. *Anthrozoös*, *23*(2): 173–184. doi: http://dx.doi.org/10.2752/175303710X12682332910051

Gee, N. R., Friedman, E., Stendahl, M., Fisk, A., & Coglitore, V. (2014). Heartrate variability during a working memory task: Does touching a dog or person effect the response. *Anthrozoös*, *27*(4): 513–528.

George, H. (1999). The role of animals in the emotional and moral development of children. In F. R. Ascione & P. Arkow (Eds.), *Child abuse, domestic violence, and animal abuse: Linking the circles of compassion for prevention and intervention* (pp. 380–392). Indiana, IN: Purdue University Press.

Ginsburg-Block, M., Rohrbeck, C., Fantuzzo, J., & Lavigne, N. C. (2006). Peer-assisted learning strategies. In G. G. Bear & K. M. Minke (Eds.), *Children's needs III: Development, prevention, and intervention* (pp. 631–645). Washington, DC: National Association of School Psychologists.

Godinez, D. A., Willcutt, E. G., Burgess, G. C., Depue, B. E., Andrews-Hanna, J., & Banich, M. T. (2015). Familial risk and ADHD-specific neural activity revealed by case-control, discordant twin pair design. *Psychiatry Research: Neuroimaging, 233*(3): 458–465. doi: http://dx.doi.org/10.1016/j.pscychresns.2015.07.019

Grzadzinski, R., Di Martino, A., Brady, E., Mairena, M. A., O'Neale, M., Petkova, … Castellanos, F. X. (2011). Examining autistic traits in children with ADHD: Does the autism spectrum extend to ADHD? *Journal of Autism Developmental Disorders, 41*: 1178–1191. doi: 10.1007/s10803-010-1135-3

Individuals with Disabilities Education Act, 20 U.S.C. § 1400 (2004).

Institute for Humane Education. (n.d.). *What is humane education?* Retrieved from http://humaneeducation.org/become-a-humane-educator/what-is-humane-education/

Intermountain Therapy Animals. (n.d.). *Reading education assistance dogs.* Retrieved from http://therapyanimals.org/Read_Team_Steps.html

Kilpatrick, L., & Cahill, L. (2003). Modulation of memory consolidation for olfactory learning by reversible inactivation of the basolateral amygdala. *Behavioral Neuroscience, 117*(1): 184–188. doi: http://dx.doi.org/10.1037/0735-7044.117.1.184

Kotkin, R. A., & Fine, A. H. (2003). Attention deficit hyperactivity disorder and learning disabilities: An overview for practitioners. In A. Fine & R. Kotkin (Eds.), *Therapist's guide to learning and attention disorder* (pp. 1–42). San Diego, CA: Academic Press. doi: http://dx.doi.org/10.1016/B978-012256430-7/50003-X

Kotrschal, K., & Ortbauer, B. (2003). Behavioral effects of the presence of a dog in a classroom. *Anthrozoös, 16*: 147–159.

Krause-Parello, C., & Friedmann, E. (2014). The effects of an animal-assisted intervention on salivary alpha amylase, salivary immunoglobulin A, and heart rate during forensic interviews in child sexual abuse cases. *Anthrozoös, 27*(4): 581–590. doi: http://dx.doi.org/10.2752/089279314X14072268688005

Lahey, B. B., Schaughency, E. A., Hynd, G. W., Carlson, C. L., & Nieves, N. (1987). Attention deficit disorder with and without hyperactivity: Comparison of behavioral characteristics of clinic-referred children. *Journal of the American Academy of Child & Adolescent Psychiatry, 26*(5): 718–723. Retrieved from http://search.proquest.com/docview/617442435?accountid=14509

Leopold, D. R., Christopher, M. E., Burns, G. L., Becker, S. P., Olson, R. K., & Willcutt, E. G. (2016). Attention-deficit/hyperactivity disorder and sluggish cognitive tempo throughout childhood: Temporal invariance and stability from preschool through ninth grade. *Journal of Child Psychology and Psychiatry, 157*(9): 1006–1074. doi: http://dx.doi.org/10.1111/jcpp.12505

le Roux, M. C., Swartz, L., & Swart, E. (2014). The effect of an animal-assisted reading program on the reading rate, accuracy and comprehension of grade 3 students: A randomized control study. *Child Youth Care Forum, 43*: 655–673. doi: 10.1007/s10566-014-9262-1

Luman, M., Oosterlaan, J., & Sergeant, J. A. (2005). The impact of reinforcement contingencies on AD/HD: A review and theoretical appraisal. *Clinical Psychology Review, 25*(2): 183–213. doi: http://dx.doi.org/10.1016/j.cpr.2004.11.001

Melson, G. F. (2003). Child development and the human-companion animal bond. *American Behavioral Scientist, 47*: 31. doi: 10.1177/0002764203255210

Molina, B. S. G., Hinshaw, S. P., Arnold, L. E., Swanson, J. M., Pelham, W. E., Hechtman, L., & Marcus, S. (2013). Adolescent substance use in the multimodal treatment study of attention-deficit/hyperactivity disorder (ADHD) (MTA) as a function of childhood ADHD, random assignment to childhood treatments, and subsequent medication. *Journal of the American Academy of Child & Adolescent Psychiatry, 52*(3): 250–263. doi: http://dx.doi.org/10.1016/j.jaac.2012.12.014

Musick, M. A., & Wilson, J. (2008). *Volunteers: A social profile.* Bloomington, IN: Indiana University Press.

National Humane Education Society. (n.d.) *So you want to be a humane educator.* Retrieved from http://nhes.org/sections/view/63

Neeper, R., & Lahey, B. B. (1986). The children's behavior rating scale: A factor analytic developmental study. *School Psychology Review, 15*(2): 277–288.

O'Haire, M. E., McKenzie, S. J., McCune, S., & Slaughter, V. (2013). The effects of animal-assisted activities with guinea pigs in the primary school classroom. *Anthrozoös, 23*(3): 445–458. doi: 10.2752/175303713X13697429463835

O'Haire, M. E., McKenzie, S. J., McCune, S., & Slaughter, V. (2014). Effects of classroom animal-assisted activities on social functioning in children with autism spectrum disorder. *The Journal of Alternative and Complementary Medicine, 20*(3): 162–168. doi: 10.1089/acm.2013.0165

Paul, E. S. (2000). Love of pets and love of people. In A. L. Podberscek, E. S. Paul, & J. A. Serpell (Eds.), *Companion animals and us: Exploring the relationships between people and pets* (pp. 168–186). Cambridge: Cambridge University Press.

Pelham, W. E., & Fabiano, G. A. (2008). Evidence-based psychosocial treatments for attention-deficit/hyperactivity disorder. *Journal of Clinical Child Adolescent Psychology, 37*: 184–214.

Phelps, E. A. (2006). Emotion and cognition: Insights from studies of the human amygdala. *Annual Review of Psychology, 57*: 27–53.

Plumer, P. J., & Stoner, G. (2005). The relative effects of classwide peer tutoring and peer coaching on the positive social behaviors of children with ADHD. *Journal of Attention Disorders, 9*(1): 290–300.

Satterfield, J. H., Faller, K. J., Crinella, F. M., Schell, A. M., Swanson, J. M., & Homer, L. D. (2007). A 30-year prospective follow-up study of hyperactive boys with conduct problems: Adult criminality. *Journal of the American Academy of Child & Adolescent Psychiatry, 46*(5): 601–610. doi: http://dx.doi.org/10.1097/chi.0b013e318033ff59

Schuck, S. E. B., Emmerson, N., Fine, A. H., & Lakes, K. D. (2015). Canine-assisted therapy for children with ADHD: Preliminary findings from The Positive Assertive Cooperative Kids Study. *Journal of Attention Disorders, 19*(2): 125–137. doi: 10.1177/1087054713502080

Schuck, S. E. B., Emmerson, N., Abdullah, M. M., Fine, A. H., Stehli, A., & Lakes, K. D. (under review). A randomized controlled trial of traditional psychosocial and canine-assisted interventions for ADHD. *Human Animal Interaction Bulletin.*

Simonoff, E., Pickles, A., Charman, T, Chandler, S., Loucas, T., & Baird, G. (2011). Psychiatric disorders in children with autism spectrum disorders: Prevalence, comorbidity, and associated factors in a population-derived sample. *Journal of the American Academy of Child & Adolescent Psychiatry, 47*(8): 921–929.

Sugai, G., & Horner, R. H. (2002). The evolution of discipline practices: School-wide positive behavior supports. *Child & Family Behavior Therapy, 24*: 23–50.

Tomasi, D., & Volkow, N. D. (2012). Abnormal functional connectivity in children with attention-deficit/hyperactivity disorder. *Biological Psychiatry, 71*(5): 443–450. doi: http://dx.doi.org/10.1016/j.biopsych.2011.11.003

Yerkes, R. M., & Dodson, J. D. (1908). The relation of strength of stimulus to rapidity of habit-formation. *Journal of Comparative Neurology & Psychology, 18*(5): 459–482.

CHAPTER 7

The Impact of Animals in Classrooms Assisting Students with Autism and Other Developmental Disorders

Marguerite E. O'Haire and Robin L. Gabriels

He is less anxious and more interested around the animals. He has started to call class members by name and has shown more of an interest in being in class and seeing what the children are doing. He is eager and excited to come to school.

Parent of child with autism, about having an animal in the classroom

Introduction

A surge in research since 2008 has examined the connection between animals and individuals with autism (O'Haire, 2013). This is paralleled by an increase in having animals integrated into clinical interventions and settings such as classrooms.

The search for effective classroom strategies is no surprise, given the growing global awareness of autism. The prevalence of autism in the US has risen from roughly 1 in 150 children in 2000 to 1 in 45 children in 2014 (Centers for Disease Control, 2014). Among those diagnosed, there is a broad range of severity, highlighted by the "spectrum" nature of the disorder, predominantly characterized by social and communication impairments along with a restricted range of interests and/or repetitive, stereotyped behaviors. Core diagnostic criteria include impairments in social-emotional reciprocity, nonverbal communication, and forming, maintaining, and understanding social relationships (American Psychiatric Association, 2013).

The school classroom is an inherently complex social environment. The characteristic impairments of autism may hinder classroom integration and academic success. In this chapter we review the learning styles of students with autism and document how animals can be incorporated into the educational environment to enhance school outcomes. We present the research evidence base to inform recommendations for education professionals, and provide a summary of the risks, and possible solutions, for having animals in classrooms with this unique population.

Autism at School

Classroom Challenges

The classroom is a critical environment for both social and academic learning, especially in the early years when children begin to spend more time away from home and are challenged to adapt to novel environments and social experiences. For children with autism, these experiences can be daunting due to their general preference for predictability and routines, along with their deficits in comprehending the inherent complexities of social relationships. For some, experiences of being bullied or ostracized can further hinder their motivation for school attendance and success (Cappadocia, Weiss, & Pepler, 2012). Teachers also have different relationships with children with autism, compared to typically-developing students (Robertson, Chamberlain,

& Kasari, 2003). Careful planning and structure are critical to enable children with autism to thrive in the classroom.

Learning Styles

Students with autism have a common set of unique learning styles, derived from neurobehavioral theories and research. These have been eloquently described by Mesibov and Shea (2005) as a "culture of autism" and have important implications for the successful incorporation of animals into education settings.

Individuals with autism tend to be visual learners. Providing clear visual cues (e.g., pictures) capitalizes on the visual processing strengths of this population, which can increase attention to task and decrease challenging behavior (e.g., Bryan & Gast, 2000; Minshew, Scherf, Behrmann, & Humphreys, 2011).

Individuals with autism have difficulties with emotion regulation. Research has demonstrated that disruptions in brain connectivity and processing are common in this population, which negatively impact emotional expression, insight, self-monitoring, cognitive flexibility, processing speed, and the ability to appropriately evaluate social situations (Mazefsky et al., 2013).

There are several other unique learning styles of students with autism that influence classroom success (for a review, see Gabriels & Hill, 2007). For example, they have a tendency to think concretely or literally, which complicates their ability to interpret spoken language. They may struggle to understand the intentions, emotions, and behaviors of others, hindering their ability to appropriately engage in social interactions or reflect on how their behaviors may impact others. Many focus on details rather than evaluating and understanding situations in context, which is essential for generalized learning. Related to this, executive functioning challenges in organization and sequencing make disorganized or unpredictable school environments particularly problematic. Finally, they are often easily distracted, despite an ability to focus intensely on their restricted range of interests. Distractions are magnified by a heightened reactivity to, or interest in, sensory input, such as smells, sounds, lights, or textures (Minshew et al., 2011).

The specific learning styles of children with autism can influence classroom success, both at the social and academic levels. Conducting interventions in schools without this knowledge can confound accurate evaluation of approaches aimed to reduce disruptive behaviors and increase skill acquisition. It is imperative to create individualized approaches tailored to the documented learning characteristics of autism.

Animals for Autism

The evidence base for animals and autism has more than doubled in size in recent years (O'Haire, 2013). A subset of this research has focused on the classroom environment, or adjuncts to the classroom through extracurricular activities.

Suggested mechanisms include the social facilitation effects of animals (e.g., McNicholas & Collis, 2000), thought to act as a means of connecting children with autism to their peers and teachers. The anxiolytic effect of animal observation and contact (e.g., Wilson, 1991) may reduce stress in the classroom environment. The positive emotional experience of interacting with animals (e.g., Funahashi, Gruebler, Aoki, Kadone, & Suzuki, 2014) is anticipated to provide a positive association with the classroom and reward appropriate school behavior. There are also hypothesized hormonal mechanisms for change, such as increased oxytocin (e.g., Nagasawa et al., 2015), though these have not been substantiated in autism populations.

In the Classroom

Animal contact in the classroom can be categorized into contact with *resident animals* (in the classroom when school is in session, such as guinea pigs or rats) and *visiting animals* (living in someone's home and visiting school on scheduled occasions, such as dogs or cats).

Resident Animals

To date, resident animal research has focused primarily on guinea pigs. O'Haire, McKenzie, McCune, and Slaughter (2014) showed that among 64 children with autism aged 5–12, parents and teachers perceived an increase in social and communication behaviors, along with a decrease in social withdrawal behaviors, following an eight-week exposure to having guinea pigs in the classroom compared to an eight-week waitlist control. Video and physiological analyses for 33 children with autism revealed that when the guinea pigs were present (compared to toys), children with autism showed more social behaviors (e.g., smiling, laughing, and talking) and less social withdrawal behaviors (e.g., playing alone; O'Haire, McKenzie, Beck, & Slaughter, 2013), as well as lower skin conductance arousal (O'Haire, McKenzie, Beck, & Slaughter, 2015), suggesting that the presence of an animal may ease arousal states and encourage positive social interactions with peers. Although academic outcomes were not directly assessed, over half of the sample of 64 children showed an increased interest in attending school when the guinea pigs were present in the classroom (O'Haire et al., 2014). Parents reported highly valuing this outcome, and indeed, school success generally depends on children's classroom presence.

Visiting Animals

Many animals are amenable to brief classroom visits, most commonly dogs. In one study, ten children with autism, ages 7–10 years, engaged in more verbal social communication in the presence of a dog, compared to toys (Fung & Leung, 2014). Another found that ten children with autism, ages 3–13 years, showed increased attention, interest, and playfulness in the presence of a dog, compared to a ball or stuffed dog (Martin & Farnum, 2002). When considered in conjunction to the studies with guinea pigs, these findings suggest that both dogs and guinea pigs in the classroom may have a beneficial effect on the social, communication, attention, and play skills of children with autism compared to alternative, more traditional classroom activities such as play with toys.

Adjuncts to the Classroom

87

Dogs and other animals may also serve as adjuncts to the classroom setting, particularly horses, who may be best incorporated via external activities such as visits to farms or equine centers.

External Activities

Horses

While autism is characterized by a lack of human social understanding, horses are highly social animals who will respond to subtle human cues. The horse's responsiveness may enhance the cause-and-effect communication learning experience of a child with autism (Gabriels et al., 2012). Riding a horse involves a heightened sensory experience (e.g., movement and warmth of the horse's body) that may lead to a calmer emotional state for the child with autism. The large size of a horse commands attention, which can create an ideal setting to experience a sense of teamwork to navigate the demands of horseback riding, which may encourage learning joint attention skills. This context may foster social communication and support social development.

In the largest clinical trial of AAI with horses to date, 127 children with autism were randomly assigned to receive either ten weeks of therapeutic horseback riding or ten weeks of similar activities in a barn with a stuffed horse (Gabriels et al., 2015). Children in the riding group showed improvements in their social cognition and social communication skills, both core areas of impairment in autism. They also showed reductions in irritability and hyperactivity behaviors on a standard behavioral measure typically used to assess the efficacy of medication in autism treatment (Aberrant Behavior Checklist; Gabriels et al., 2015). These changes were generalized beyond their time at the riding arena, indicating that even though the AAI with horses may take place outside of school, the changes can translate to improved behavior and functioning in multiple areas of children's lives.

Dogs

Children with autism generally partake in various therapeutic services, such as speech, occupational, and applied behavioral analysis therapies. Clinicians in these modalities sometimes decide to include an animal in their practice. Findings from research on AAI with dogs for individuals with autism reflect those findings from the classroom setting, such as increased social interaction behaviors (e.g., Grigore & Rusu, 2014). These outcomes may serve to enhance the targeted outcomes of these "typical" therapeutic interventions, which could also have implications for the school setting.

Home Activities

Including animals in the home is a common form of HAI among families with children and typically involves companion animals or service animals.

Companion Animals

One study interviewed 70 parents of children with autism, aged 8–18 years. Children with dogs at home showed strong attachments to the dogs and increases in age appropriate social skills, compared to children without dogs at home (Carlisle, 2014a). Another study showed the arrival of a pet was related to increased pro-social behaviors (such as a willingness to share and offer comfort) among children with autism aged 4–5 years old, compared to before the pet's arrival and to age-matched individuals with no pets (Grandgeorge et al., 2012). It should be noted that, despite social benefits, several drawbacks to companion animals were also reported by parents, such as the time and cost required for appropriate care (Carlisle, 2014b).

Service Animals

The topic of service animals for autism is controversial. Though research has demonstrated promising benefits for human well-being, such as reduced stress levels via cortisol (Viau et al., 2010) and increased feelings of safety and competence among families (e.g., Burgoyne et al., 2014), it is unclear whether this practice is appropriate for the welfare of the animal. In some cases, children with autism are tethered to the animal to prevent bolting or running off. This practice may have a negative impact on the relationship between the child and the animal, and may limit the ability of the animal to seek refuge or rest when needed (Burrows, Adams, & Millman, 2008). Even without tethering, a major concern is determining who will monitor the animal for signs of comfort or fear. Animals included in AAI require thoughtful attention to their behavior to ensure that they are amenable to the interactions, or to remove them from stressful situations. Without a caregiver who can attend to these, we do not recommend this practice until further research on efficacy, screening, and safety has been conducted. If the appropriate supervision, protocols, and procedures are established, it is possible that service animals could effectively assist some, though not all, individuals with autism in the home and classroom environments.

89

Benefits and Risks

Based on existing research and anecdotal experience in clinical and school settings, the following are two summary tables of the potential benefits (Table 7.1) and risks (Table 7.2) of including animals in education settings.

To maximize benefits and minimize risks, careful planning and ongoing attention to the individualized needs of both the animal and the human are required. Priority research questions relate to the refinement of techniques for maximally efficient and effective protocols, outcomes, and standards to enhance animal welfare (see also Chapter 14) and human well-being, along with predictive screening tools to determine who will benefit and under what circumstances.

Recommendations for Teachers

Animal Welfare

Our primary recommendation for teachers is to focus on safety and animal welfare. Animals that are not comfortable with human interactions will show signs of stress, which are not only a problem for

Table 7.1 Evidence-based benefits of animals for children with autism and relevant examples

Benefits	Examples
Increased social interaction and social skills	Talking, smiling, and laughing with peers and teachers (e.g., O'Haire et al., 2013), displaying appropriate social skills (e.g., Carlisle, 2014b).
Increased language and communication	More language output and greater verbal fluency (e.g., Gabriels et al., 2015; Sams, Fortney, & Willenbring, 2006).
Increased pro-social behavior	Greater willingness to share and help (e.g., Grandgeorge et al., 2012).
Positive attitude about school	Increased interest in school attendance (e.g., O'Haire et al., 2014).
Reduced anxious arousal and social anxiety	Reduced arousal or stress levels that lead to an openness to positive social engagement (e.g., O'Haire et al., 2015; Viau et al., 2010).
Reduced problem behaviors	Less irritability and hyperactivity (e.g., Gabriels et al., 2015).
Less social withdrawal	Less solitary play, more engagement with peers (e.g., Ward, Whalon, Rusnak, Wendell, & Paschall, 2013).
Improvements in sensory integration and executive function	Reduced distraction by sensory stimuli and more focused problem solving skills (e.g., Bass, Duchowny, & Llabre, 2009; Borgi et al., 2015).

the animal, but may also detract from efficacious human outcomes and create an unsafe learning environment. Prior to introducing an animal into the classroom setting, teachers should select a certified animal-handler team to visit the classroom to assess the appropriateness of the environment for the animal and engage the animal in a process of gradual exposure to the classroom environment to assess for signs of stress in the animal. A key predictor of animal inclusion success is positive socialization, which can be accomplished for both children who experience animals in the classroom environment from a young age and for those who experience animals through gradual exposure over time. Once introduced to the

Table 7.2 Potential risks of animals for children with autism and strategies to ameliorate problems

Risks	Suggested solutions
Distraction from classwork	• Implement animal as a contingent reward (e.g., following completion of a less preferred work task).
Harm or danger to animals	• Only allow interactions for students with appropriate motor/impulse control under careful teacher supervision. • Develop scheduled times for structured interactions including supervised animal care chores.
Fear or dislike of animals	• Recognize and accept that not all students will enjoy or benefit. • Foster positive interactions where possible, but do not force it on everyone.
Allergies to animals	• Select hypoallergenic animals such as fish or reptiles. • Maintain a high standard of classroom hygiene (e.g., cage cleaning, hand washing before and after interactions). • Encourage non-contact interactions such as observation of natural animal behavior.
Time required for care and potential for animal neglect	• Enlist volunteer assistance from capable students or families. • Create an animal interaction and care schedule and checklist. • Carefully consider whether you can commit to the care required *before* introducing an animal to the classroom.

91

classroom, the goal is for the teacher to facilitate an experience that is engaging and safe for all involved. Facilitation includes providing close supervision of the child-animal interactions and allowing both parties to take breaks away from each other to prevent over-stimulation and promote positive associations.

Individualized Approach

HAI is an inherently bi-directional process that can be mutually beneficial when managed correctly. Even if the animal is well suited to the setting and population, the human side of the equation also brings nuances. Not all children with autism will enjoy or benefit from interacting with animals. The spectrum nature of the disorder nearly guarantees that one size will not fit all. Thus, teachers and other educators should take an individualized approach to animals in the classroom, closely monitoring both the children and the animal. Some children may have an overwhelming fear of animals or have sensory sensitivities that make the smell, sound, or motion of the animal disconcerting (Grandin et al., 2015). If the animal is a strong deterrent (e.g., child is fearful of the animal), the child may not be amenable to the interaction and it should not be forced. There are several evidence-based strategies to enhance the classroom environment; AAI should be viewed as a unique part of this rich milieu, which will be highly effective for some and not applicable for others.

Strategies for Success

For individuals who appear to enjoy or seek out contact with the animals, we recommend the following strategies (shown in Table 7.3) to enhance learning and school success.

Table 7.3 Animal-assisted intervention strategies for autism learning styles

Autism learning style	AAI strategy
Concrete or literal thinking	• Provide examples of concrete, visual cues in animal behavior and environment to explain concepts about animal care and contact. • Provide pictures and references to observed animal behaviors to teach how to recognize signs of distress in the animal (e.g., giving picture or video examples or highlighting when the animal has a response to the child's touch).

Difficulty understanding others' intentions, emotional states, and behaviors	• Teach specific strategies to identify the emotional states of the animals via their behaviors (e.g., eating as a sign of comfort or hiding as a sign of fear). • Use examples to help the child understand and identify one's own and others' emotional behavioral signals.
Focus on the details rather than the big picture	• Use a cause-and-effect teaching strategy. For example, "first cut the carrots, and then hold one in front of the guinea pig to feed him" or "first call the dog's name or a command the dog knows, and then observe the dog's response."
Difficulty with organization and sequencing	• Use picture schedules to signal animal interaction activities or multi-step tasks (e.g., steps to clean a cage). • Organize the animal supplies with picture labels. • Develop visual schedules for practicing routines for feeding, grooming, interacting, and putting materials away.
Distractible yet intensely focused on areas of interest	• Select a quiet, clean environment for HAI to reduce sensory distractions during animal interaction. • Engage in child-directed areas of interest, then expand to other parts of the HAI. • Highlight to the child how the animal also does not like distractions or loud chaotic environments. • Give the child pictures of safe rules with the animal, including using a quiet voice and nice touch.

93

Conclusion

The inclusion of animals in educational services can be a motivating and hands-on sensory learning experience for some individuals with autism. Success will be enhanced by thoughtful attention to the unique learning styles of autism, via visual schedules, controlled environments, and practiced routines. Potential positive outcomes include increased social and communication engagement with classroom peers and educational professionals, reduced anxious arousal in the school setting, and increased motivation to attend and learn. Risks may include danger to the animal or child, without appropriate planning, supervision, and selection. Not all children with autism will enjoy, benefit, or be safe with the provision of AAI. Yet for those who do make a connection with the animal, benefits should follow. The key to effective classroom AAI for students with autism is to create a thoughtful and individualized approach that values the needs and skills of both the human and the animal.

References

American Psychiatric Association. (2013). *Diagnostic and statistical manual of mental disorders: DSM-V* (5th edn). Washington, DC: Author.

Bass, M. M., Duchowny, C. A., & Llabre, M. M. (2009). The effect of therapeutic horseback riding on social functioning in children with autism. *Journal of Autism and Developmental Disorders, 39*(9): 1261–1267. doi: 10.1007/s10803-009-0734-3

Borgi, M., Loliva, D., Cerino, S., Chiarotti, F., Venerosi, A., Bramini, M., … Cirulli, F. (2015). Effectiveness of a standardized equine-assisted therapy program for children with Autism Spectrum Disorder. *Journal of Autism and Developmental Disorders, 46*(1): 1–9. doi: 10.1007/s10803-015-2530-6

Bryan, L. C., & Gast, D. L. (2000). Teaching on-task and on-schedule behaviors to high-functioning children with autism via picture activity schedules. *Journal of Autism and Developmental Disorders, 30*(6): 553–567.

Burgoyne, L., Dowling, L., Fitzgerald, A., Connolly, M., P Browne, J., & Perry, I. J. (2014). Parents' perspectives on the value of assistance dogs for children with autism spectrum disorder: A cross-sectional study. *BMJ Open, 4*(6). doi: 10.1136/bmjopen-2014-004786

Burrows, K. E., Adams, C. L., & Millman, S. T. (2008). Factors affecting behavior and welfare of service dogs for children with autism spectrum disorder. *Journal of Applied Animal Welfare Science, 11*(1): 42–62.

Cappadocia, M. C., Weiss, J. A., & Pepler, D. (2012). Bullying experiences among children and youth with autism spectrum disorders. *Journal of Autism and Developmental Disorders, 42*(2): 266–277. doi: 10.1007/s10803-011-1241-x

Carlisle, G. K. (2014a). Pet dog ownership decisions for parents of children with autism spectrum disorder. *Journal of Pediatric Nursing, 29*(2): 114.

Carlisle, G. K. (2014b). The social skills and attachment to dogs of children with autism spectrum disorder. *Journal of Autism and Developmental Disorders*: 1–9. doi: 10.1007/s10803-014-2267-7

Centers for Disease Control. (2014). Prevalence of autism spectrum disorders among children aged 8 years: Autism and developmental disabilities monitoring network, 11 sites, United States, 2010. *MMWR Surveillance Summaries, 63*(2): 1–22.

Funahashi, A., Gruebler, A., Aoki, T., Kadone, H., & Suzuki, K. (2014). Brief report: The smiles of a child with autism spectrum disorder during an animal-assisted activity may facilitate social positive behaviors-Quantitative analysis with smile-detecting interface. *Journal of Autism and Developmental Disorders, 44*: 685–693. doi: 10.1007/s10803-013-1898-4

Fung, S.-C., & Leung, A. S.-M. (2014). Pilot study investigating the role of therapy dogs in facilitating social interaction among children with autism. *Journal of Contemporary Psychotherapy, 44*(4): 253–262.

Gabriels, R. L., Agnew, J. A., Holt, K. D., Shoffner, A., Zhaoxing, P., Ruzzano, S., ... Mesibov, G. (2012). Pilot study measuring the effects of therapeutic horseback riding on school-age children and adolescents with autism spectrum disorders. *Research in Autism Spectrum Disorders, 6*(2): 578–588. doi: 10.1016/j.rasd.2011.09.007

Gabriels, R. L., & Hill, D. E. (Eds.). (2007). *Growing up with autism: Working with school-age children and adolescents*. New York: The Guilford Press.

Gabriels, R. L., Zhaoxing, P., DeChant, B., Agnew, J. A., Brim, N., & Mesibov, G. (2015). Randomized controlled trial of therapeutic horseback riding in children and adolescents with autism spectrum disorder. *Journal of the American Academy of Child & Adolescent Psychiatry, 55*(7): 541–549.

Grandgeorge, M., Tordjman, S., Lazartigues, A., Lemonnier, E., Deleau, M., & Hausberger, M. (2012). Does pet arrival trigger prosocial behaviors in individuals with autism? *PLoS ONE, 7*(8): e41739.

Grandin, T., Fine, A. H., O'Haire, M. E., Carlisle, G. K., & Bowers, C. M. (2015). The role of animals for individuals with autism spectrum disorder. In A. H. Fine (Ed.), *Handbook on animal-assisted therapy: Foundations and guidelines for animal-assisted interventions* (4th edn, pp. 225–236). San Diego, CA: Academic Press.

Grigore, A. A., & Rusu, A. S. (2014). Interaction with a therapy dog enhances the effects of social story method in autistic children. *Society & Animals, 1*: 21.

Martin, F., & Farnum, J. (2002). Animal-assisted therapy for children with pervasive developmental disorders. *Western Journal of Nursing Research, 24*(6): 657–670. doi: 10.1177/019394502320555403

95

Mazefsky, C. A., Herrington, J., Siegel, M., Scarpa, A., Maddox, B. B., Scahill, L., & White, S. W. (2013). The role of emotion regulation in autism spectrum disorder. *Journal of the American Academy of Child & Adolescent Psychiatry, 52*(7): 679–688.

McNicholas, J., & Collis, G. M. (2000). Dogs as catalysts for social interaction: Robustness of the effect. *British Journal of Psychology, 91*(1): 61–70.

Mesibov, G. B., & Shea, V. (2005). The culture of autism. In G. B. Mesibov, E. Schopler, & V. Shea (Eds.), *The TEACCH approach to autism spectrum disorders* (pp. 19–32). New York: Springer.

Minshew, N. J., Scherf, K. S., Behrmann, M., & Humphreys, K. (2011). Autism as a developmental neurobiological disorder: New insights from functional neuroimaging. In D. G. Amarel, G. Dawson, & D. H. Geschwind (Eds.), *Autism spectrum disorders* (pp. 632–650). New York: Oxford University Press.

Nagasawa, M., Mitsui, S., En, S., Ohtani, N., Ohta, M., Sakuma, Y., … Kikusui, T. (2015). Oxytocin-gaze positive loop and the coevolution of human-dog bonds. *Science, 348*(6232): 333–336. doi: 10.1126/science.1261022

O'Haire, M. E. (2013). Animal-assisted intervention for autism spectrum disorder: A systematic literature review. *Journal of Autism and Developmental Disorders, 43*(7): 1606–1622. doi: 10.1007/s10803-012-1707-5

O'Haire, M. E., McKenzie, S. J., Beck, A. M., & Slaughter, V. (2013). Social behaviors increase in children with autism in the presence of animals compared to toys. *PLoS ONE, 8*(2): e57010. doi: 10.1371/journal.pone.0057010

O'Haire, M. E., McKenzie, S. J., Beck, A. M., & Slaughter, V. (2015). Animals may act as social buffers: Skin conductance arousal in children with autism spectrum disorder in a social context. *Developmental Psychobiology,* Advance online publication. doi: 10.1002/dev.21310

O'Haire, M. E., McKenzie, S. J., McCune, S., & Slaughter, V. (2014). Effects of classroom animal-assisted activities on social functioning in children with autism spectrum disorder. *Journal of Alternative and Complementary Medicine, 20*(3): 162–168. doi: 10.1089/acm.2013.0165

Robertson, K., Chamberlain, B., & Kasari, C. (2003). General education teachers' relationships with included students with autism. *Journal of Autism and Developmental Disorders, 33*(2): 123–130.

Sams, M. J., Fortney, E. V., & Willenbring, S. (2006). Occupational therapy incorporating animals for children with autism: A pilot investigation.

American Journal of Occupational Therapy, 60(3): 268–274. doi: 10.5014/ ajot.60.3.268

Viau, R., Arsenault-Lapierre, G., Fecteau, S., Champagne, N., Walker, C.-D., & Lupien, S. (2010). Effect of service dogs on salivary cortisol secretion in autistic children. *Psychoneuroendocrinology, 35*(8): 1187–1193. doi: 10.1016/j.psyneuen.2010.02.004

Ward, S. C., Whalon, K., Rusnak, K., Wendell, K., & Paschall, N. (2013). The association between therapeutic horseback riding and the social communication and sensory reactions of children with autism. *Journal of Autism and Developmental Disorders, 43*: 2190–2198. doi: 10.1007/ s10803-013-1773-3

Wilson, C. C. (1991). The pet as an anxiolytic intervention. *Journal of Nervous and Mental Disease, 179*(8): 482–489.

97

CHAPTER 8

Companion Animals as Moderators of Stress Responses

Implications for Academic Performance, Testing, and Achievement

Erika Friedmann and Nancy R. Gee

Introduction

The presence of companion animals in an education environment may improve outcomes based on the animals' contributions to stress reduction, which is expected to lead to better behavior, more attentiveness, and even greater academic success. After presenting an overview of human physiological response to both acute and chronic stress, this chapter focuses on the potential impact of companion animals as moderators of acute stressors specific to challenging tasks in the classroom setting. We conclude with suggestions for additional research to clarify the circumstances under which academic stress reduction, tied to the presence of companion animals, might be most effective.

Physiological Responses to Stress

A biopsychosocial model (illustrated in Figure 8.1) provides a frame-work for understanding how multiple contributors can be related to chronic disease outcomes. In this model, challenges, insults, or posi-tive supports in each of the three realms (biological, social, and psychological) lead to consequences in both of the other realms, and all realms collectively combine to determine health outcomes. This model illustrates how psychological challenges can lead to bio-logical challenges and how biological measures can be used to assess psychological status (Engel, 1981).

The stress response is the body's method of reacting to a perceived challenge in which physical activity may be required and bodily damage may occur. Inappropriately activated and unreleased, the stress response is a premier illustration of the biopsychosocial model. Understanding the stress response and its relationship to social and psychological factors is crucial for understanding the research evaluating the ability of companion animals to moderate it.

The stress response begins when the brain's limbic system inte-grates input from the medial pre-frontal cortex, hippocampus,

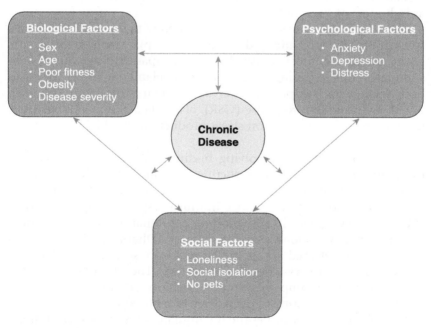

Figure 8.1 The biopsychosocial model

amygdala, and sensory and memory inputs (Ulrich-Lai & Herman, 2009) and interprets the situation as stressful or dangerous. The limbic system signals the hypothalamus, which activates the autonomic nervous system (ANS).

The ANS activation in stress mainly stimulates the sympathetic nervous system and suppresses the parasympathetic nervous system. This activates the sympathetic-adrenal-medullary (SAM) axis to secrete epinephrine and norepinephrine into the blood (Ulrich-Lai & Herman, 2009), stimulates the lymph and other organs through their sympathetic innervation, and ultimately leads to increased respiratory rate, heart rate (HR), blood pressure (BP), and cardiac output, decreased high frequency and high/low frequency ratio HR variability (Ulrich-Lai & Herman, 2009), decreased body surface temperature, and increased blood sugar. Direct sympathetic innervation of the salivary glands stimulates release of α amylase (Nater & Rohleder, 2009). Other hormonal changes cause the adrenal cortex to secrete glucocorticoids, mainly cortisol, and the adrenal medulla to secrete epinephrine and norepinephrine into the blood (Ulrich-Lai & Herman, 2009). Arginine vasopressin, secreted into the blood by the hypothalamus, causes the kidneys to retain water; that causes increases in blood volume, BP, and cardiac output. Most of these physiological endpoints have been used as indicators of stress in HAI studies.

The stress response typically is associated with sweat in the palms, soles of the feet, face, and underarms (axilla), places where the eccrine sweat glands are most dense. The parasympathetic nervous system stimulates this sweating while apocrine gland sweating increases body-wide with sympathetic nervous system stimulation (Harker, 2013). Galvanic skin response (GSR), also called skin conductance, is used to assess stress based on sweat production; the higher the stress, the higher the GSR.

A complex interplay involving bi-directional regulation between the central nervous system, endocrine, and immune systems controls immune function during the stress response (Glaser & Kiecolt-Glaser, 2005). Acute stress may enhance immune response whereas chronic stress can dysregulate it and promote proinflammatory and type-2 cytokine driven responses to the stressor (Dhabhar, 2009). Glucocorticoids are released when the stress response is activated in the hypothalamic-pituitary-adrenal (HPA) axis. The stimulation of the HPA and SAM axes impairs immune function; other hormones interfere with it as well. Cortisol degrades white blood cells, blocks T cells from proliferating, and stifles the inflammatory response by inhibiting histamine secretion by immune system cells. If the endogenous hormone has a physiologic concentration in response to stress, it actually enhances the immune system. If the endogenous hormone is in a pharmacological concentration or is synthetic, then the response to stress is actually immunosuppression (Dhabhar, 2009). The timing of the exposure to the stressor and the activation of the immune response is important, as well as the timing of the overall time course of the immune response. An enhanced response of the immune system occurs with acute stress, but immunosuppression occurs in later stages of the immune response to stress. Cytokines have been used in some research to assess stress levels.

Thus, based on the physiology of the stress response, many indicators are used to assess short-term (acute) and long-term (chronic) stress. Some of the responses mediated by the SAM axis, like BP and HR, change from second to second, while cortisol, mediated by the HPA axis, takes tens of minutes, and thyroid hormones take days (Ulrich-Lai & Herman, 2009). Cortisol is an excellent example of why natural variation must be considered when using biomarkers for stress assessment. Cortisol varies naturally over the course of the day, with a spike when awakening and lowest levels at bedtime. A flattened slope in diurnal variation in cortisol from its peak to its trough is a useful measure of chronic stress, even in young children (van Andel, Jansen, Grietens, Knorth, & van der Gaag, 2014). Cortisol can be assessed in blood, saliva, and urine; each has different time courses after exposure to an acute stressor, and therefore may be more valid as an indicator of long term or chronic, rather than acute, stress (Hellhammer, Wust, & Kudielka, 2009).

This elaborate, coordinated "fight-or-flight" stress response is adaptive for responding to emergencies. Long-term chronic activation, or frequent repeated acute activation, of the stress response without the concomitant intense activity leads to chronic arousal, which can impair the ability to function and thereby facilitate the development/progression of chronic disease. As predicted by the biopsychosocial model, chronic stress provides the ambient stress levels for each individual and will impact physiology and learning ability in a more general sense.

Studies of HAI and Stress Reduction

The first research examining the presence of a companion animal as a moderator of stress responses was an extension of research on the stress response related to interpersonal communication. A series of studies determined that when a person was talking, as compared to sitting quietly (the QTQ, or quiet-talk-quiet, protocol), a 10 to 50% increases in systolic (SBP) and diastolic (DBP) blood pressure and HR occurred; these returned to baseline within one minute of cessation of speech or reading (Lynch, Long, Thomas, Malinow, & Katcher, 1981; Lynch et al., 1982; Malinow, Lynch, Thomas, Friedmann, & Long, 1982). Reading to another person provides a more standard stressful manipulation in a QTQ protocol, since conversations, having higher affect, lead to greater stress responses (Lynch et al., 1981). In a study involving reading aloud in the low stress environment of a neighbor's home, the presence of a friendly dog was associated with lower BP responses in elementary school children. Each child completed the QTQ both with and without a dog present; interestingly, BP was lower overall when the dog was present in the first half of the protocol rather than the latter half (Friedmann, Katcher, Thomas, Lynch, & Messent, 1983).

Several studies in college students, and the general adult population, confirmed and extended the finding that the presence of a friendly companion animal, whether or not the pet of the participant, led to reduced stress responses as compared with a friend or supportive person. In college students taking the Trier Social Stress Test in the presence of a novel dog, a human friend, or a control situation, the presence of the dog attenuated salivary cortisol and HR stress responses (Polheber & Matchock, 2014). A pet's presence also moderated adults' autonomic (BP, HR, GSR) stress responses to mental arithmetic better than a spouse's (Allen, Blascovich, & Mendes, 2002) or friend's presence, even one specifically chosen for support (Allen, Blascovich, Tomaka, & Kelsey, 1991). By contrast, although they reported significantly lower subjective distress in the presence of a dog or friendly person, female college students who watched a "traumatic film" did not differ in physiological measures of stress (salivary cortisol, BP, or HR) when a friendly human, a live dog, a toy dog, or no companion was present (Lass-Hennemann, Peyk, Streb, Holz, & Michael, 2014). In the only randomized trial of pet acquisition (Allen, Shykoff, & Izzo, 2001), individuals in a high-stress occupation and receiving therapy for hypertension who were willing to adopt a pet were assigned to obtain pets (dog or cat as they preferred), or to remain under their usual care (the control group). All patients received standard of care angiotensin converting enzyme (ACE) inhibitor anti-hypertensive medication. Cardiovascular responses to mental stress were measured before assignment to experimental groups and six months later. Resting BPs for participants in both the pet and no pet groups were lower after six months than at the beginning of the study. However, while BP responses to mental arithmetic did not differ between the two groups prior to the study, after intervention the BP stress responses were lower among pet owners with the pet present than among those who did not receive a pet.

Attitudes toward animals in general, attachment to a particular animal, and pet ownership may be related to pets' stress-moderating effect. In research using the QTQ protocol, in the presence of a dog, college students with more positive attitudes toward dogs had lower cardiovascular stress responses than those who had less positive attitudes, but were not afraid of dogs (Friedmann, Locker, & Lockwood, 1993). In another study, both the presence of, and thinking about, their dogs, moderated dog owners' stress responses to a difficult cognitive task. Owners who were more securely attached experienced reduced SBP and DBP stress responses, while those who were not highly attached did not (Zilcha-Mano, Mikulincer, & Shaver, 2012). Oxytocin and cortisol levels have been associated with some characteristics of dog-owners' relationships with their dogs; for example, higher oxytocin and lower cortisol are associated with liking to kiss their dogs (Handlin, Nilsson, Ejdeback, Hydbring-Sandberg, & Uvnas-Moberg, 2012). During a modified Stroop test, the presence of a friendly, unfamiliar dog produced a better cardiac autonomic profile for pet owners than the absence of the dog, while the reverse was true of non-pet owners (Kingwell, Lomdahl, & Anderson, 2001).

In contrast to these studies indicating positive physiological responses, three experimental cognitive studies that required touching an animal did not result in stress response moderation. In two, where animals sat on the laps of participants during a stressful activity, the BP and HR stress responses were not moderated (Somervill, Kruglikova, Robertson, Hanson, & MacLin, 2008; Straatman, Hanson, Endenburg, & Mol, 1997). Similarly, in our study of young adults performing a working memory task, touching a dog did not moderate their stress responses (Gee, Friedmann, Stendahl, Fisk, & Coglitore, 2014) and there was no difference in heart rate variability (HRV) while touching a dog, a person, or a toy dog.

In studies using experimental paradigms in environments designed to resemble natural settings, children's stress responses were moderated by the presence of a companion animal. Systolic and mean arterial BP and HR responses to a mock pediatric examination were moderated when children had a dog present (Nagengast, Baun, Megel, & Leibowitz, 1997). In male children with insecure attachment, stress responses to the Trier Social Stress Test for Children were moderated by the presence of a dog (Beetz, Julius,

103

Turner, & Kotrschal, 2012). In a mock classroom, the salivary cortisol response was lower when an unfamiliar therapy dog was present during the stressful activity than when a toy dog or a person was present. The more the children stroked the dog the lower their stress responses. In a study comparing children with autism spectrum disorder (ASD) and typically developing children, the presence of a guinea pig was particularly effective at moderating the social stress experience for children with ASD (O'Haire, McKenzie, Beck, & Slaughter, 2015).

In two studies of physiological responses to stressors in natural health care settings, children's stress responses were moderated by the presence of a dog in one but not the other. During clinically prescribed venipuncture, children had lower serum cortisol while physically interacting with a dog (petting, stroking, brushing) than without a dog present (Vagnoli et al., 2015). When 2–6-year-old children were randomly assigned to pediatric examinations with a dog present, and touch was permitted but not required, the dog did not moderate the physiological stress responses as compared with when the dog was not present, although the presence of the dog was effective at reducing behavioral signs of distress (i.e., Hansen, Messinger, Baun, & Megel, 1999).

Research Summarized

The results of these varied studies indicate that companion animals can moderate stress responses in many situations, including classroom activities such as reading aloud, mental arithmetic, and stressful cognitive tasks. These tasks were presumed to be stressors related to social pressure associated with the participant's desire to perform well and not appear incompetent to the researcher or others present. In other studies, either standardized social stressor tests or natural stressors were used to test the stress-moderating effects of the presence of an animal. Each of these tasks can create more or less stress for specific individuals, and thus variability in stress responses and their moderation would be expected in different study conditions.

Future Directions

A major challenge for future research is to determine for whom, and in what situation, an animal could moderate the stress response. A few critical questions drawn from research we cite might help focus research on stress moderation.

Question 1

Is physical interaction or just presence of an animal necessary or optimal for stress response moderation? The answer could depend on the situation causing the stress response or the structure of the experimental protocol; studies have produced mixed results. Specific groups may benefit from touch while others may not. For instance, in male children with insecure attachment, the more they stroked a dog, the lower their stress responses (Beetz et al., 2012).

It may be that the artificiality of the requirement to touch an animal or keep an animal on one's lap is in itself stressful and masks any stress response moderation that might occur. Further, the response may be difficult to quantify due to variability in situations, so the moderation is not apparent when the responses are not assessed in the same individuals in both conditions – animal present and not present (i.e., Hansen et al., 1999). It is important to recognize that if stress responses are mild, it is unlikely that the presence of an animal will reduce the responses further.

Question 2

Are previous experiences with companion animals or attitudes toward animals related to stress response moderation? Evidence suggests that attitudes toward dogs are related to their stress-response reducing effects (Friedmann et al., 1993). Participants in research studies are volunteers who, in the informed consent process, have agreed to be in the presence of animals. Therefore, one presumes they are not afraid. If attitudes toward animals are closely related to the potential for stress reduction when an animal is present, the animal intervention may not be generalizable to all children. Exploration of the interrelationships among attitudes, experience, and stress reduction with other animals is needed.

Question 3

Do animals moderate stress responses over the long term in individuals' daily lives or is this a novelty effect in experimental manipulations? At least one study (Friedmann, Thomas, Son, Chapa, & McCune, 2013) suggests that the presence of an animal can moderate stress responses in some situations in people's daily lives. More research is needed to understand the situations, types of behavioral interactions, and proximity that are required to produce stress moderation over sustained periods as compared to novel one-time experiences. Most classroom studies do not evaluate whether the beneficial effect of the animal intervention continues over months of exposure, whether it extends beyond the time when the animal is present, and if so, how long it might last before a new "inoculation" is required.

Question 4

Is stress moderation always the most desirable outcome? Some degree of stress (or stimulation) might be a reasonable goal for optimal functioning in the classroom and in other academic situations. According to the Yerkes-Dodson Law there is an inverted U-shaped relationship between arousal and performance, such that performance increases as arousal increases, to an optimal level, represented by the peak on the curve (Salehi, Cordero, & Sandi, 2010; Teigen, 1994). A further increase in arousal beyond the peak or optimal level results in corresponding decreases in performance. Maintaining an optimal level of arousal facilitates higher order cognitive functions such as executive functioning (EF) (Blair & Dennis, 2010). EF is important for a variety of aspects of learning such as goal directed behaviors like working memory, attentional flexibility, and inhibitory control (Vilgis, Silk, & Vance, 2015). One example of this relationship is the impact of increasing amounts of test anxiety on academic performance. Low test anxiety facilitates performance (e.g., Hardy, Beattie, & Woodman, 2007), while high test anxiety may disrupt mental processes, especially during formal academic assessments (Wachelka & Katz, 1999).

In most of the studies discussed in this chapter an animal's presence moderates stress responses. By reducing stress and anxiety, animal presence may improve performance in academic tasks. Nursing students who visited with and petted a dog while studying prior to taking an exam had better test performance and lower test anxiety than their compatriots who did not engage with dogs while studying (Young, 2012). But we know of no studies linking moderation of physiological indicators of stress when a pet is present to improved academic performance. As children progress from kindergarten through high school, there are differences in developmental states. Therefore, in evaluating the potential of the presence of an animal prior to or during testing as a method to decrease test anxiety and improve performance, it would be useful to study students at various grade levels.

It is important to note that depending on the population, a companion animal may positively moderate stress responses, increasing, rather than decreasing, stress hormones. For example, in individuals with ADHD poor EF (mental control skills) is related to under-arousal (Schuck, Emmerson, Fine, & Lakes, 2015). In this population, the presence of a companion animal can improve focus by stimulating arousal. Students with ADHD who participated in cognitive behavioral therapy with a pet experienced greater improvement in pro-social behaviors and decreases in ADHD-symptomatic behaviors than those who received the therapy without the animal. This increased arousal contrasts with the decreased stress responses in children with ASD (O'Haire, McKenzie, Beck, & Slaughter, 2013; O'Haire et al., 2015).

Practical Conclusions

Clearly, the identification of how HAI can benefit student learning is complex; evidence suggests that stress reduction may play a key role in its effectiveness. The addition of a companion animal to a classroom may result in an environment more conducive to learning by reducing student stress and improving student behavior. The benefits for individual students are likely related to their attitudes toward animals. It also is important to respect students in the classroom setting who may not be comfortable with animals. Similarly, for some students interacting with a companion animal prior to a test will decrease test anxiety; for others having the animal present during the actual test may be necessary. It is important to recognize that an animal's presence during a test may be distracting for all, which may offset test anxiety reduction or even increase it for those who do not appreciate having an animal present.

As evidence-based practices evolve, it becomes apparent that it is crucial to identify goals specific to the individual and the situation when evaluating the impact of HAI and eventually when choosing a type of interaction to offer to a specific individual. For practitioners and researchers interested in the intersection of HAI and education, it is an exciting beginning of discovery.

References

Allen, K., Blascovich, J., & Mendes, W. B. (2002). Cardiovascular reactivity and the presence of pets, friends, and spouses: The truth about cats and dogs. *Psychosomatic Medicine, 64*: 727–739.

Allen, K. M., Blascovich, J., Tomaka, J., & Kelsey, R. M. (1991). Presence of human friends and pet dogs as moderators of autonomic responses to stress in women. *Journal of Personality and Social Psychology, 61*: 582.

Allen, K., Shykoff, B. E., & Izzo, J. L. (2001). Pet ownership, but not ACE inhibitor therapy, blunts home blood pressure responses to mental stress. *Hypertension, 38*: 815–820.

Beetz, A., Julius, H., Turner, D., & Kotrschal, K. (2012). Effects of social support by a dog on stress modulation in male children with insecure attachment. *Frontiers in Psychology, 3*: 352.

Blair, C., & Dennis, T. (2010). An optimal balance: The integration of emotion and cognition in context. In Calkins, S. & Bell, M. A. (Eds.), *Child development at the intersection of emotion and cognition* (pp. 17–35). Washington: DC: American Psychaological Association.

Dhabhar, F. S. (2009). Enhancing versus suppressive effects of stress on immune function: Implications for immunoprotection and immunopathology. *Neuroimmunomodulation, 16*: 300–317.

Engel, G. L. (1981). The clinical application of the biopsychosocial model. *Journal of Medicine and Philosophy, 6*: 101–124.

Friedmann, E., Katcher, A. H., Thomas, S. A., Lynch, J. J., & Messent, P. R. (1983). Social interaction and blood pressure. Influence of animal companions. *Jounal of Nervous and Mental Disease, 171*: 461–465.

Friedmann, E., Locker, B. Z., & Lockwood, R. (1993). Perception of animals and cardiovascular responses during verbalization with an animal present. *Anthrozoös, 6*: 115–134.

Friedmann, E., Thomas, S. A., Son, H., Chapa, D., & McCune, S. (2013). Pet's presence and owner's blood pressures during the daily lives of pet owners with pre-to mild hypertension. *Anthrozoös, 26*: 535–550.

Gee, N. R., Friedmann, E., Stendahl, M., Fisk, A., & Coglitore, V. (2014). Heart rate variability during a working memory task: Does touching a dog or person affect the response? *Anthrozoös, 27*: 513–528.

Glaser, R., & Kiecolt-Glaser, J. K. (2005). Stress-induced immune dysfunction: Implications for health. *Nature Reviews Immunology, 5*: 243–251.

Handlin, L., Nilsson, A., Ejdeback, M., Hydbring-Sandberg, E., & Uvnas-Moberg, K. (2012). Associations between the psychological characteristics of the human-dog relationship and oxytocin and cortisol levels. *Anthrozoös, 25*: 215–228.

Hansen, K. M., Messinger, C. J., Baun, M. M., & Megel, M. (1999). Companion animals alleviating distress in children. *Anthrozoös, 12*: 142–148.

Hardy, L., Beattie, S., & Woodman, T. (2007). Anxiety-induced performance catastrophes: Investigating effort required as an asymmetry factor. *British Journal of Psychology, 98*: 15–31.

Harker, M. (2013). Psychological sweating: A systematic review focused on aetiology and cutaneous response. *Skin Pharmacology and Physiology, 26*: 92–100.

Hellhammer, D. H., Wust, S., & Kudielka, B. M. (2009). Salivary cortisol as a biomarker in stress research. *Psychoneuroendocrinology, 34*: 163–171.

Kingwell, B. A., Lomdahl, A., & Anderson, W. P. (2001). Presence of a pet dog and human cardiovascular responses to mild mental stress. *Clinical Autonomic Research, 11*: 313–317.

Lass-Hennemann, J., Peyk, P., Streb, M., Holz, E., & Michael, T. (2014). Presence of a dog reduces subjective but not physiological stress responses to an analog trauma. *Frontiers in Psychology, 5*: 1010.

Lynch, J. J., Long, J. M., Thomas, S. A., Malinow, K. L., & Katcher, A. H. (1981). The effects of talking on the blood pressure of hypertensive and normotensive individuals. *Psychosomatic Medicine, 43*: 25–33.

Lynch, J. J., Thomas, S. A., Long, J. M., Malinow, K. L., Friedmann, E., & Katcher, A. H. (1982). Blood pressure changes while talking. *Israeli Journal of Medical Science, 18*: 575–579.

Malinow, K. L., Lynch, J. J., Thomas, S. A., Friedmann, E., & Long, J. M. (1982). Automated blood pressure recording: The phenomenon of blood pressure elevations during speech. *Angiology, 33*: 474–479.

Nagengast, S. L., Baun, M. M., Megel, M., & Leibowitz, J. M. (1997). The effects of the presence of a companion animal on physiological arousal and behavioral distress in children during a physical examination. *Journal of Pediatric Nursing, 12*: 323–330.

Nater, U. M. & Rohleder, N. (2009). Salivary alpha-amylase as a non-invasive biomarker for the sympathetic nervous system: Current state of research. *Psychoneuroendocrinology, 34*: 486–496.

O'Haire, M. E., McKenzie, S. J., Beck, A. M., & Slaughter, V. (2013). Social behaviors increase in children with autism in the presence of animals compared to toys. *PloS ONE, 8*: e57010.

O'Haire, M. E., McKenzie, S. J., Beck, A. M., & Slaughter, V. (2015). Animals may act as social buffers: Skin conductance arousal in children with autism spectrum disorder in a social context. *Developmental Psychobiology, 57*(5): 584–595.

Polheber, J. P., & Matchock, R. L. (2014). The presence of a dog attenuates cortisol and heart rate in the Trier Social Stress Test compared to human friends. *Journal of Behavioral Medicine, 37*: 860–867.

Salehi, B., Cordero, M. I., & Sandi, C. (2010). Learning under stress: The inverted-U-shape function revisited. *Learning & Memory, 17*: 522–530.

Schuck, S. E., Emmerson, N. A., Fine, A. H., & Lakes, K. D. (2015). Canine-assisted therapy for children with ADHD: Preliminary findings from the positive assertive cooperative kids study. *Journal of Attention Disorders, 19*: 125–137.

109

Somervill, J. W., Kruglikova, Y. A., Robertson, R. L., Hanson, L. M., & MacLin, O. H. (2008). Physiological responses by college students to a dog and a cat: Implications for pet therapy. *North American Journal of Psychology, 10*: 519–528.

Straatman, I., Hanson, E. K., Endenburg, N., & Mol, J. A. (1997). The influence of a dog on male students during a stressor. *Anthrozoös, 10*: 191–197.

Teigen, K. H. (1994). Yerkes-Dodson: A law for all seasons. *Theory & Psychology, 4*: 525–547.

Ulrich-Lai, Y. M., & Herman, J. P. (2009). Neural regulation of endocrine and autonomic stress responses. *Nature Reviews Neuroscience, 10*: 397–409.

Vagnoli, L., Caprilli, S., Vernucci, C., Zagni, S., Mugnai, F., & Messeri, A. (2015). Can presence of a dog reduce pain and distress in children during venipuncture? *Pain Management Nursing, 16*: 89–95.

van Andel, H. W., Jansen, L. M., Grietens, H., Knorth, E. J., & van der Gaag, R. J. (2014). Salivary cortisol: A possible biomarker in evaluating stress and effects of interventions in young foster children? *European Child & Adolescent Psychiatry, 23*: 3–12.

Vilgis, V., Silk, T. J., & Vance, A. (2015). Executive function and attention in children and adolescents with depressive disorders: A systematic review. *European Child & Adolescent Psychiatry, 24*: 365–384.

Wachelka, D., & Katz, R. C. (1999). Reducing test anxiety and improving academic self-esteem in high school and college students with learning disabilities. *Journal of Behavior Therapy and Experimental Psychiatry, 30*: 191–198.

Young, J. S. (2012). Pet therapy: Dogs de-stress students. *Journal of Christian Nursing, 29*: 217–221.

Zilcha-Mano, S., Mikulincer, M., & Shaver, P. R. (2012). Pets as safe havens and secure bases: The moderating role of pet attachment orientations. *Journal of Research in Personality, 46*: 571–580.

CHAPTER 9

Does Reading to a Dog Affect Reading Skills?

Andrea Beetz and Peggy McCardle

Introduction

Reading programs including animals, mostly dogs, have become quite popular in the US and Europe since the introduction of this animal-assisted education approach by Intermountain Therapy Animals in 1999 (Intermountain Therapy, n.d.). Today, two different forms of dog-assisted reading exist. In the first, children read to a dog mainly in a one-to-one setting, with the dog-handler there to ensure safety for all parties without being intensely involved in the reading process. The child should merely enjoy reading to a non-judgmental listener, the dog, in a relaxed environment. In the second, a teacher or education expert provides reading training over the course of several weeks, mainly for small groups of students with low reading skills, including a trained (school-) dog in the process. Students receive reading instruction, discuss what they have read, learn reading strategies and more, while the dog serves to make the setting more relaxed, fun, and motivating and is actively involved in tasks such as handing out worksheets. According to the definitions of AAI by the International Association of Human-Animal Interaction Organizations (Jegatheesan et al., 2015), the first approach should be counted as an animal-assisted activity, due to the frequently encountered lack of the educational expertise of the dog-handler and his/her non-involvement, while the dog-assisted reading training represents a form of animal-assisted education.

In this chapter, we provide a short introduction to factors important in the process of learning to read, then present available data on the effects of reading with dogs. We also address some theories, mechanisms, and general effects of HAI that could explain the positive effects of reading with dogs and what is needed to promote this practice as a valid educational approach.

Important Issues in Learning to Read

Reading is a complex endeavor, and we know that it requires explicit instruction (National Institute of Child Health and Human Development (NICHD), 2000), opportunities to practice, and early intervention when students struggle to master the necessary skills. The five major components of reading instruction are phonemic awareness (learning that words can consist of smaller segments of sound, phonemes, which can change the meaning of words – e.g., *cat* versus *bat* or *can* versus *car*), phonics (learning that the letters of the alphabet represent phonemes, that can be blended together to form words), fluency (reading quickly, accurately, and with expression), vocabulary, and reading comprehension (NICHD, 2000). Motivation and self-efficacy are also important, and students who struggle can become discouraged over time and begin to avoid reading, thus denying themselves important practice and information gained through reading.

Instruction and Intervention

In most countries, children learn to read when they begin kindergarten or primary school, and may be learning letter names and sounds even earlier. They learn to "sound out" words (phonics, or "decoding"), and they are on the way to reading. By about 6–7 years of age, they are reading words and sentences; now the goals are reading fluency and the ultimate goal of reading – reading comprehension, the ability to understand what is read, be able to repeat and explain the main ideas, link what they have read to their knowledge of the world, and eventually to draw inferences. One important part of learning to read is practicing reading. Mastery in any domain consists both of developing skills and then using them; this is also true for reading. As students get better at decoding, it becomes automatized, and they are able to read more quickly – this comes through mastering decoding and through practice. They need to know what words mean – so vocabulary is crucially important, too, and many words are learned through wide reading.

112

Explicit instruction in reading should be ongoing, as everything increases in complexity. Vocabulary requires continuing instruction: even though reading helps increase vocabulary, instruction in new words and their morphology and syntax is important, and whole new sets of words are encountered, e.g., in science, geography, social studies. Sentences increase in length and structure, and the ideas presented are more complex. Even fluency requires instructional support. Both independent practice, and practice with corrective feedback, as well as explicit models of fluent reading are important for struggling readers (for a synthesis of fluency research, see Chard, Vaughn, & Tyler, 2002).

Motivation and Self-efficacy

Psychologists differentiate between intrinsic motivation (acting for one's own satisfaction) and extrinsic motivation (acting to gain rewards or avoid punishments or negative outcomes). A review of the literature on motivation and self-efficacy is beyond the scope of this article. However, those interested in examining possible mechanisms for effects of reading-to-animals programs might note the following. Researchers have argued that motivated readers read more and feel more positive toward the activity; based on this, Wigfield conceptualized dimensions and a theory of motivation for reading (Wigfield, 1997). Wigfield and Guthrie (1997) found that 4th and 5th grade children's intrinsic motivation predicted both the amount and breadth of their reading more strongly than did extrinsic motivation, and Baker and Wigfield (1999) demonstrated that dimensions of motivation for reading could be reliably measured. Logan, Medford, and Hughes (2011) found low intrinsic motivation to contribute to low-ability readers' poor reading comprehension. Finally, researchers have demonstrated that it is possible to improve both intrinsic motivation and self-efficacy for reading (Wigfield, Guthrie, Tonks, & Perencevich, 2004), although few, if any, have studied the impact of reading-to-animals programs on motivation or self-efficacy (see Beetz, 2012; Heyer & Beetz, 2014). Guthrie et al. (2006) did report that a high number of stimulating tasks (such as hands-on science activities) increased reading comprehension, but this was mediated by motivation; they concluded that situational interest was increased by stimulating tasks, and that this positively affected both longer-term intrinsic motivation and reading comprehension. This at least raises the question as to whether a similar study of reading-to-animals programs might show positive effects on reading motivation.

113

Research on Reading with Dogs

The positive effects of involving dogs in reading settings, which are assumed by the AAI-practitioners, have been investigated via various research designs. Not all are published studies, but given the limited amount of research, we report both published work and poster presentations.

Experimental Research – Spontaneous Effects of Dogs on Reading

In the following experimental studies, the reading performance of the same children was tested twice; once in a situation without a dog present, and once with a friendly but unfamiliar dog present. The order of the settings was counterbalanced; half of the sample always started out with the dog, the other half without the dog. Strasser, Kelly-Vance, Dredge, and Juilfs (2013) assessed the reading performance of 40 students from grades 1 to 7 in each reading setting twice, and measured salivary cortisol after each 1-minute reading situation. All children had improved in the short reading assessment over the course of the four sessions, with no significant differences between settings. However, the children who had a dog at home showed lower cortisol levels after sessions reading with the (unfamiliar) dog as compared to reading without the dog.

Similarly, Jäger and Hirschenhauser (2014) assessed salivary cortisol in nine children, reading once with and once without an unfamiliar dog present. While the entire group tended towards lower cortisol levels in the dog's presence, two children had higher cortisol levels with the dog. This indicates that individual differences need to be observed closely in practice and research and, in the course of individual optimization, indications and contra-indications for reading with dogs as well as the appropriate amount of time for familiarization with the animal need to be identified. And finally, Wohlfarth, Mutschler, Beetz, and Schleider (2014) investigated the reading performance of 12 children aged 6–7, assessing the amount of text read in a fixed period of time in the presence, or absence, of an unfamiliar dog. In the presence of the dog, the children read significantly more words and reached a higher number of line breaks.

All of these experiments involved children without significant deficits in reading skills. This makes the generalization of positive findings to the actual target group somewhat questionable, since children with low reading skills, experiences and fears of failure, and low motivation might react differently with regard to reading performance as well as stress regulation in a dog's presence. In contrast, Schretzmeyer, Beetz, Amon, and Kotrschal (2014) applied the same experimental design to 36 3rd graders (50% male) with reading skills notably below average. In the second session of two, the group reading in the presence of the dog reached higher scores in a standardized reading test, although when taking both sessions together, no significant differences between settings were observed. However, the children showed lower cortisol levels when reading with the dog present. These findings indicate that it is possible that dogs might provide a physiological advantage, and, once students are accustomed to the experimenter or the reading test situation, they may experience a spontaneous advantage for reading performance.

Evaluations of Reading-with-Dogs Programs

In contrast to these experiments investigating spontaneous effects of dog presence on reading, the following evaluations captured effects of reading-with-dogs programs over several weeks, using pre/post measurement control-group designs.

Smith (2010) investigated the reading skills of 26 children in the 3rd grade, who were schooled at home and read aloud to a dog once a week for 30 minutes, while the control group read alone. While both groups improved in reading, the increase of reading skills was significantly greater in the dog-group. Similarly, Emmert (2013) assessed effects of reading-with-dogs for 15 minutes over the course of ten weeks in afternoon school in 64 children with below average reading skills. In contrast to a control group, which read without a dog, the dog-group had improved significantly in reading fluency. Also, the children voluntarily read longer than the required time with the dog, which points to a potential positive influence of the dog setting on motivation and practice. Finally, le Roux, Swartz, and Swartz (2014) reported a controlled ten-week trial in which poor 3rd grade readers were randomly assigned to groups that read to a dog, an adult, or a teddy bear, or received no intervention. While no formal instruction was provided in the three treatment conditions, all volunteers were "encouraged to correct the errors of students and support the students" (p. 662). Le Roux and colleagues reported improved reading comprehension in the group reading to a dog.

Evaluations of Dog-assisted Reading Intervention

Today, training for dog-assisted reading seems to be found mainly in German-speaking countries. This might be due to the fact that school dogs are quite common there (see Beetz, 2013; Kotrschal & Ortbauer,

115

2003). School dogs usually belong to the teacher and are especially trained and tested for working in a classroom setting with children, and it is easy to integrate them in the extra reading instruction these teachers provide throughout the school year for students with low reading skills. The following research consisted of pre/post and follow-up measurement with control groups, employing standardized and validated reading tests, and included more peer-reviewed research than the two previous categories.

In a pilot-study, Beetz (2012) evaluated the effect of a 12-week dog-assisted reading program on six students in the 6th grade with low reading skills, and a control group of seven students receiving the usual reading instruction without a dog. Each session lasted 45 minutes once a week and included reading a book together, working with worksheets, and discussing reading strategies and the content of the text. Groups were not balanced for gender. Both groups improved in reading skills over the course of the 12 weeks, with no significant group differences. However, at the post-measurement (eight weeks after the end of the intervention, including six weeks of summer holiday which usually lead to a drop in academic scores), the dog-group had improved even more in reading skills while the scores of the control-group had declined. That is, on the follow-up measurement, the dog-group showed a significantly larger increase in reading competence. This result also indirectly suggests positive effects on reading motivation as well as an improved reader self-concept. All children in the dog-group reported that they had read on their own during the summer holidays.

Heyer and Beetz (2014) assessed the effects of 12 sessions of a dog-assisted reading program for 3rd graders (four male and four female) in contrast to a control group (four male and four female) receiving the same reading instruction with a life-size dog hand puppet that resembled the employed school dog. Sessions were held weekly in groups of four. At the end of the training and at follow-up eight weeks later (after the six-week summer holiday), the dog-group had improved significantly more in reading skills, including the understanding of sentences and text content. In addition, seven of the eight children in the dog-group reported having read by themselves during the holidays, while no child in the control-group reported this. Again, this suggests a motivational effect and more sustainable improvements in the dog-assisted reading training. Regarding the overall socio-emotional experiences in school, the dog-group reported better class climate in their regular classrooms, and more enjoyment of learning, and feelings of acceptance by teachers and peers. These improvements positively correlated with the improvements in reading skills.

Summary of Research on Reading with Dogs

Overall, the results of these different studies suggest a positive effect for reading with dogs and dog-assisted reading programs. However, as many of the studies, with the exception of Beetz (2012), Heyer and Beetz (2014), le Roux et al. (2014), and Wohlfarth et al. (2014), have not yet been published in peer-reviewed journals, they should be interpreted with caution. Definitely, more peer-reviewed published research with larger samples is needed before one can argue in general for the effectiveness of reading with dogs. In addition, indications and contra-indications of these programs for individual students should be investigated. The possible underlying mechanisms explaining why dogs might effectively support learning to read, are clearly important, as discussed in the next section.

How Can Dogs Support Reading Skills?

Different theories and potential mechanisms have been discussed with regard to positive effects of HAI in general (Beetz, Julius, Turner, & Kotrschal, 2012; Freund, McCune, Esposito, & McCardle, 2016; Julius, Beetz, Kotrschal, Turner, & Uvnäs-Moberg 2013; Wohlfarth et al., 2014), of which some might be applicable also to reading with dogs.

Motivation

Working with animals, in particular dogs, seems to increase motivation with regard to the skill to be trained. Several authors (Beetz, 2012; Emmert, 2013; Heyer & Beetz, 2014) have interpreted their observations as an increased motivation to read in the dog-groups. In a sports program for overweight children, Wohlfarth et al. (2014) proposed that a dog increased intrinsic motivation, indirectly indicated by a higher amount of movement in the dog setting; the authors refer to motivation theory, following the distinction between extrinsic and intrinsic motivation, which often are in conflict. For example, with reading, participation is often externally motivated, required by school, while due to experiences of failure the child may lack intrinsic motivation to read.

Wohlfarth and colleagues (2014), citing various authors, describe motivation as follows: Intrinsic motivation is subconsciously aroused, associated with task enjoyment, and builds on natural incentives; they are closely associated with processing and learning via actual experiences rather than symbols and language, while explicit motivation is aroused consciously and via verbal stimuli. Wohlfarth and colleagues propose that animals have the potential to activate implicit motives, since interacting with them automatically activates the experiential or sensory system (smells, actions, sights, touch), at least to a larger extent than paper-and-pencil tasks. Therefore, the situation, the stimuli provided by the animal, is "coded" by the human in terms of positive emotional and motivational states (joy, curiosity). Overall, they suggest, animals can serve as "hot stimuli" (Wohlfarth et al., 2014) in challenging situations, eliciting implicit motivation and enjoyment of the tasks.

Biophilia

Why animals can be "hot stimuli" may be explained at least partly via the concept of biophilia (Wilson, 1984). Biophilia is an affinity to nature, life, and life-like processes, including animals, which developed in the course of evolution as humans lived with animals in a shared environment. Paying attention to animals, be it positive (caring, appreciation of aesthetics) or negative (fear of predators, disgust) had survival value for humans. Animals could indicate danger, which is probably the reason calm and relaxed animals in our surroundings can promote a feeling of safety and relaxation (biophilia-effect; Julius et al., 2013). On the other hand, attention to animals and interest in interacting with friendly animals seem to increase motivation and activation. Human attachment demonstrated by caregiving behavior toward animals, activated particularly by friendly animals perceived as cute, may also play a role in promoting interaction (Julius et al., 2013).

Attachment and Stress Reduction via Social Support

Based on humans' early experiences with their caregivers, humans develop attachment behaviors, which also influence strongly how well a person can regulate stress reactions via social support (Julius et al., 2013). Those with insecure attachment do not profit as much from social support from another person as do securely attached individuals, with regard to stress regulation. For example, children with insecure attachment may not be able to use friendly teacher support to help them regulate their stress. Insecure attachment is found in up to 90% of children with special education needs, and in challenging situations like reading intervention, with a subjectively high chance of failure, and potentially heightened levels of fear and stress, these children therefore are less likely to be optimally supported in their stress regulation by another person. In contrast, children with insecure attachment can spontaneously profit from social support by a friendly dog, and have been shown to have lower cortisol levels during challenging tasks when a dog is present (Beetz et al., 2011; Beetz, Julius, et al., 2012). This also seems to be true to some extent for reading with dogs (Jäger & Hirschenhauser, 2014; Strasser et al., 2013).

Activation of the Oxytocin System

Irrespective of attachment, down-regulation of stress reactions via HAI is probably also achieved via the activation of the oxytocin system (Beetz & Bales, 2016; Beetz, Uvnäs-Moberg, Julius, & Kotrschal, 2012; Carter & Porges, 2016). The hormone oxytocin reduces stress reactions (cortisol levels, heart rate, blood pressure) and fear. The oxytocin system can be activated via pleasant touch, a factor which usually prominent in HAI, but less so interpersonally outside parent-child or intimate partner relationships. Therefore, reading with dogs can provide the advantage of easily achieved pleasant touching of the dog resulting in reduction of stress and fear. That oxytocin is indeed released due to the pleasant touch of a friendly or familiar dog has been documented by several studies. Oxytocin also promotes positive mood, trust, and social interaction including communication, all effects observed in HAI.

119

Dogs Promote Learning Prerequisites

It is an accepted fact that successful and sustainable learning experiences require attention, concentration, motivation, absence of fear and stress, and neutral-to-positive mood. As noted, interactions with dogs (and friendly animals in HAIs in general) have the potential to promote these factors and therefore contribute to the prerequisites for successful learning. This is even more important for students who already have had negative experiences with a subject or skill; expectancy of failure usually induces avoidance, negativity, fear, and stress, which negatively affect executive functions (Diamond & Lee, 2011; Miyake et al., 2000), which include, e.g., impulse control, self-reflection, self-motivation, working memory, and concentration. Studies have documented that the involvement of dogs can indeed promote concentration and motivation (Gee, Church, & Altobelli, 2010; Gee, Crist, & Carr, 2010; Hediger & Turner, 2014).

Overall, these concepts and mechanisms provide a broad explanatory basis for the potential positive effects of integrating dogs in reading programs for children with low reading skills. However, motivation, activation of the oxytocin system, reduction of stress and fear, all need to be more closely investigated in reading settings with more controlled studies and larger samples.

Conclusion

While theory and data provide a rationale for including dogs in interventions to improve reading skills, more research is needed as well as a consideration of the suitability of the approach for each child. In conducting this research, reading measures should be carefully chosen, with more than one where possible, and information on other factors (practicing reading at home, pet ownership, tutoring received, presence of learning disabilities) that might affect the outcomes considered. Since motivation and stress reduction are potential mechanisms, these too should be measured both pre and post. Given what is known about the process of learning to read, it is relatively obvious that reading-to-dogs programs without teaching involvement are only suitable for children who already have achieved a certain level of reading skills (decoding) and predominantly need to practice reading fluency. For children with insufficient basic reading skills, dog-assisted reading interventions that include instruction are more appropriate. A dog can support the prerequisites of learning, but certainly cannot teach a child to read. In addition, the acceptance and credibility of including dogs in reading programs will only increase if such programs include concerns for child and animal safety and well-being, appropriate instruction, and thoughtful structure with clear goals and well-documented outcomes.

References

Baker, L., & Wigfield, A. (1999). Dimensions of children's motivation for reading and their relations to reading activity and reading achievement. *Reading Research Quarterly, 34*(4): 452–477.

Beetz, A. (2012). Leseförderung mit Hund – Eine Pilot-Studie. *Heilpädagogik, 56*(1): 17–25.

Beetz, A. (2013). Socio-emotional correlates of a schooldog-teacher-team in the classroom. *Frontiers in Psychology* (*Frontiers in Educational Psychology*), 4: 886. doi: 10.3389/fpsyg.2013.00886

Beetz, A., & Bales, K. (2016). Affiliation in human-animal interaction. In L. S. Freund, S. McCune, L. Esposito, N. Gee, & P. McCardle (Eds.), *Social neuroscience and human-animal interaction* (pp. 107–126). Washington, DC: American Psychological Association.

Beetz, A., Julius, H., Turner, D., & Kotrschal, K. (2012). Effects of social support by a dog on stress modulation in male children with insecure attachment. *Frontiers in Psychology*, *3*: 352. doi: 10.3389/fpsyg.2012. 00352

Beetz, A., Kotrschal, K., Hediger, K., Turner, D., Uvnäs-Moberg, K., & Julius, H. (2011). The effect of a real dog, toy dog and friendly person on insecurely attached children during a stressful task: An exploratory study. *Anthrozoös*, *24*(4): 349–368.

Beetz, A., Uvnäs-Moberg, K., Julius, H., & Kotrschal, K. (2012). Psychosocial and psychophysiological effects of human-animal interactions: The possible role of oxytocin. *Frontiers in Psychology*, *12*(3): 234. doi: 10.3389/ fpsyg.2012.00234

Carter, C. S., & Porges, S. W. (2016). Neural mechanisms underlying human-animal interaction: An evolutionary perspective. In L. S. Freund, S. McCune, L. Esposito, N. Gee, & P. McCardle (Eds.), *Social neuroscience and human-animal interaction* (pp. 89–106). Washington, DC: American Psychological Association.

Chard, D. J., Vaughn, S., & Tyler, B. (2002). Effective interventions for building reading fluency with elementary student with learning disabilities. *Journal of Learning Disabilities*, *35*(5): 386–406.

Diamond, A., & Lee, K. (2011). Interventions shown to aid executive function development in children 4 to 12 years old. *Science*, *333*: 959–964.

Emmert, J. (2013). Quantifying the impact of incorporating therapy dogs in an afternoon school program: A comparison of net change in reading fluency. Oral Presentation at the ISAZ Conference, Chicago, IL, July 17–19, 2013.

Freund, L. S., McCune, S., Esposito, L., Gee, N., & McCardle, P. (Eds.) (2016). *Social neuroscience and human-animal interaction*. Washington, DC: American Psychological Association.

Gee, N. R., Church, M. T., & Altobelli, C. L. (2010). Preschoolers make fewer errors on an object categorization task in the presence of a dog. *Anthrozoös*, *23*(3): 223–230.

Gee, N. R., Crist, E. N., & Carr, D. N. (2010). Preschool children require fewer instructional prompts to perform a memory task in the presence of a dog. *Anthrozoös*, *23*(2): 173–184.

Guthrie, J. T., Wigfield, A., Humenick, N. M., Perencevich, K. C., Taboada, A., & Barbosa, P. (2006). Influences of stimulating tasks on reading motivation and comprehension. *The Journal of Educational Research*, *99*(4): 232–246.

Hediger, K., & Turner, D. (2014). Can dogs increase children's attention and concentration performance? A randomized controlled trial. *Human-Animal Interaction Bulletin, 2*(2): 21–39.

Heyer, M., & Beetz, A. (2014). Grundlagen und Effekte einer hundegestützten Leseförderung. *Empirische Sonderpädagogik, 2*: 172–188.

Intermountain Therapy Animals. (n.d.). Pets helping people: Reading Education Assistance Dogs (R.E.A.D.). Retrieved from http://therapyanimals.org/R.E.A.D.html

Jäger, N., & Hirschenhauser, K. (2014). Stress hormone patterns of nine-year-old children during dog-assisted reading: Which factors predict individual responsiveness. Poster, 23rd Annual Meeting of the International Society for Anthrozoology (ISAZ). Vienna, Austria, July 19–21, 2014.

Jegatheesan, B., Beetz, A., Ormerod, E., Johnson, R., Fine, A. H., Yamazaki, K., ... Choi, G. (2015). *The IAHAIO definitions for animal assisted intervention and guidelines for wellness of animals involved.* In A. H. Fine (Ed.), *Handbook on animal-assisted therapy* (pp. 415–418). New York: Academic Press,.

Julius, H., Beetz, A., Kotrschal, K., Turner, D., & Uvnäs-Moberg, K. (2013). *Attachment to pets – An integrative view of human-animal relationships with implications for therapeutic practice.* New York: Hogrefe.

Kotrschal, K., & Ortbauer, B. (2003). Behavioral effects of the presence of a dog in a classroom. *Anthrozoös, 16*(2): 147–159.

le Roux, M. C., Swartz, L., & Swartz, E. (2014). The effect of an animal-assisted reading program on the reading rate, accuracy and comprehension of grad 3 students: A randomized controlled study. *Child Youth Care Forum, 43*: 655–673. doi: 10.1007/s10566-014-9262-1

Logan, S., Medford, E., & Hughes, N. (2011). The importance of intrinsic motivation for high and low ability readers' reading comprehension performance. *Learning and Individual Differences, 21*(1): 124–128.

Miyake, A., Friedman, N. P., Emerson, M. J., Witzki, A. H., Howerter, A., & Wager, T. D. (2000). The unity and diversity of executive functions and their contributions to complex frontal lobe tasks: A latent variable analysis. *Cognitive Psycholrlgy, 41*(1): 49–100.

National Institute of Child Health and Human Development (NICHD). (2000). *Report of the National Reading Panel. Teaching children to read: An evidence-based assessment of the scientific research literature on reading and its implications for reading instruction: Reports of the subgroups* (NIH Publication No. 00-4754). Washington, DC: U.S. Government Printing Office.

Schretzmeyer, L., Beetz, A., Amon, S., & Kotrschal, K. (2014).
Psychophysiologic benefits of dog-assistance for reading performance?
Poster, 23rd Annual Meeting of the International Society for
Anthrozoology (ISAZ). Vienna, Austria, July 19–21, 2014.

Smith, K. A. (2010). *Impact of animal assisted therapy reading instruction on
reading performance of homeschooled students.* ProQuest LLC, Ed.D.
Dissertation, Northcentral University.

Strasser, R., Kelly-Vance, L., Dredge, S., & Juilfs, K. (2013). Animal-assisted
intervention: Impact on children's stress hormone levels and reading
scores. Poster, IAHAIO Conference 2013, Chicago, IL, July 20–22, 2013.

Wigfield, A. (1997). Children's motivation for reading and reading
engagement. In J. T. Guthrie & A. Wigfield (Eds.), *Reading engagement:
Motivating readers through integrated instruction* (pp. 14–33). Newark, DE:
International Reading Association.

Wigfield, A., & Guthrie, J. T. (1997). Relations of children's motivation for
reading to the amount and breadth of their reading. *Journal of
Educational Psychology, 89*(3): 420–432.

Wigfield, A., Guthrie, J. T., Tonks, S., & Perencevich, K. C. (2004). Children's
motivation for reading: Domain specificity and instructional influences.
The Journal of Educational Research, 97(6): 299–310.

Wilson, E. O. (1984). *Biophilia.* Cambridge, MA: Harvard University Press.

Wohlfarth, R., Mutschler, B., Beetz, A., & Schleider, K. (2014). An
investigation into the efficacy of therapy dogs on reading performance
in 6–7 year old children. *Human-Animal Interaction Bulletin, 2* (2):
60–73.

CHAPTER 10

Children's Play, Self-Regulation, and Human-Animal Interaction in Early Childhood Learning

*Vinaya Rajan, Nancy R. Gee,
Roberta Michnick Golinkoff, and
Kathy Hirsh-Pasek*

Lisa can't wait to get to school! Today it's her turn to take care of the class pets, Burt and Ernie. At the start of the year everyone in Ms. Taylor's classroom learned how to care for guinea pigs: What they eat, how they like to be handled, how to clean their cage, when they like to sleep, and much more. The students who showed the teacher they were capable of taking on the responsibility were each assigned a week to care for Burt and Ernie. Lisa loves Burt and Ernie and considers it an honor to care for them. She

also gets to select responsible helpers to assist her with the job. This experi-
ence has taught Lisa and her classmates about responsibility, empathy,
ecology, animal behavior, and respect for living creatures.

Introduction

Classrooms such as Ms. Taylor's, where animals are integral to the educational experience and learning is made enjoyable through active participation tied to meaningful information, easily fit the vision of a high-quality preschool classroom. Unfortunately, the preschool class-room has changed drastically in recent years. Focused narrowly on academic performance, today's preschools are determined to ensure that each child is ready for school – a cliché that translates into ready to perform in math and reading. Indeed, a recent article bemoans the "academization" of early learning classrooms over the last two decades (Bassok, Latham, & Rorem, 2016). In 1998, 31% of kindergar-ten teachers thought their children should know how to read; that number has more than doubled to 80% in 2005. Classrooms once flush with art supplies, pets, and music are now more formalized hotbeds for "learning." Time spent on art and music has dropped by 16 and 18 percentage points, respectively (Bassok et al., 2016).

There is no doubt that having exposure to a rich curriculum is central to later learning, especially for children not receiving this exposure in their home or community. Attention to curricular goals advances preschool education. But attention to curricular goals in the absence of an age-appropriate pedagogy is ill-founded (Hirsh-Pasek & Golinkoff, 2011; Hirsh-Pasek, Golinkoff, Berk, & Singer, 2009). A narrow focus on academics to the exclusion of social skills, enriched language knowledge, and creative expression will not prepare our children well (Golinkoff & Hirsh-Pasek, 2016).

Christakis (2016) argues that the modern preschool has lost its way, becoming an artificial habitat for children – a place where the animals are made of plastic. In this chapter, we suggest that it is possible to con-struct a rich curriculum for preschool learning delivered within a playful learning pedagogy. We argue that in the new culture of preschools, we can teach children a rich palate of twenty-first-century skills. To the extent that we want to "craft environments that promote healthy, think-ing, caring and social children who will become collaborative, creative, competent and responsible citizens tomorrow" (Golinkoff & Hirsh-Pasek, 2016), we must offer children a richer palate of learning opportu-nities from the youngest ages. This vision paves the way for the return of the class pet as a central ingredient in a high-quality classroom.

125

Human-Animal Interaction and Principles for Effective Learning

Human-animal interaction (HAI) is a relatively young field of inquiry for developmental scientists (Esposito, McCune, Griffin, & Maholmes, 2011). Researchers have recently begun to more seriously examine the physical, social, and emotional benefits of HAI on child health and development in everyday life, classroom settings, and therapeutic contexts (see Chapters 4–10 in this volume). HAI has promise as a mechanism to foster children's learning because it embraces principles of effective learning from the science of learning (Bransford, Brown, & Cocking, 1999; Meltzoff, Kuhl, Movellan, & Sejnowski, 2009), which states that children learn best when (1) they are *active* rather than passive; (2) they are *engaged*, not distracted; (3) the information or activity is *meaningful*; and (4) the activity is socially *interactive* (Hirsh-Pasek et al., 2015; Toub, Rajan, Golinkoff, & Hirsh-Pasek, 2016). These principles are evident when teachers incorporate animals in the classroom as part of the educational experience, although this area deserves more empirical research.

Incorporating animals in the classroom can capitalize on children's interests and attention, keeping them actively engaged with content and providing meaningful educational experiences. Teachers incorporate animals in the classroom to provide hands-on, active learning experiences in academic subjects and creative projects. For example, Rud and Beck (2000, 2003) found that teachers use animals in the classroom to teach concepts such as biological content related to the life cycle or ethical and financial issues with respect to pet care. Such practices align with the research literature on early childhood learning, which shows that children actively involved and cognitively engaged with the material experience superior learning (Fisher, Hirsh-Pasek, Newcombe, & Golinkoff, 2013; Haden, 2002; Sénéchal, Thomas, & Monker, 1995). Animals in the classroom can enhance a lesson, allowing children to make meaningful connections between newly acquired information and their personal experiences or pre-existing knowledge, another characteristic of an effective learning environment (Bransford et al., 1999). Endenburg and van Lith (2011) suggest that companion animals can serve as powerful motivators for learning for two reasons: (1) when children have an emotional investment in a subject, they will learn and retain more about it; and (2) learning is optimized when it occurs within the context of meaningful relationships. Thus, it appears that teachers can involve classroom pets as a way to enhance the curriculum, allow for active participation in the learning context, and provide opportunities to make meaningful connections with new material (Gee, 2010).

Effective learning environments should also keep children's attention task-focused. Children learn best in environments with limited distractions. For example, play with electronic toys decreases the quality of parent-child interaction compared to traditional toys, as less on-topic language is used (Parish-Morris, Mahajan, Hirsh-Pasek, Golinkoff, & Collins, 2013; Sosa, 2015; Zosh et al., 2015). Children learn best in environments that allow them to focus on relevant information, and there is some evidence that children's memory (Gee, Belcher, Grabski, DeJesus, & Riley, 2012) and concentration improve in the presence of an animal (Chapter 5, this volume) and that they are less likely to make mistakes on a categorization task (Gee, Church, & Altobelli, 2010).

The best learning contexts are not just active or constructive but also interactive and contingent (Chi, 2009). The presence of a social partner interacting in a contingent manner results in superior object retrieval (Troseth, Saylor, & Archer, 2006) and word learning (Krcmar, Grela, & Lin, 2007; Roseberry, Hirsh-Pasek, & Golinkoff, 2014) in young children. In fact, children can benefit from having parasocial relationships with on-screen characters (Hirsh-Pasek et al., 2015). To elaborate, Lauricella, Gola, and Calvert (2011) found that toddlers learned better from a video demonstration of an early math task when the onscreen character (i.e., Elmo) was socially meaningful rather than unfamiliar. If children can show educational gains from the relationships they build with media characters, then it is likely that they can learn and acquire important cognitive and socio-emotional skills from their interactions with live animals.

Levinson (1962, 1964) was one of the first to suggest that the presence of an animal might function as a social facilitator. Furthermore, caring for an animal increases children's empathic responses (Daly & Suggs, 2010), something essential for having our children become caring people who can take the perspective of others. O'Haire, McKenzie, McCune, and Slaughter (2013) found that a primary school animal-assisted activity program involving guinea pigs led to improved social functioning (see also Chapter 7, this volume). Therefore, contexts that promote positive social interaction (e.g., classrooms including animals) may be especially beneficial for student learning. Indeed, Kotrschal and Ortbauer (2003) found that the presence of a dog increased 1st graders' attention to the teacher. To summarize, HAI has promise as a mechanism to foster children's learning because it embraces the four principles of effective learning, creating environments that are active, engaging, meaningful, and socially interactive.

Correlates of Self-Regulation in Early Childhood

As previously noted, the focus of early childhood education should not be narrowly constrained to academic outcomes, but should also emphasize key social and emotional skills that impact school readiness and later school success. One such skill is self-regulation, the volitional control of attention, emotion, and executive functions (EFs) in service of a goal (Blair & Ursache, 2011; Chapter 5, this volume). Mastery of self-regulation in early childhood affects later academic and life trajectories, predicting important adult outcomes 30 years later (i.e., physical health status, substance dependence, wealth, and crime rates; Moffitt et al., 2011).

Self-regulation is foundational for positive school adaptation. A child who can pay attention, stay engaged, inhibit impulsive behavior, and manage frustration is better able to benefit from the learning environment (Blair & Raver, 2015). An accumulating body of research highlights the importance of self-regulation. Cognitive aspects of self-regulation, often referred to as EFs, predict emergent numeracy and literacy skills and later reading and math achievement (Blair & Razza, 2007; Clark, Pritchard, & Woodward, 2010).

Young children who are more adept at regulating their emotions are more likely to acquire early academic skills, adapt to routines, follow rules, and form positive relationships, thus adjusting better to the classroom context (Shields et al., 2001) and performing better academically (Graziano, Reavis, Keane, & Calkins, 2007). In contrast, lower levels or inadequate mastery of self-regulation places students at educational risk (Blair & Diamond, 2008; Raver, 2002). Children who exhibited classroom misconduct, aggression, and were disengaged were found more likely to underachieve and have negative attitudes about school (Ladd & Burgess, 2001). Therefore, children experiencing difficulty effectively managing frustration and negative emotions may have trouble regulating classroom learning behaviors and, thus, have lower academic achievement (Howse, Calkins, Anastopoulos, Keane, & Shelton, 2003).

How HAI might Influence Self-regulation

Taken together, these findings suggest that self-regulation serves as an antecedent for school readiness, and educators should focus on fostering its development. Preschool curricula, such as *Tools of the Mind* (Bodrova & Leong, 2007), shown to improve self-regulation and positively affect academic progress (Blair & Raver, 2014), may prove amenable to the inclusion of HAI. One potential way HAI could influence the development of self-regulation is through stress regulation. EFs, which include the core skills of working memory, inhibitory control, and cognitive flexibility (Miyake et al., 2000), depend on the prefrontal cortex and are negatively impacted by chronic stress (Diamond, 2013; Liston, McEwen, & Casey, 2009; Morasch, Raj, & Bell, 2013). Programs that enhance emotional well-being and help us feel calm and socially supported can potentially improve EFs (Diamond, 2015), and children's play or interaction with a classroom pet has the potential to boost EF skills. For example, when children are required to retain multi-step directions with respect to the proper care and handling procedures for taking care of an animal, it may lead to gains in working memory. Teachers can incorporate animals in play by allowing each child to take turns handling the classroom pet. Through their interaction, children practice inhibiting certain behaviors (e.g., habitual response of trying to grab or hug the animal) and practice delaying gratification by learning how to wait their turn or waiting for a time when the animal is receptive or initiates contact. The presence of an animal also promotes calmness and reduces stress, fear, and anxiety (see Beetz, Uvnas-Moberg, Julius, & Kotrschal, 2012, for a review). HAI can also influence the emotional aspects of self-regulation by increasing social skills and decreasing problem behaviors such as classroom aggression (Hergovich, Monshi, Semmler, & Zieglmayer, 2002).

HAI may also influence self-regulation indirectly via physical activity. We know physical activity is beneficial to human health and well-being, and relatively recent investigations reveal its benefits for cognitive development (e.g., Churchill et al., 2002; Ploughman, 2008). In a review expanding on a meta-analysis of 44 studies, Tomporowski, Davis, Miller, and Naglieri (2008) reported that, while exercise was positively related to child intelligence, cognition, and academic achievement, those gains were most clearly seen on EF tasks. Best (2010) discusses the convergence of an assortment of studies showing that moderate to vigorous aerobic exercise promotes EF in children; the greater cognitive engagement required (team cooperation, strategizing, task switching), the more likely it was to influence cognitive development, specifically EF. Diamond's (2000) review of the literature presented evidence that specific brain structures (the cerebellum and prefrontal cortex) are important for the execution of both complex cognitive and motor functions, opening the possibility that physical activity causes physiological changes to specific brain structures underlying both cognition and motor behavior.

Both researchers and the popular press have focused on the relationship between dog ownership and physical activity; e.g., in a survey of 1,813 adults, the adjusted odds of achieving sufficient physical activity and walking were 57% to 77% higher among dog owners compared with non-dog owners (Cutt, Giles-Corti, Knuiman, Timperio, & Bull, 2008). Although little of this research focused on children, in one observational study one-third of 1,097 Australian primary school children were physically active with their dogs (Martin, Wood, Christian, & Trapp, 2015), suggesting dog walking/play as a viable means of supporting child health. Diamond (2015) noted that physical activity and play with animals is cognitively engaging and may have a strong impact on boosting EF.

Future Directions

Educational practices that integrate HAI and play into early curricula show promise in promoting children's early learning and self-regulation development. However, this area can benefit from more sound, methodologically rigorous experimental designs. Future studies should examine whether hands-on activities using animals in the classroom lead to greater gains in academic knowledge beyond more passive methods of instruction. For example, Hummel and Randler (2012) found that the presence of living animals in a middle school classroom increased student retention relative to a control group, but found comparable rates between the live animal and film condition. However, students in the live animal condition reported increased interest. In contrast, another study found that using live zoo animals in the classroom for science education improved 1st grade students' writing; students in the live-animal classroom produced longer, more coherent texts and included more references to science concepts compared to students taught using traditional methods (Wilson, Trainin, Laughridge, Brooks, & Wickless, 2011). Clearly, more work is needed to understand whether gains in cognitive achievement can be directly linked to the inclusion of live animals. Moreover, if benefits are established in experimental designs, the mechanisms whereby these effects are created must be studied. What is it about a live animal that promotes greater attention and focus in the classroom? Or do animals trigger increased motivation to perform?

In addition to the safety, liability, and health concerns of incorporating animals in classrooms (Chapters 2 and 3, this volume), special consideration must be given to providing teachers with adequate training in incorporating play with animals in order to achieve a specific learning goal. For guidelines on the use of animals in the classroom for educational purposes, we refer the reader to Gee, Fine, and Shuck (2015) and Chapter 14 of this volume. Of critical importance is the extent to which the presence of animals in the classroom helps students stay engaged and focused on specific learning objectives *without* interfering. According to Gee (2010), teachers reported that animals in the classroom could be a distraction; incorporating an animal as an effective motivator to learning would require a delicate balance. Gee, Sherlock, Bennett, and Harris (2009) examined motor skills in preschoolers, under three conditions: the presence of a live dog, stuffed dog, or adult. Children adhered to instructions better when the real dog served as co-performer (relative to other co-performers) in modeling tasks, indicating that there may be something uniquely motivational for preschoolers watching a dog perform a task and then doing that same task. However, in a tandem task (requiring the same behaviors are executed at the same time) their best performance was with an adult present, and the children sought clarification more when a dog was present; having a live animal present may help children restrict their attention to task demands, but also can create an additional challenge for some tasks. Further research is needed to determine the circumstances under which the presence of an animal may be beneficial, detrimental, or irrelevant for preschool children.

In conclusion, although the guinea pigs are small, the lessons that Burt and Ernie impart in Ms. Taylor's classroom are massive. They can bring a new level of enthusiasm and interest to enhance lessons in vocabulary (e.g., what words describe a guinea pig?), mathematics (e.g., how much does it weigh?), and science (e.g., what is the guinea pig's natural habitat?), while also encouraging the development of self-regulation and social skills by creating a calming presence in the classroom and instilling a sense of responsibility and compassion when caring for another living creature. All of this can be accomplished age-appropriately to maximally promote the twenty-first-century skills children need to succeed (Golinkoff & Hirsh-Pasek, 2016). Incorporating animals may provide a promising approach to hands-on, active, playful educational experiences in early childhood learning.

References

Bassok, D., Latham, S., & Rorem, A. (2016). Is kindergarten the new first grade? *AERA Open*, 1(4): 1–31. doi: 10.1177/2332858415616358

Beetz, A., Uvnas-Moberg, K., Julius, H., & Kotrschal, K. (2012). Psychosocial and psychophysiological effects of human-animal interactions: The possible role of oxytocin. *Frontiers in Psychology*, *3*: 352. doi: 10.3389/fpsyg.2012.00352

Best, J. R. (2010). Effects of physical activity on children's executive function: Contributions of experimental research on aerobic exercise. *Developmental Review*, *30*: 331–351. doi: 10.1016/j.dr.2010.08.001

Blair, C., & Diamond, A. (2008). Biological processes in prevention and intervention: The promotion of self-regulation as a means of preventing school failure. *Developmental Psychopathology*, *20*(3): 899–911.

Blair, C., & Raver, C. C. (2014). Closing the achievement gap through modification of neurocognitive and neuroendocrine function: Results from a cluster randomized controlled trial of an innovative approach to the education of children in kindergarten. *PloS one*, *9*(11): e112393–e112393. doi: 10.1371/journal.pone.0112393

Blair, C., & Raver, C. C. (2015). School readiness and self-regulation: A developmental psychobiological approach. *Annual Review of Psychology*, *66*: 711–731. doi: 10.1146/annurev-psych-010814-015221

Blair, C., & Razza, R. P. (2007). Relating effortful control, executive function, and false belief understanding to emerging math and literacy ability in kindergarten. *Child Development*, *78*(2): 647–663 doi: 10.1111/j.1467-8624.2007.01019.x

Blair, C., & Ursache, A. (2011). A bidirectional model of executive functions and self-regulation. In K. D. Vohs & R. F. Baumeister (Eds.), *Handbook of self-regulation* (2nd edn, pp. 300–320). New York: Guilford.

Bodrova, E., & Leong, D. J. (2007). *Tools of the mind: A Vygotskian approach to early childhood education* (2nd edn). Columbus, OH: Merrill/Prentice Hall.

Bransford, J., Brown, A., & Cocking, R. (Eds.) (1999). *How people learn: Brain, mind, experience and school*. Washington, DC: National Academy of Sciences.

Chi, M. T. H. (2009). Active-Constructive-Interactive: A conceptual framework for differentiating learning activities. *Topics in Cognitive Science*, *1*: 73–105. doi: 10.1111/j.1756-8765.2008.01005

Christakis, E. (2016). *The importance of being little*. New York: Viking.

Churchill, J. D., Galvez, R., Colcombe, S., Swain, R. A., Kramer, A. F., & Greenough, W. T. (2002). Exercise, experience and the aging brain. *Neurobiology of Aging*, *23*: 941–955. doi: 10.1016/S0197-4580(02)00028-3

Clark, C. A., Pritchard, V. E., & Woodward, L. J. (2010). Preschool executive functioning abilities predict early mathematics achievement. *Developmental Psychology, 46*(5): 1176–1191. doi: 10.1037/a0019672

Cutt, H., Giles-Corti, B., Knuiman, M., Timperio, A., & Bull, F. (2008). Understanding dog owners' increased levels of physical activity: Results from RESIDE. *American Journal of Public Health, 98*: 66–69. doi: 10.2105/AJPH.2006.103499

Daly, B., & Suggs, S. (2010). Teachers' experiences with humane education and animals in the elementary classroom: Implications for empathy development. *Journal of Moral Education, 39*(1): 101–112. doi: 10.1080/03057240903528733

Diamond, A. (2000). Close interrelation of motor development and cognitive development and of the cerebellum and prefrontal cortex. *Child Development, 71*: 44–56. doi: 10.1111/1467-8624.00117

Diamond, A. (2013). Executive functions. *Annual Review of Psychology, 64*: 135–168. doi: 10.1146/annurev-psych-113011-143750

Diamond, A. (2015). Effects of physical exercise on executive functions: Going beyond simply moving to moving with thought. *Annals of Sports Medicine and Research, 2*(1): 1011.

Endenburg, N., & van Lith, H. A. (2011). The influence of animals on the development of children. *The Veterinary Journal, 190*: 208–214. doi: 10.1016/j.tvjl.2010.11.020

Esposito, L., McCune, S., Griffin, J. A., & Maholmes, V. (2011). Directions in human-animal interaction research: Child development, health, and therapeutic interventions. *Child Development Perspectives, 5*(3): 205–211. doi: 10.1111/j.1750-8606.2011.00175.x

Fisher, K. R., Hirsh-Pasek, K., Newcombe, N., & Golinkoff, R. M. (2013). Taking shape: Supporting preschoolers' acquisition of geometric knowledge through guided play. *Child Development, 84*(6): 1872–1878. doi: 10.1111/cdev.12091

Gee, N. R. (2010). The role of pets in the classroom. In P. McCardle, S. McCune, J. Griffin, L. Esposito, & L. Freund (Eds.), *Animals in our lives: Human-animal interaction in family, community, & therapeutic settings* (pp. 117–141). Baltimore, MD: Brookes Publishing.

Gee. N. R., Belcher, J. M., Grabski, J. L., DeJesus, M., & Riley, W. (2012). The presence of a therapy dog results in improved object recognition performance in preschool children. *Anthrozoös, 25*(3): 289–300. doi: 10.2752/175303712X13403555186172

Gee, N. R., Church, M. T., & Altobelli, C. L. (2010). Preschoolers make fewer errors on an object categorization task in the presence of a dog. *Anthrozoös, 23*(3): 223–230. doi: 10.2752/175303710X12750451258896

Gee, N. R., Fine, A., & Shuck, S. (2015). Animals in educational settings: Research and application. In A. Fine (Ed.), *Animal assisted therapy: Theoretical foundations and guidelines for practice* (4th edn, pp. 195–210). New York: Academic Press.

Gee, N. R., Sherlock, T. R., Bennett, E. A., & Harris, S. L. (2009). Preschoolers' adherence to instructions as a function of the presence of a dog, and motor skills task. *Anthrozoös, 22*: 267–276. doi: 10.2752/175303709X457603

Golinkoff, R. M., & Hirsh-Pasek, K. (2016). *Becoming brilliant: What science tells us about raising successful children.* Washington, DC: APA Press.

Graziano, P. A., Reavis, R. D., Keane, S. P., & Calkins, S. D. (2007). The role of emotion regulation in children's early academic success. *Journal of School Psychology, 45*(1): 3–19. doi: 10.1016/j.jsp.2006.09.002

Haden, C. A. (2002). Talking about science in museums. *Child Development, 4*: 62–67. doi: 10.1111/j.1750-8606.2009.00119.x

Hergovich, A., Monshi, B., Semmler, G., & Zieglmayer, V. (2002). The effects of the presence of a dog in the classroom. *Anthrozoös, 15*: 37–50. doi: 10.2752/089279302786992775

Hirsh-Pasek, K., & Golinkoff, R. M. (2011). The great balancing act: Optimizing core curricula through playful learning. In E. Zigler, W. S. Gilliam, & W. S. Barnett (Eds.), *The pre-K debates: Current controversies and issues* (pp. 110–115). Baltimore, MD: Brookes Publishing Company.

Hirsh-Pasek, K., Golinkoff, R. M., Berk, L. E., & Singer, D. G. (2009). *A mandate for playful learning in school: Presenting the evidence.* New York: Oxford University Press.

Hirsh-Pasek, K., Zosh, J., Golinkoff, R. M., Gray, J., Robb, M., & Kaufman, J. (2015). Putting education in "educational" apps: Lessons from the science of learning. *Psychological Science in the Public Interest, 16*(1): 3–34. doi: 10.1177/1529100615569721

Howse, R. B., Calkins, S. D., Anastopoulus, A. D., Keane, S. P., & Shelton, T. L. (2003). Regulatory contributors to children's kindergarten achievement. *Early Education and Development, 14*(1): 101–120. doi: 10.1207/s15566935eed1401_7

Hummel, E., & Randler, C. (2012). Living animals in the classroom: A meta-analysis on learning outcome and a treatment-control study focusing on knowledge and motivation. *Journal of Science Education and Technology, 21*(1): 95–105. doi: 0.1007/s10956-011-9285-4

Kotrschal, K., & Ortbauer, B. (2003). Behavioral effects of the presence of a dog in a classroom. *Anthrozoös, 16*: 147–159. doi: 10.2752/089279303786992170

Krcmar, M., Grela, B., & Lin, K. (2007). Can toddlers learn vocabulary from television? An experimental approach. *Media Psychology, 10*(1): 41–63. doi: 10.1080/15213260701300931

Ladd, G. W., & Burgess, K. B. (2001). Do relational risks and protective factors moderate the linkages between childhood aggression and early psychological and school adjustment? *Child Development, 72*(5): 1579–1601. doi: 10.1111/1467-8624.00366

Lauricella, A. R., Gola, A. A. H., & Calvert, S. L. (2011). Toddlers' learning from socially meaningful video characters. *Media Psychology, 14*: 216–232. doi: 10.1080/15213269.2011.573465

Levinson, B. M. (1962). The dog as "co-therapist." *Mental Hygiene, 46*: 59–65.

Levinson, B. M. (1964). Pets: A special technique in child psychotherapy. *Mental Hygiene, 48*: 243–248.

Liston, C., McEwen, B. S., & Casey, B. J. (2009). Psychosocial stress reversibly disrupts prefrontal processing and attentional control. *Proceedings of the National Academy of Sciences, 106*: 912–917. doi: 10.1073/pnas.0807041106

Martin, K. E., Wood, L., Christian, H., & Trapp, G. S. A. (2015). Not just "A Walking the Dog": Dog walking and pet play and their association with recommended physical activity among adolescents. *American Journal of Health Promotion, 29*(6): 353–356. doi: 10.4278/ ajhp.130522-ARB-262

Meltzoff, A. N., Kuhl, P. K., Movellan, J., & Sejnowski, T. J. (2009). Foundations for a new science of learning. *Science, 325*(5938): 284–288. doi: 10.1126/science.1175626

Miyake, A., Friedman, N. P., Emerson, M. J., Witzki, A. H., Howerter, A., & Wager, T. D. (2000). The unity and diversity of executive functions and their contributions to complex "frontal lobe" tasks: A latent variable analysis. *Cognitive Psychology, 41*(1): 49–100. doi: 10.1006/cogp. 1999.0734

Moffitt, T. E., Arseneault, L., Belsky, D., Dickson, N., Hancox, R. J., Harrington, H., … Caspi, A. (2011). A gradient of self-control predicts health, wealth and public safety. *Proceedings of the National Academy of Sciences, 108*(7): 2693–2698. doi: 10.1073/pnas.1010076108

Morasch, K. C., Raj, V., & Bell, M. A. (2013). The development of cognitive control from infancy through early childhood. In D. Reisberg (Ed.), *Oxford handbook of cognitive psychology* (pp. 989–999). New York: Oxford University Press.

O'Haire, M. E., McKenzie, S. J., McCune, S., & Slaughter, V. (2013). Effects of animal-assisted activities with guinea pigs in the primary school classroom. *Anthrozoös, 26*(3): 445–458 doi: 10.2752/175303713X13697 429463835

Parish-Morris, J., Mahajan, N., Hirsh-Pasek, K., Golinkoff, R. M., & Collins, M. F. (2013). Once upon a time: Parent-child dialogue and storybook reading in the electronic era. *Mind, Brain, and Education, 7*(3): 200–211. doi: 10.1111/mbe.12028

Ploughman, M. (2008). Exercise is brain food: The effects of physical activity on cognitive function. *Developmental Neurorehabilitation, 11*: 236–240. doi: 10.1080/17518420801997007

Raver, C. C. (2002). Emotions matter: Making the case for the role of young children's emotional development for early school readiness. *Social Policy Report, 16*(3): 3–19.

Roseberry, S., Hirsh-Pasek, K., & Golinkoff, R. M. (2014). Skype me! Socially contingent interactions help toddlers learn language. *Child Development, 85*(3): 956–970. doi: 10.1111/cdev.12166

Rud, A. G., Jr., & Beck, A. M. (2000). Kids and critters in class together. *Phi Delta Kappan, 82*(4): 313–315. doi: 10.1177/003172170008200417

Rud, A. G., Jr., & Beck, A. M. (2003). Companion animals in Indiana elementary schools. *Anthrozoös, 16*(3): 241–251. doi: 10.2752/089279303786992134

Sénéchal, M., Thomas, E., & Monker, J. (1995). Individual differences in 4-year-old children's acquisition of vocabulary during storybook reading. *Journal of Educational Psychology, 87*(2): 218–229. doi: 10.1037/0022-0663.87.2.218

Shields, A., Dickstein, S., Seifer, R., Giusti, L., Dodge Magee, K., & Spritz, B. (2001). Emotional competence and early school adjustment: A study of preschoolers at risk. *Early Education and Development, 12*(1): 73–96. doi: 10.1207/s15566935eed1201_5

Sosa, A. V. (2015). Association of the type of toy used during play with the quantity and quality of parent-infant communication. *Journal of the American Medical Association Pediatrics.* Advance online publication. doi: 10.1001/jamapediatrics.2015.3753

Tomporowski, P. D., Davis, C. L., Miller, P. H., & Naglieri, J. A. (2008). Exercise and children's intelligence, cognition, and academic achievement. *Educational & Psychological Review, 20*: 111–131. doi: 10.1007/s10648-007-9057-0

Toub, T. S., Rajan, V., Golinkoff, R. M., & Hirsh-Pasek, K. (2016). Guided play: A solution to the play versus learning dichotomy. In D. Geary & D. Berch (Eds.), *Evolutionary perspectives on child development and education* (pp. 117–141). New York: Springer.

Troseth, G. L., Saylor, M. M., & Archer, A. H. (2006). Young children's use of video as a source of socially relevant information. *Child Development, 77*(3): 786–799. doi: 10.1111/j.1467-8624.2006.00903.x

Wilson, K., Trainin, G., Laughridge, V., Brooks, D., & Wickless, M. (2011). Our zoo to you: The link between zoo animals in the classroom and science and literacy concepts in first-grade journal writing. *Journal of Early Childhood Literacy, 11*(3): 275–306. doi: 10.1177/1468798410390898

Zosh, J. M., Verdine, B. N., Filipowicz, A., Golinkoff, R. M., Hirsh-Pasek, K., & Newcombe, N. S. (2015). Talking shape: Parental language with electronic versus traditional shape sorters. *Mind, Brain, and Education, 9*(3): 136–144. doi: 10.1111/mbe.12082

The Methods and Approaches

CHAPTER 11

Methods for Bridging Human-Animal Interactions and Education Research

Carol McDonald Connor and Harold Herzog

Introduction

As many have noted, research on HAI has suffered from a number of serious flaws (e.g., Chur-Hansen, Stern, & Winefield, 2010; Herzog, 2015), including small sample sizes, inadequate or no control groups, lack of standardization of intervention procedures, no controls for researcher expectations, lack of long-term follow-up, and positive publication bias. At the same time, research methods and reporting are improving. In this chapter we offer guidance in designing and conducting HAI studies in schools; describe best practices in conducting research in schools, the challenges and potential pitfalls researchers may face; and suggestions for conducting HAI research in classrooms, from correlational and longitudinal studies to randomized controlled trials (RCTs). We also cover *What Works Clearinghouse* standards for conducting RCTs in education, and appropriate data analyses.

What is Your Research Question?

In any study, the design and methods will be driven by the researchers' questions. Is so little known about the question that it is best answered using qualitative methods, or is enough known that a quasi-experiment or RCT is warranted? Or is the purpose of the research to design and test a specific intervention? In this chapter, we focus on questions of "what works?" Arguably, these are the kinds of studies most needed in the field, as can be seen by the previous chapters and concerns about the robustness of existing HAI research.

Making Causal Claims

To say that something – e.g., the use of animals to improve learning – has a positive effect on student outcomes (say, science learning), three conditions are required: (1) predictor (animals) and outcome (science learning) must be correlated; (2) the predictor must chronologically precede the outcome; and (3) there can be no other plausible explanation for the relation between the them. For example, a researcher wants to know whether the use of live animals, such as worms, in a science unit on soil ecology and animal habitats, helps children learn the science content (Connor et al., 2010). A number of teachers are teaching this unit; some are using worms whereas others are not. The researcher compares students' scores on the science unit post-test in classrooms with and without worms. Students in classrooms where teachers used worms had stronger scores on the post-test compared to students in classrooms where the teacher did not use worms. Can the researcher conclude that using worms in the unit improved learning? That is, were all three conditions met to make this causal claim?

Unfortunately, no. The first claim was met – use of worms and student outcomes were correlated. The second claim, that using worms preceded measuring the student outcome, was only partially met. A stronger design would have measured students' knowledge of soil ecology before the unit. It is possible that students in the classrooms where worms were used already had more understanding of worms and soil ecology. Without a pre-test, we cannot conclude that performance on the post-test actually represented student learning. This is a serious limitation of concurrent data.

Finally, the researcher could not claim there were no other plausible explanations for the relation between using worms and students' post-test scores. It is conceivable that generally more effective teachers are more likely to go to the time and trouble of using animals to teach science; their students would have learned more science whether the teacher used worms or not. Using worms might have presented an expense higher-poverty schools could not afford. Hence classrooms not using worms might have also served more children living in poverty, who also may have had fewer opportunities to learn science outside the home (Duncan & Murnane, 2011). The researchers can claim that using worms correlates with science learning but not that it *caused* better learning, a useful first step. If using worms and student outcomes had not been related, the expense and trouble of using worms would be unwarranted. Such opportunistic studies are useful but have clear limitations.

Designing Studies that Meet all Three Requirements to Make a Causal Claim

143

Developing Research Questions

Requirement 1, that the predictor and outcome are related, is fairly straightforward, but depends on the research question. Our example of whether or not to use worms in a science unit has an easy-to-manipulate variable – worms – and clear and easy-to-measure outcomes – gains in the unit test scores from before to after the unit was taught. However, some comparisons are not as easy (or cheap). What if the question was about the impact of service dogs in the classroom? Dogs can be trained to sense the impending onset of hypoglycemic attacks in individuals suffering from Type I diabetes; people with diabetic alert dogs report decreased emergency room calls, fewer bouts of unconsciousness, and improved independence (Rooney, Morant, & Guest, 2013). It is certainly possible that these dogs could help diabetic children adapt to educational settings, but is this the case? There are a number of serious challenges when framing the research questions and designing this study. Service animals such as diabetic alert dogs are typically highly trained and relatively rare. What "effect" do we measure? Are questions centered around the student who wants to bring the dog to school? What about the other students in the class? Is the health of the student (e.g., reducing the number of days absent; maintaining consistent blood sugar levels) or the effect on classmates (e.g., frequency of disruptions) to be measured? Observing the classroom with the dog present might offer some ideas. To begin to make causal claims, however, specific measureable predictors and outcomes are required. Assume that there are two important research questions: (1) does the presence of service dogs reduce school absences for the target student?; and (2) does the number of classroom disruptions change when the dog is present? Although this seems to oversimplify the question, in fact, making sure that we ask answerable questions is critical to making causal claims. Careful conversations with stakeholders (students, parents, teachers, school administrators) will help frame research questions worth answering. Indeed, stakeholders at a specific school are likely to be more interested in results at their school than at schools in general. In this case, carefully considering which covariates to measure will improve generalizability as well as help educators make informed decisions about service animals at their school. Case studies at a single school may be a good place to start but it is unlikely that the findings will generalize to other schools. For example, our target student with the diabetic alert dog might attend an affluent school in a suburb where home and school resources ensure that the dog does not increase disruptions, and the student's attendance might have been high with or without the service dog. A diabetic alert dog might have a very different impact at a school serving higher poverty or more remote communities where resources are different.

The two questions in our example are designed to provide clear answers about the potential benefits (lower absenteeism) accorded target students and potential costs (increased disruptions) to peers. The predictors, intervention, and outcomes are measurable, so it is straightforward to examine the associations among the use of service dogs, target student attendance, and class disruptions (e.g., number of minutes students are off task). But correlation is not causation. Causal claims require carefully designed studies.

Designing the Study

To meet requirement 2, that the predictor chronologically precedes the outcome, requires a longitudinal design. For the worms, as discussed, assessing students' knowledge prior to the beginning of the unit, teaching the unit with or without worms, and assessing students' knowledge afterward is a straightforward longitudinal design that meets requirement 2 – the predictor, worms or no worms, precedes the outcome, plus there is some understanding of conditions prior to intervention.

But what about our diabetic alert dog study? Because service dogs are highly trained, there may be no more than one per school. Plus, diabetic alert dogs may serve a number of purposes (Gonder-Frederick, Rice, Warren, Vajda, & Shepard, 2013). Designing a study of the impact of service dogs more generally requires a different design – longitudinal, with pre- and post-intervention assessments and a diverse sample of schools. The number of days students were absent prior to receiving a dog or before the dogs were allowed in school, as well as the number of minutes of disruption in the class-room before the dog was allowed in the classroom, are important baseline measures. Then, once the dog has been allowed in the class-room for a specified amount of time (e.g., 3 months), the outcomes are assessed – the number of days the target student was absent and the number of minutes of disruption while the dog was in the class-room. This design will meet requirements 1 and 2 for causal infer-ences but will not allow us to claim that diabetic alert dogs reduce absenteeism and do not disrupt the classroom, because there are still many other plausible explanations. Service dogs are expensive and, thus, are more likely to be available to children with more resources (both economic and social capital). Children with service dogs are likely to have parents who are more responsive and caring generally and have the time and resources to help children train and care for the service dog. Additionally, schools where discipline and behavior are chronic problems might be less likely to participate in the study. Thus, service dogs might seem to be more effective only because the schools and families participating are more likely to support school attendance and discipline with or without a service dog. As we will discuss, random assignment to treatment and control conditions is one of the most efficient ways to remove this kind of selection bias.

145

Theory of Change and Logic Models

A well-articulated theory of change (TOC, also called theory of action) greatly improves research design. The TOC provides a clear explanation for what the intervention does and why it should have the intended effects. Returning to our worm example, TOCs are cha-racterized by a foundation in theory and prior research, identify the intended target population, and specify the intended outcomes that will be affected. From this, protocols, manuals, measures of fidelity, materials, training, etc. can be developed.

Using our worm example, the nature of the problem is that many students in the early grades fail to learn important science content well (NAEP, 2015). One reason is that science knowledge is not presented compellingly and with real-world information. The underlying theory is that the use of live worms and the opportunity to build and observe a habitat for them will help students learn about soil ecology and how worms help support a thriving soil ecology (Lawrence Hall of Science, 2007). The control condition would use photos and pictures instead of live worms to present the same materials. The contrast between treatment and control conditions reflects the essence of the research question and the TOC. Additionally, without a well-articulated TOC, findings (null or otherwise) are not interpretable.

Figure 11.1 presents the logic model for our worm study. It starts with the population (oval) – 2nd graders learning about habitats. This guides our selection of participating schools, classrooms, and students, that leads to the intervention – use of worms – (rounded-corner square). The squares present expected intervention outcomes. The hypothesis is that the use of worms will more closely portray what happens than can be shown in pictures and photos, and that using live worms will improve students' experience in directly observing soil ecology and the role of worms (e.g., by building and

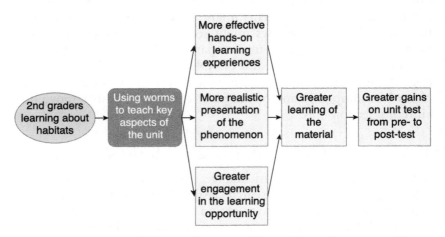

Figure 11.1 Theory of change for research question about using live worms to improve science learning

146

observing a worm terrarium with specific types of soil). Thus, the proximal outcomes offer more effective hands-on learning experiences, more realistic presentation of the phenomenon, and greater student engagement in the learning opportunity. These can be assessed through observation. In turn, these proximal outcomes will result in better learning of the material, reflected in stronger scores on the post-test and greater pre-to-post-test gains. The TOC and logic model will also help clarify which moderators (e.g., student prior science knowledge, school poverty level, teacher years of experience) will be important to include.

Randomized Controlled Field Trials (RCT)

RCTs, also called clinical trials, are considered the gold standard for making causal inferences (Shadish, Cook, & Campbell, 2002; Shavelson & Towne, 2002), because no other design is as efficient or effective in meeting requirement 3 – that there are no other plausible explanations for the association. RCTs reduce both known and unknown biases (e.g., children with service dogs are likely to attend more affluent schools and come from more affluent families). When trying to decide whether, for example, using worms in the science unit causes stronger student learning of the science concepts being taught, we are trying to observe whether a given student learns better with or without live worms. However, the student cannot do both. Once the lesson is taught, the student cannot go back and do the unit again in the other condition – the learning does not go away. Instead, the student is randomly assigned to one condition or the other, so whichever lesson they get is purely by chance. With enough participating students, it is possible to infer what would have happened to the particular student if he or she had been in the other condition. This is the essence of random assignment. The *What Works Clearinghouse* (What Works Clearinghouse (WWC), 2014) offers guidelines for the elements of a rigorous RCT: (1) random assignment, at the student, classroom, school or district level; (2) low overall attrition; (3) baseline equivalency if attrition is high; (4) valid and reliable outcomes aligned with the intervention and collected in the same way for treatment and control groups; (5) reported effect sizes; and (6) appropriate analyses – multi-level if required and correcting for multiple comparisons if needed.

Our worm example provides a straightforward RCT design. Teachers and their students are randomly assigned within schools to one of two conditions: using live worms or using photos and

147

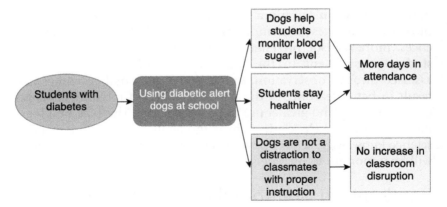

Figure 11.2 Theory of change for study on diabetic alert dogs in schools

pictures. Some studies use a business as usual control group which may be problematic because some teachers in the business as usual control might use worms as part of their standard practice. The alternative treatment is the stronger design: the unit is the same except that either live worms or pictures are used to teach the material.

Our service dog example provides more challenges to designing an RCT; this is where well-considered TOCs and logic models are critical. Figure 11.2 provides the logic model. The target population is students with diabetes. In our example, we include only students with diabetes and randomly assign diabetes alert dogs to some students and not others.

A number of designs would work. Two of the most useful designs when conducting school research are using (1) a waitlist control or (2) a delayed treatment design (see Figure 11.3). Because the number of students who might benefit from a diabetes alert dog is greater than the number of dogs available, we might create a natural experiment where students are randomly assigned to receive a dog or be placed on a waiting list. If there will be enough dogs eventually, then a delayed treatment design where children are randomly assigned to receive a dog right away or later might be the better design; the mid-test provides the RCT and the post-test shows how well the intervention outcomes are maintained over time. The advantage of delayed treatment is that all eligible students receive a diabetic alert dog. In Figure 11.3, for a waitlist control design, the

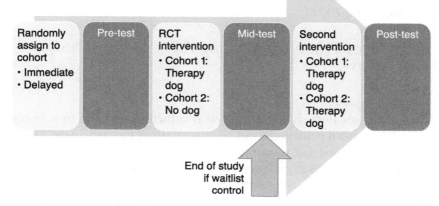

Figure 11.3 Example of a delayed treatment randomized controlled trial design

mid-test would be the post-test and the study would be over. The delayed treatment design is more expensive but tends to be more accepted in schools because all eligible students receive the intervention.

Another challenge for any design is recruiting a large enough sample size to have sufficient statistical power to find differences between treatment and control group outcomes (i.e., power). A well-designed study will include a representative sample large enough to detect an effect that suggests that the intervention is worth the cost. Most school researchers do not use Cohen's guidelines for interpreting effect sizes. Rather, they use more recent guidelines (e.g., Hill, Bloom, Black, & Lipsey, 2008) that consider the students' grade and age as well as the outcome of interest. A study may find null effects only because the size of the sample was too small and not because the treatment was ineffective. In addition, studies with insufficient sample sizes are more likely to produce false positive results (Button et al., 2013). A number of publications discuss estimating the minimally detectable effect size (Hill et al., 2008; Sink & Stroh, 2006). There are also freely available web resources, including Optimal Design software (Raudenbush et al., 2011), which can be used for determining appropriate sample sizes.

It has been argued that well-designed quasi-experiments can be used to make causal inferences, but this is still under debate and there are only a few study designs that will meet the WWC standards with reservations (WWC, 2014). We encourage readers to consult a number of excellent books on quasi-experiment designs (e.g., Shadish et al., 2002).

Challenges When Conducting RCTs (or any Study) in Schools

Recruiting

One of the greatest challenges when conducting research in schools is finding school principals and teachers willing to participate. There are many reasons for refusing – a busy school day, accountability issues, bad previous experiences, and lack of interest. Schools located near universities are frequently research weary or have too many researchers to accommodate. Others schools have never participated in research and are hesitant. Still others may be dysfunctional, so even if they are willing to participate, there are serious challenges to conducting research at the school (e.g., teacher mobility, changing leadership).

One effective paradigm for recruiting schools is fostering researcher-school partnerships (Coburn, Penuel, & Geil, 2013). Coburn and colleagues describe these partnerships as "long term, mutualistic collaborations between practitioners and researchers that are intentionally organized to investigate problems of practice and solutions for improving [student] outcomes" (p. 2). These partnerships differ from more typical researcher-school relationships in five important ways: (1) they are long term and do not stop when the study is completed; (2) they focus specifically on practice and how to improve practice; (3) researchers and practitioners both bring value to the partnership (i.e., mutualism); (4) the strategies for fostering the partnership are intentional; and (5) the results of the partnership affect theory and practice. Studies where researchers pop in, conduct their study, and then disappear are problematic to schools and to other researchers who want to partner with them. Fostering long-term partnerships creates win–win situations where both researchers and practitioners are able to answer their research questions.

Compelling and relevant research questions facilitate participant recruitment. Working closely with stakeholders and school partners before designing the study is important. In our example, the researchers are most interested in whether or not diabetic alert dogs improve the health and school attendance of students whereas teachers and principals are more interested in whether the dogs will present a disruption to learning; both are important and can be included in the overall study.

Designing a Win–Win Study

The sad truth is that practitioners hate control groups. Even though the honest researcher knows that the intervention might not work, the perception is that students in the control group will be denied a potentially effective intervention. The greater the need, the greater the resistance to control groups. This is likely to be the case for many HAI studies.

We have started avoiding any study design that has an untreated control group, as they make it difficult to identify why the intervention is effective, or, if there is no treatment effect, why not. The worm study is designed with an alternative treatment – live worms versus photos – and the rest of the science unit is taught the same way, so all children have the opportunity to learn about worms and soil ecology. If there is no difference between the treatment and control groups, then teachers can use worms at their discretion. (We have already described two other highly useful research designs – waitlist control and delayed treatment.)

151

Selecting Outcomes Useful to Both Practitioners and Researchers

Schools are under pressure to ensure that all students are provided sufficient time in effective learning opportunities, and are held accountable for student outcomes. To the extent that the study design incorporates outcomes that would be useful to practitioners, recruiting and retaining school partners will be easier. For example, in addition to the science unit test, the researchers might also administer a standardized assessment of reading that can be shared with the school. Hence, schools have access to data they can use and the researchers have tested a potentially important moderator of the intervention.

Preserving Study Integrity

Schools are dynamic and challenging environments, which can make it difficult to preserve the integrity of the study while it is being conducted. As discussed, high attrition can destroy the integrity of a well-designed RCT or quasi-experiment. The dynamics of the school community tends to exacerbate attrition: teachers move from grade to grade, sometimes during the school year; students move in and out of the school and district. Such mobility is typically greater at higher-poverty schools. Changes in leadership at the school and district levels can also change a partner into a non-participant. In general, losing more than 25% of the sample, particularly if this attrition is not distributed evenly between treatment and control conditions, changes an RCT to a quasi-experiment. This is why forging strong relationships with school personnel is so important.

How the study is designed and conducted can ameliorate some of the most serious threats to study integrity. First, be conscious of when random assignment is conducted. Wait until the school year has started and rosters are stable before randomly assigning teachers or students to treatment and control conditions. This also avoids the problem of "joiners." This happens when random assignment is conducted before the rosters are stable. If teachers and principals know which teacher is in the treatment and which in the control group, they may move students they perceive to have greater need for the intervention to the treatment classrooms, introducing selection bias and jeopardizing random assignment.

Another threat is "contamination," that teachers in the control group could use key aspects of the intervention. For example, teachers in the worm picture control group might go out and buy their own live worms. Thus, carefully explaining the purpose of the study and carefully observing instruction in both treatment and control conditions is important.

Assessing Fidelity

In any intervention study, making sure the intervention and alternative treatment are implemented as intended is important for making causal inferences. If the interventions are not conducted as intended (e.g., following the science unit protocol with or without worms), then it is not clear what the findings mean. Using the diabetic alert dog study as an example, if the students in the treatment condition never bring their dogs to school, then the intervention was not conducted as intended and so no inferences about service dogs in the classroom can be made. There can also be drift of the intervention so that implementation changes over time.

As noted previously, an important part of fidelity is examining whether there is contamination or drift. Ongoing observations to insure fidelity in both treatment and control groups help to maintain study integrity. There are a number of ways to assess fidelity, which will depend on the research questions and study design. For example, in the worm study, a checklist completed during weekly classroom observations is probably sufficient. On the other hand, because classroom disruptions are an important outcome of the diabetic alert dog study, video-taping and coding disruptions over multiple observations provides a stronger measure of fidelity, as well as a reliable and valid measure of the outcome (i.e., disruptions) before, during, and after the study. For examples of the use of video-tapes and coding in assessing classroom animal interventions, see Kotrschal and Ortbauer (2003) and O'Haire, McKenzie, Beck, and Slaughter (2013).

When considering intervention effects, there are intent-to-treat analyses where the treatment and control groups are compared without consideration of fidelity. In treatment-effects-on-the-treated analyses, the fidelity measure is used and/or only students who actually received the intervention are considered in the analyses (Shadish et al., 2002). Hence, all studies – particularly RCTs and well-designed quasi-experiments – require careful consideration of fidelity, how it is measured in both treatment and control classrooms, and how it is used in analyses.

Mediators and Moderators
Increasingly, researchers want to know not only whether the intervention works but for whom, and when, by examining treatment X child characteristic interaction effects. For example, service dogs might be more effective for children with social-emotional challenges than for more typical children (a treatment X social-emotional status interaction effect). Carefully considering questions about moderation and mediation when developing the research protocol will strengthen the study and the inferences that can be made. Additionally, including key moderators in the analyses will improve the power to find treatment effects.

Analyzing the Data
Simple t-tests are not optimal for school-based research because students are in classrooms, located in schools and communities – the data are nested (Raudenbush & Bryk, 2002). Thus, students who share a classroom are likely to have similar characteristics just because they attend the same classroom. For example, the teacher might be particularly effective teaching science (effects of teaching); more of the children might be gifted (effects of peers); the school might be located in an affluent community (effects of neighborhood), so that the children are likely to learn more science, make

greater gains by interacting with classmates, and have greater resources. In contrast, students who attend schools in high-poverty neighborhoods are likely to share a different set of characteristics. When data are nested, failing to take into account the specific variance of classrooms and schools will tend to misestimate standard errors and p-values. A number of statistical packages can analyze multi-level models including HLM (Raudenbush, Bryk, Cheong, Congdon, & du Toit, 2004), SPSS, and MPlus.

Another consideration in analyzing multi-level data from school research is deciding at which level to enter the variable that represents the treatment effect. If teachers are randomly assigned (e.g., worms or pictures), then the treatment variable should be entered at the classroom level. If schools are randomly assigned, the variable would be entered at the school level; entering the treatment variable at the student level would tend to overestimate the treatment effect and would not meet WWC standards.

Being Honest about Findings and Publishing No Matter What

Increasingly, researchers are becoming aware of publication bias – that studies that find significant treatment effects are more likely to be published than studies with null findings. Thus, it is important for all researchers to attempt to publish all of their findings whether or not the results were as anticipated. Null findings for a well-designed RCT are informative and suggest that some aspect of the TOC is wrong and should be changed. This is how knowledge is created. When researchers leave disappointing findings on their computer or in the filing cabinet, practitioner and researcher communities are short-changed, ineffective interventions continue to be implemented in schools instead of more effective interventions, and students underachieve. There are an increasing number of venues for publishing null findings. For example, the *Journal of Research on Effective Interventions* (https://sree.org/pages/publications/journal.php) and *AERA Open* (http://aera.net/Publications/Journals/tabid/10232/Default.aspx) have specific missions to publish null findings and replications of well-designed studies.

Summary

As is evident from the chapters in this book, funding and conducting rigorous HAI research is becoming a priority. While challenging, rigorous research in schools can answer important questions about HAI and improve our understanding of the role animals play in students' achievement, health, behavior, and social-emotional well-being.

References

Button, K. S., Ioannidis, J. P., Mokrysz, C., Nosek, B. A., Flint, J., Robinson, E. S., & Munafò, M. R. (2013). Power failure: Why small sample size undermines the reliability of neuroscience. *Nature Reviews Neuroscience, 14*(5): 365–376.

Chur-Hansen, A., Stern, C., & Winefield, H. (2010). Commentary: Gaps in the evidence about companion animals and human health: Some suggestions for progress. *International Journal of Evidence-Based Healthcare, 8*(3): 140–146.

Coburn, C. E., Penuel, W. R., & Geil, K. E. (2013). Research-practice partnerships: A strategy for leveraging research for educational improvement in school districts. Retrieved from http://forumfyi.org/files/R-P%20Partnerships%20White%20Paper%20%20Jan%202013%20%20Coburn%20Penuel%20&%20Geil.pdf

Connor, C. M., Kaya, S., Luck, M., Toste, J., Canto, A., Rice, D. C., ... Underwood, P. (2010). Content-area literacy: Individualizing student instruction in second grade science. *Reading Teacher, 63*(6): 474–485.

Duncan, G. J., & Murnane, R. J. (Eds.) (2011). *Whither opportunity? Rising inequality, schools, and children's life changes.* New York: Russel Sage.

Gonder-Frederick, L., Rice, P., Warren, D., Vajda, K., & Shepard, J. (2013). Diabetic alert dogs: A preliminary survey of current users. *Diabetes Care, 36*(4): e47.

Herzog, H. (2015). The research challenge: Threats to the validity of animal-assisted therapy studies and suggestion for improvements. In A. H. Fine (Ed.), *Handbook on animal-assisted therapy: Theoretical foundations and guidelines for practice* (4th edn, pp. 402–407). New York: Academic Press.

Hill, C., Bloome, H., Black, A. R., & Lipsey, M. W. (2008). Empirical benchmarks for interpreting effect sizes in research. *Child Development Perspectives, 2*(3): 172–177.

Kotrschal, K., & Ortbauer, B. (2003). Behavioral effects of the presence of a dog in a classroom. *Anthrozoös, 16*(2): 147–159.

Lawrence Hall of Science. (2007). *Seeds of science/roots of reading.* Nashua, NH: Delta Education LLC & Regents of the University of California.

NAEP. (2015). National Assessment of Educational Progress: The nation's report card. Retrieved from http://nces.ed.gov/nationsreportcard/

O'Haire, M. E., McKenzie, S. J., Beck, A. M., & Slaughter, A. (2013). Social behaviors increase in children with autism in the presence of animals compared to toys. *PLOS One, 8*(2): e57010. doi: 10.1371/journal/pone.0057010

Raudenbush, S. W., & Bryk, A. S. (2002). *Hierarchical linear models: Applications and data analysis methods* (2nd edn). Thousand Oaks, CA: Sage.

Raudenbush, S. W., Bryk, A. S., Cheong, Y. F., Congdon, R., & du Toit, M. (2004). *HLM6: Hierarchical linear and nonlinear modeling*. Lincolnwood, IL: Scientific Software International.

Raudenbush, S. W., Spybrook, J., Congdon, R., Liu, X., Martinez, A., Bloom, H., & Hill, C. (2011). *Optimal design plus empirical evidence* (Version 3.0). Retrieved from http://wtgrantfoundation.org/focusareas#tools-for-group-randomized-trials

Rooney, N. J., Morant, S., & Guest, C. (2013). Investigation into the value of trained glycaemia alert dogs to clients with type I diabetes. *PloS One, 8*(8): 1–12.

Shadish, W. R., Cook, T. D., & Campbell, J. R. (2002). *Experimental and quasi-experimental designs for generalized causal inference*. New York: Houghton Mifflin Company.

Shavelson, R. J., & Towne, L. (Eds.) (2002). *Scientific research in education*. Washington, DC: National Academy Press.

Sink, C., & Stroh, H. (2006). Practical significance: The use of effect sizes in school counseling research. *Professional School Counseling, 9*(4): 401–411. doi: 10.5330/prsc.9.4.283746k664204023

What Works Clearinghouse (WWC) (2014). *WWC procedures and standards handbook* (Version 3.0). Retrieved from http://ies.ed.gov/ncee/wwc/references/idocviewer/Doc.aspx?docId=19&tocId=4

CHAPTER 12

Recommendations for Measuring the Impact of Animals in Education Settings

Nancy R. Gee and
Alexis N. W. Schulenburg

Introduction

In research on human-animal interaction (HAI), one theme echoes throughout the literature. This theme is not new, and has been heralded by many voices (e.g., Fine, 2015; Nimer & Lundahl, 2007). It is simply that high-quality, rigorous research is needed to establish a scientific evidence base for HAI and to support evidence-based practice (Kazdin, 2011). In this volume, authors refer specifically to research on the subject of animals in education settings. In order to recommend to the boards of education and school administrators that animals can, or should, be incorporated into classrooms, we must first establish the pedagogical efficacy of such practices. We need a clear, science-based understanding of when, where, and how animals impact students, teachers, or classroom environments.

Further, we must understand the clinical significance or therapeutic dosage (how much and how often) associated with incorporating diverse animal species in varying contexts and activities. This information will allow us to objectively weigh the practical costs and benefits associated with animal inclusion in education settings.

We are not suggesting that educators wait for a stronger evidence base to be established before incorporating animals into the classroom. In fact, Chapter 1 discusses the frequency of animal inclusion as recently reported, and in many cases underreported due to school policies that ban animals from some schools. Instead we call on researchers to conduct more rigorous investigations and on educators to connect with researchers to participate in ongoing research, and to consider gathering information for themselves, in their own classrooms.

To that end, this chapter provides, at a glance, a resource summarizing key aspects of several assessment tools that are likely to be useful to researchers and educators interested in exploring the intersection of HAI and education. The list is not exhaustive; rather, it highlights and builds on previous resources such as Anderson's (2007) compendium of HAI measures, Wilson and Nettings' (2012) discussion of instrument development in HAI and Strauss, Sherman, and Spreen's (2006) comprehensive sourcebook of critical reviews of neuropsychological assessment tools. We provide information such as reliability, validity, type of test, age range, cost, and administration time and method, for a variety of measures which we have grouped generally into four categories: 1) Academic outcomes: tests of reading, language, and mathematics; 2) Cognition: tools measuring constructs such as general intelligence, working memory and reasoning, presumed to underpin academic achievement and executive functions (EF); 3) Emotional health: measures of psychological constructs such as depression, anxiety, social competency, and positive and negative affect; and 4) Relational health: measures focusing on social interactions, emotional awareness, and social skills.

Academic Outcomes

Arguably, the most direct method of examining the pedagogical efficacy of a particular intervention is to assess academic learning outcomes. The measures listed in Table 12.1 directly assess fundamental aspects of academic attainment: reading, language, and mathematics. The use of direct assessments of academic learning outcomes can render the results largely transparent. One example is a study

158

Table 12.1 Assessments of academic outcomes

Measures	Reliability[a]	Validity[b]	What is measured	Response type, administration time and score[c]	Age range	Information regarding disabilities – appropriate for, or sensitive to	Cost[d]
Expressive One-Word Picture Vocabulary Test, Fourth Edition (EOWPVT-4) Martin & Brownell (2011)	IC: 0.93–0.97 TR: 0.98	n/a	• Examines expressive vocabulary	OR 15–25 minutes Yields RS	2 years 0 months – 70+ years	• Early language delay • Aphasia	A
Expressive Vocabulary Test, Second Edition (EVT-2) Williams (2007)	IC: 0.93–0.94 AR: M = 0.87 across age TR: M = 0.95 across age	CV: 0.81–0.82	• Expressive vocabulary • Word retrieval • Standardized scores provided in manual	OR 10–20 minutes Yields RS	2 years 6 months – 90+ years	• Multiple developmental disabilities • Gifted, and some adult speech-language disorders • Nonverbal, across various ages	B, WM, $R

(continued)

Table 12.1 Assessments of academic outcomes (*continued*)

Measures	Reliability[a]	Validity[b]	What is measured	Response type, administration time and score[c]	Age range	Information regarding disabilities – appropriate for, or sensitive to	Cost[d]
Gray Oral Reading Test 5 (GORT-5) Wiederholt & Bryant (2012)	IR: r ≥ 0.99 TR: r = 0.82–0.90	CV: 0.33–0.77	• Rate • Accuracy • Fluency • Comprehension	WR 15–45 minutes Yields SS	6 years 0 months – 23 years 11 months	• Poor readers	B
Peabody Picture Vocabulary Test, Fourth Edition (PPVT-4) Dunn & Dunn (2007)	TR: M = 0.93 IC: 0.94–0.95 AR: 0.89	CV: 0.82–0.84	• Receptive vocabulary	OR or pointing 10–15 minutes Yields RS	2 years 6 months – 90+ years	• Nonverbal • Various exceptionalities	B, WM, $R
Neale Analysis of Reading Ability (NARA) Neale (n.d.)	AR: 0.93–0.96 McKay (1996)	CCV: 0.91–0.93	• Accuracy • Comprehension • Rate of reading	OR 20 minutes Yields SS	6–12 years	n/a	B

Test	Reliability	Validity	Areas measured	Administration	Age range	Uses	C-WB
Wechsler Individual Achievement Test III (WIAT-III) Wechsler (2009)	IR: 91%–99% TR: 0.87–0.96 IC: 0.46–0.98	n/a	• Oral language • Total reading • Basic reading • Reading comprehension and fluency • Written expression • Mathematics • Math fluency • Total achievement	WR or OR or pointing, web based or in person 29–144 minutes Yields SS	4 years 0 months – 19 years 11 months	• Differentiates between special groups (e.g., gifted, learning problems) and matched controls	
Wide-Range Achievement Test 4 (WRAT-4) Wilkinson & Robertson (2006)	IC: 0.87–0.93	CV: see manual	• Word reading • Sentence comprehension • Spelling • Mathematics	WR 10–45 minutes Yields SS	5–94 years	• Learning disabled • High and low cognitive ability	B

(continued)

Table 12.1 Assessments of academic outcomes (continued)

Measures	Reliability[a]	Validity[b]	What is measured	Response type, administration time and score[c]	Age range	Information regarding disabilities – appropriate for, or sensitive to	Cost[d]
Woodcock-Johnson IV – Tests of Achievement (WJ IV ACH) Schrank, McGrew, & Mather (2014)	TR: 0.83–0.95 IC: 0.89–0.96 LaForte, McGrew, & Schrank (2014)	CV: 0.85–0.93 AR: 0.79–0.95	• Reading • Mathematics • Writing	WR, web based Yields SS	2–90+ years	n/a	A-WB

Academic outcomes refer to reading, writing, language, and mathematics. The measures listed are directly administered to individual students, and all require trained administrators.

Abbreviations used: [a] IR (Interrater Reliability), TR (Test-Retest Reliability), IC (Internal Consistency), AR (Alternate Forms Reliability). [b] Validity: CV (construct validity), CVV (convergent validity), CCV (concurrent validity), EV (ecological validity), FV (factorial validity), DV (divergent validity), CTV (content validity). [c] WR (written response by individual student), OR (oral response by student), SS (Standardized Score), RS (Raw Score compared to standardized norms). [d] A (kit ranges up to $199), B (kit $299–$499), C (kit $500 or more), WB (web based kit available), $R (fee charged for reports).

conducted by le Roux, Swartz, and Swart (2014) evaluating a reading-to-dogs intervention for grade 3 children classified as poor readers; this randomized controlled trial using a standardized measure of reading, the Neale Analysis of Reading Ability (NARA; Neale, n.d.) shows how an assessment tool can be used to examine the pedagogical impact of a specific animal in a specific educational context. The NARA provides standardized measures of reading rate, accuracy, and comprehension for students aged 6–12 years (although see McKay, 1996). The combination of design type, and a reliable and valid assessment, allowed the researchers to draw well-supported conclusions regarding the efficacy of the intervention for the children being evaluated. In brief, they found that children in the "dog group" scored significantly higher on reading comprehension than children in the other three conditions: reading to an adult, a teddy bear, or no intervention. Although the study is not without limitations, it does represent the type of research that is needed to begin to accumulate the evidence base underpinning the intersection between education and HAI and as a first step to determining whether a deeper investigation into mechanisms that might underlie these effects is warranted.

163

Cognition

The assessment tools in Table 12.2 measure skills and abilities necessary for academic achievement, including verbal and nonverbal abilities, working memory, and reasoning. There is now a body of research indicating that these are associated with academic success and general success in life (Qehaja, 2013). In a systematic review of the literature, Jacob and Parkinson (2015) reported a moderate unconditional association between EF and student achievement; broadly speaking EF can be conceptualized as a set of cognitive skills required to direct behavior towards a goal, including working memory, inhibitory control, and attentional flexibility among others, and many of these skills are assessed in the measures listed. Fundamentally, the ability to direct behavior towards the attainment of a goal is key to most academic tasks. Although it may seem intuitive that a causal relationship exists between EF and academic achievement, there is currently no compelling evidence to support such a link. However, in general, the assessments in this section of the table measure globally relevant aspects of human cognition that are associated with, and may potentially be causally related to, academic achievement. Previous research has shown that the presence of a

Table 12.2 Assessments of cognition

Measures	Reliability[a]	Validity[b]	Specific subtests	Response type, administration time and score[c]	Age range	Information regarding disabilities – appropriate for, or sensitive to	Cost[d]
Bayley Scales of Infant and Toddler Development: Third Edition: Cognitive, Language, and Motor Scales Bayley (2005)	IC: 0.86–0.93 TR: 0.67–0.94	CV: 0.49–0.83	• Cognitive • Language: Receptive and expressive • Motor: Eye movements, perceptual-motor integration, motor planning, and motor speed	MR Complete battery: 50–90 minutes Yields SS	1–42 months	Children with Down Syndrome, PDD, CP, SLI, DD, asphyxiation at birth, and prenatal alcohol exposure and children who are small for gestational age or who were born premature or with low birth weight	C

Test	Reliability	Validity	Content	Administration	Age	Population	C-WB
Differential Ability Scales – Second Edition (DAS-II) Elliott (2007)	IC: 0.74–0.96 TR: 0.63–0.93 IR: 0.95–0.99	n/a	• Verbal ability • Nonverbal ability • Nonverbal reasoning ability • Spatial ability • Additional subtests with information regarding memory, processing speed, and foundational abilities	MR Can be web based Core battery: 45–60 minutes Diagnostic subtests: 30 minutes Yields SS	2 years 6 months – 17 years 11 months	Children with learning or hearing impairments, intellectual impairments, and behavior disorders and children with limited English proficiency, intellectual giftedness and disability	
Rivermead Behavioral Memory Test, Third Edition (RBMT-III) Wilson et al. (2008)	IR: ≥ 0.90 AR: 0.57–0.86 IC: 0.87	EV: 0.43–0.44	• Names • Belongings • Appointments • Picture and face recognition • Story • Route • Messages • Orientation and date • Novel tasks	OR 25–30 minutes Yields SS	16–96 years	Clinical memory problems	B

(continued)

165

Table 12.2 Assessments of cognition (continued)

Measures	Reliability[a]	Validity[b]	Specific subtests	Response type, administration time and score[c]	Age range	Information regarding disabilities – appropriate for, or sensitive to	Cost[d]
Social Skills Rating System (SSRS): Academic Competence Community-University Partnership for the Study of Children, Youth, and Families (2011)	IC: 0.95 TR: 0.84–0.93 DiPerna & Volpe (2005)	CV: 0.75	n/a	Teacher completes questionnaire on each student; inputs and receives response from software 15–25 minutes per rating form	3–18 years	Learning impairments, intellectual impairments, and behavior disorders	A-WB
Wechsler Intelligence Scale for Children – Fifth Edition (WISC-V) Wechsler (2014)	IR: 0.90–0.99 TR: 0.63–0.91 IC: 0.81–0.94	CV: 0.74–0.84	• Verbal comprehension • Visual-spatial ability • Fluid reasoning • Working memory • Processing speed	WR, web based 60 minutes Yields SS	6 years 0 months – 16 years 11 months	Intellectual disabilities, learning disabilities and impairments, and giftedness	C-WB

Measure	Reliability & Validity	Domains	Administration	Age range	Purpose	Cost
Wechsler Memory Scale – Fourth UK Edition (WMS-IV UK) Wechsler (2010)	IC: 0.83–0.97 TR: 0.59–0.83 IR: 96–97% CV: 0.50–0.81	• Auditory memory • Visual memory • Visual-working memory • Immediate memory • Delayed memory	OR, WR, MR, Administrator scores manually or using computer entry 80–116 minutes Yields SS	16–69 years	Information available in purchasable manual	C
Wechsler Preschool and Primary Scale of Intelligence – Fourth Edition (WPPSI-IV) Wechsler (2012)	IC: 0.86–0.90 TR: 0.75–0.90 IR: 0.98–0.99 DV: 0.54–0.86	• Verbal: Comprehension, visual spatial, fluid reasoning working memory, processing speed, verbal acquisition • Nonverbal: General ability, cognitive proficiency	MR 30–60 minutes Yields SS	2 years 6 months – 7 years 7 months	Intellectual giftedness, delays, or disability	C

The measures listed are directly administered to individual students, and all require trained administrators.

Abbreviations used: [a] IR (Interrater Reliability), TR (Test-Retest Reliability), IC (Internal Consistency), AR (Alternate Forms Reliability). [b] Validity: CV (construct validity), CVV (convergent validity), CCV (concurrent validity), EV (ecological validity), FV (factorial validity), DV (divergent validity), CTV (content validity). [c] WR (written response by individual student), OR (oral response by student), MR (manual response), SS (Standardized Score), RS (Raw Score compared to standardized norms). [d] A (kit ranges up to $199), B (kit $299–$499), C (kit $500 or more), WB (web based kit available), $R (fee charged for reports).

therapy dog can have a positive effect on preschoolers performing a non-standardized memory task (Gee, Crist, & Carr, 2010). Future research incorporating the cognitive assessment tools in this table could build on that early work.

Emotional Health

The focus of the measures listed in Table 12.3 is on constructs of emotional health, including depression, anxiety, social competence, loneliness, and positive and negative affect, each of which is likely to affect overall student engagement and/or the classroom emotional climate. Student engagement is critical to academic achievement (Reyes, Brackett, Rivers, White, & Salovey, 2012). Students who are engaged are attentive, actively participate in class, and exhibit interest and motivation to learn. However, when disengaged, students tend to become disruptive, have lower educational goals and aspirations, have lower grades and higher drop-out rates, and report being bored, anxious, or even angry about being in class. Student engagement, often viewed as an individual attribute, is also a product of the student's proximal classroom environment and the context in which the student interacts with the teacher and other students in the classroom (Reyes et al., 2012). The tools presented in Table 12.3 provide a window through which researchers and educators can glimpse the way in which the presence of an animal might impact the student as an individual or potentially the entire class as an educational microcosm.

Relational Health

Expanding on the concepts discussed above with regard to emotional health, the measures in Table 12.4 (pp. 174–177) can extend the scope of potential analysis to include all types of relationships a student might have and how the landscape of those relationships might impact student engagement, the extended emotional climate of the classroom, and ultimately academic achievement. There is mounting evidence that a child's overall adjustment and school success depend upon the ability to meet social, as well as academic, challenges (Wentzel, 1998). Student perceptions of social and emotional support from parents and peers have been shown to be associated with motivation, academic effort, and interest in school. Further, Shim and Finch (2014) have shown that academic and social concerns can interact and may jointly influence adjustment at school; they found that students with moderate levels of academic

Table 12.3 Assessments of emotional health

Measures	Reliability[a]	Validity[b]	What is measured	Administration manner, time, and score[c]	Age range	Information regarding disabilities – sensitive to	Cost[d]
Beck Anxiety Inventory (BAI) Beck (1990, 1993)	TR: 0.62–0.83 IC: 0.90–0.94 AR: 0.93	CVV: 0.44–0.85	• Symptoms specific to anxiety and unrelated to depression	TA, WR, web based 5–10 minutes Yields SS	17–80 years	• Anxiety disorders	WB-A
Emotional and Social Competency Inventory-University Edition (ESCI-U) Boyatzis & Goleman (n.d.)	n/a	CV: 0.376	• Self-awareness • Self-management • Social awareness • Relationship management	WR Participant completes questionnaire and self-interprets using guide 20–30 minutes	University-aged students	n/a	A

(continued)

Table 12.3 Assessments of emotional health (continued)

Measures	Reliability[a]	Validity[b]	What is measured	Administration manner, time, and score[c]	Age range	Information regarding disabilities – sensitive to	Cost[d]
Positive and Negative Affect Schedule (PANAS) Watson, Clark, & Tellegen (1988)	IC: 0.84–0.90 PA: 0.47–0.68 NA: 0.39–0.71	FV: 0.89–0.95 CVV: 0.92	• Positive affect • Negative affect	WR Participant completes questionnaire and self-interprets using guide No information on time	University-aged students	n/a	Questionnaire and scoring guide available online for free
Revised UCLA Loneliness Scale Russell, Peplau, & Cutrona (1980)	IC: 0.94	CCV: 0.28–0.62 Russell, Peplau, & Cutrona (1980)	n/a	WR Participant completed questionnaire No information available about scoring or time	n/a	n/a	Free

Revised Children's Anxiety and Depression Scales (RCADS) Chorpita, Ebustani, & Spence (2015)	IC: 0.78–0.88 Chorpita, Moffitt, & Gray (2005) CVV: 0.34–0.65	• Separation anxiety disorder • Social phobia • Generalized anxiety disorder • Panic disorder • Obsessive compulsive disorder • Major depressive disorder	TA, WR, web based No information on time Yields SS	7.5 years – 17.9 years (based on norm sample)	• Major depressive • Obsessive anxiety • Compulsive anxiety • Generalized anxiety • Separation anxiety • Panic disorders • Social phobia	User's Guide and Test: free from website

(continued)

Table 12.3 Assessments of emotional health *(continued)*

Measures	Reliability[a]	Validity[b]	What is measured	Administration manner, time, and score[c]	Age range	Information regarding disabilities – sensitive to	Cost[d]
State-Trait Anxiety Inventory (STAI) Spielberger, Gorsuch, Lushene, Vagg, & Jacobs (1983)	TR: 0.16–0.86 IC: 0.38–0.69 AR: 0.95	CVV: 0.75–0.83 DV: 0.63–0.78 FV: 0.70–0.80	• State anxiety • Trait anxiety	TA, WR, web based 10 minutes Yields SS	15+ years	• Anxiety disorders	Free from the Mind Garden company

Note that unless otherwise noted these are individually administered.

Abbreviations used: [a] IR (Interrater Reliability), TR (Test-Retest Reliability), IC (Internal Consistency), AR (Alternate Forms Reliability). [b] Validity: CV (construct validity), CVV (convergent validity), CCV (concurrent validity), EV (ecological validity), DV (divergent validity), FV (factorial validity). [c] TA (requires training administrator), WR (written response by individual student), OR (oral response by student), SS (Standardized Score). [d] A (kit ranges up to $199), B (kit $299–$499), C (kit $500 or more), WB (web based kit available), $R (fee charged for reports).

achievement can improve overall level of engagement by working on social achievement goals at school. By contrast, students driven by a mastery focus may be sufficiently engaged by academic tasks to not need the additional boost.

This topical area probably boasts the largest number of studies relevant to the intersection of HAI and education, many of which have used standardized measures. For example, see O'Haire's work with animal-assisted activities involving guinea pigs in classrooms with children diagnosed with autism spectrum disorder (O'Haire, McKenzie, Beck, & Slaughter, 2015; O'Haire, McKenzie, McCune, & Slaughter, 2014) and Pendry's work on equine-facilitated learning in adolescents (Pendry & Roeter, 2013; Pendry, Smith, & Roeter, 2014). Each of these studies reported beneficial impacts of animals on some aspect of social skills or competence as measured by standardized assessments.

Conclusion

This chapter provides a summary of key aspects of assessment tools likely to be useful to researchers and educators interested in exploring the intersection of HAI and education. The four categories used are not intended to delineate the only potential groupings; they are meant to be exemplary rather than exhaustive, and build on previous resources. We encourage readers to examine Anderson's (2007) compendium of HAI measures for ready access to a number of tools frequently used by HAI researchers, such as measures of attachment, bonding, and attitudes toward animals. We also recommend Strauss, Sherman, and Spreen's (2006) comprehensive sourcebook of neuropsychological assessment tools, which provides a massive amount of useful information about a large number of standardized measures used in education and psychology. Most importantly, we intend this chapter to be used as a resource to help researchers and educators locate the tools they need to conduct rigorous investigations into the pedagogical efficacy of animals in classrooms or to determine firsthand the degree to which having an animal in the classroom may be beneficial relative to the associated costs.

Table 12.4 Assessments of relational health

Measures	Reliability[a]	Validity[b]	Specific subtests	Administration manner, time, and score[c]	Age range	Information regarding disabilities – sensitive to	Cost[d]
Personal Strengths Inventory (PSI) Liau, Chow, Tan, & Senf (2011)	IC: 0.70–0.89	n/a	• Social competence • Emotional awareness • Goal setting • Emotional regulation • Empathy	WR Participants complete questionnaire No information about scoring or time	1–16 years	• Aggression • Academic anxiety or achievement • Depression	Information not provided
Pervasive Developmental Disorder Behavior Inventory (PDDBI) Cohen, Schmidt-Lackner,	IC: 0.73–0.97 TR: 0.38–0.99	CV: −0.40–0.73	• Adaptive behaviors that predict responsiveness to intervention (e.g., joint attention skills)	WR Parents or teachers complete questionnaire about children/students and use score sheet to interpret 20–45 minutes Yield SS	2–12 years	• Problem and appropriate behaviors for children with ASD	B

Measure	Reliability	Validity	Constructs	Age	Population	Administration	Cost
Romanczyk, & Sudhalter (2003); Cohen & Sudhalter (2012) *Social Competence Inventory (SCI)* Rydell, Hagekull, & Bohlin (1997)	TR: 0.77–0.81 IR: 0.17–0.47	CCV: 0.29	• Prosocial orientation • Social initiative	7–10 years	n/a	WR Parents or teachers complete form No information about scoring or time available	Free, WB
Social Skills Improvement System–Revised Scales (SSIS-RS): Social Skills and Problem Behaviors Gresham & Elliott (2008)	TR: 0.59–upper 0.80s IR: 0.50s–0.60s	CTV: −0.42–0.65 DePerna & Volpe (2005)	• Social skills (e.g., communication, cooperation) • Problem behaviors (e.g., bullying)	3–18 years	• Learning and intellectual impairments • Behavior disorders	WR Parents or teachers complete questionnaires TA 15–25 minutes per form Yields SS	A

175

(continued)

Table 12.4 Assessments of relational health (*continued*)

Measures	Reliability[a]	Validity[b]	Specific subtests	Administration manner, time, and score[c]	Age range	Information regarding disabilities – sensitive to	Cost[d]
Social Skills Rating System (SSRS): Social Skills and Problem Behaviors Note: This is the original version of the SSIS-RS, but is included because of its continued use in research.	IC: 0.84–0.90 TR: 0.65–0.93	CV: 0.20s–0.70s	• Social skills (e.g., cooperation) • Problem behaviors (e.g., hyperactivity)	WR Parents or teachers complete questionnaires TA 15–25 minutes per form Yields SS	3–18 years	• Learning and intellectual impairments • Behavior disorders	A, WB

Community-University Partnership for the Study of Children, Youth, and Families (2011)

Note that unless otherwise noted these are individually administered.

[a] Abbreviations used: IR (Interrater Reliability), TR (Test-Retest Reliability), IC (Internal Consistency), AR (Alternate Forms Reliability). [b] Validity: CV (construct validity), CVV (convergent validity), CCV (concurrent validity), CTV (content validity), EV (ecological validity), DV (divergent validity), FV (factorial validity). [c] TA (requires training administrator), WR (written response by individual student), OR (oral response by student), SS (Standardized Score). [d] A (kit ranges up to $199), B (kit $299–$499), WB (web based kit available).

References

Anderson, D. C. (2007). *Assessing the human-animal bond: A compendium of actual measures.* West Lafayette, IN: Purdue University Press.

Bayley, N. (2005). *Bayley scales of infant and toddler development, third edition (Bayley III).* Minneapolis, MN: Pearson Education, Inc.

Beck, A. T. (1990, 1993). *Beck anxiety inventory (BAI).* Minneapolis, MN: PsychCorp, Pearson Education, Inc.

Boyatzis, R., & Goleman, D. (n.d.). Emotional and social competency inventory – university edition (ESCI-U) online. The Hay Group. Retrieved from http://haygroup.com/leadershipandtalentondemand/ourproducts/item_details.aspx?itemid=43&type=7

Chorpita, B. F., Ebesutani, C., & Spence, S. H. (2015). *Revised children's anxiety and depression scale user's guide.* Los Angeles, CA: UCLA ChildFirst. Retrieved from http:// childfirst.ucla.edu/RCADSUsersGuide20150701.pdf

Chorpita, B. F., Moffitt, C. E., & Gray, J. (2005). Psychometric properties of the revised child anxiety and depression scale in a clinical sample. *Behaviour Research and Therapy, 43*: 309–322.

Cohen, I. L, & Sudhalter, V. (2012). *PDD behavior inventory (PDDBI).* Lutz, FL: PAR Inc.

Cohen, I. L., Schmidt-Lackner, S., Romanczyk, R., & Sudhalter, V. (2003). The PDD behavior inventory: A rating scale for assessing response to intervention in children with pervasive developmental disorder. *Journal of Autism and Developmental Disorders, 33*(1): 31–45.

Community-University Partnership for the Study of Children, Youth, and Families. (2011). *Review of the social skills rating system (SSRS).* Edmonton, Alberta, Canada.

DiPerna, J. C., & Volpe, R. J. (2005). Self-report on the social skills rating system: Analysis of reliability and validity for an elementary sample. *Psychology in the Schools, 42*(4): 345–354.

Dunn, L. M., & Dunn, D. M. (2007). *Peabody picture vocabulary test, fourth edition (PPVT-4).* Minneapolis, MN: PsychCorp, Pearson Learning, Inc.

Elliott, C. D. (2007). *Differential ability scales—II (DAS-II).* Minneapolis, MN: PsychCorp, Pearson Education, Inc.

Fine, A. H. (2015). *Handbook on animal-assisted therapy: Foundations and guidelines for animal-assisted interventions.* San Francisco, CA: Elsevier.

Gee, N. R., Crist, E. N., & Carr, D. N. (2010). Preschool children require fewer instructional prompts to perform a memory task in the presence of a dog. *Anthrozoös, 23*: 178–184.

Gresham, F., & Elliott, S. N. (2008). *Social skills improvement system—revised scales (SSIS-RS)*. Minneapolis, MN: PsychCorp, Pearson Learning, Inc.

Jacob, R., & Parkinson, J. (2015). The potential for school-based interventions that target executive function to improve academic achievement: A review. *Review of Educational Research, 85*(4): 512–552. doi: 10.3102/0034654314561338

Kazdin, A. E. (2011). Establishing the effectiveness of animal-assisted therapies: Methodological standards, issues, and strategies. In P. McCardle, S. McCune, J. A. Griffin, & V. Maholmes (Eds.), *How animals affect us: Examining the influence of human-animal interaction on child development and human health* (pp. 35–52). Washington, DC: American Psychological Association.

LaForte, E. M., McGrew, K. S., & Schrank, F. A. (2014). *WJ IV technical abstract (Woodcock-Johnson IV assessment service bulletin no. 2)*. Rolling Meadows, IL: Riverside.

le Roux, M. C., Swartz, L., & Swart, E. (2014). The effect of an animal-assisted reading program on the reading rate, accuracy and comprehension of grade 3 students: A randomized control study. *Child and Youth Care Forum, 43*: 655–673. doi: 10.1007/s10566-014-9262-1

Liau, A. K., Chow, D., Tan, T. K., & Senf, K. (2011). Development and validation of the personal strengths inventory using exploratory and confirmatory factor analyses. *Journal of Psychoeducational Assessment, 29*(1): 14–26.

Martin, N., & Brownell, R. (2011). *EOWPVT-4: Expressive one-word picture vocabulary test, fourth edition*. Austin, TX: PRO-ED, Inc.

McKay, M. (1996). The Neale analysis of reading ability revised – systematically biased? *British Journal of Educational Psychology, 66*(2): 259–266.

Neale, M. D. (n.d.). *Neale analysis of reading ability (NARA)*. London: GL Assessment.

Nimer, J., & Lundahl, B. (2007). Animal-assisted therapy: A meta-analysis. *Anthrozoös, 20*: 225–238.

O'Haire, M. E., McKenzie, S. J., Beck, A. M., & Slaughter, V. (2015). Animals may act as social buffers: Skin conductance arousal in children with autism spectrum disorder in a social context. *Developmental Psychobiology, 57*(5): 584–595.

O'Haire, M. E., McKenzie, S. J., McCune, S., & Slaughter, V. (2014). Effects of classroom animal-assisted activities on social functioning in children with autism spectrum disorder. *The Journal of Alternative and Complementary Medicine, 20*(3): 162–168.

Pendry, P., & Roeter, S. (2013). Experimental trial demonstrates positive effects of equine facilitated learning on child social competence. *Human-Animal Interaction Bulletin, 1*: 1–19.

Pendry, P., Smith, A. N., & Roeter, S. (2014). Randomized trial examines effects of equine facilitated learning on adolescents' basal cortisol levels. *Human-Animal Interaction Bulletin, 2*: 80–95.

Qehaja, F. (2013). Executive functions and life success. *International Stability, 15*(1): 247–249. doi: 10.3182/20130606-3-XK-4037.00039

Reyes, M. R., Brackett, M. A., Rivers, S. E., White, M., & Salovey, P. (2012). Classroom emotional climate, student engagement and academic achievement. *Journal of Educational Psychology, 104*(3): 700.

Russell, D., Peplau, L. A., & Cutrona, C. E. (1980). The revised UCLA loneliness scale: Concurrent and discriminant validity evidence. *Journal of Personality and Social Psychology, 39*(3): 472–480.

Rydell, A. M., Hagekull, B., & Bohlin, G. (1997). Measurement of two social competence aspects in middle childhood. *Developmental Psychology, 33*(5): 824–833.

Schrank, F. A., McGrew, K. S., & Mather, N. (2014). *Woodcock-Johnson IV.* Rolling Meadows, IL: Riverside. Now available from Houghton Mifflin Harcourt.

Shim, S. S., & Finch, W. H. (2014). Academic and social achievement goals and early adolescents' adjustment: A latent class approach. *Learning and Individual Differences, 30*: 98–105.

Spielberger, C. D., Gorsuch, R. L., Lushene, R., Vagg, P. R., & Jacobs, G. A. (1983). *Manual for the State-Trait Anxiety Inventory.* Palo Alto, CA: Consulting Psychologists Press.

Strauss, E., Sherman, E. M. S., & Spreen, O. (2006). *A compendium of neuropsychological tests: Administration, norms and commentary.* London: Oxford University Press.

Watson, D., Clark, L. A., & Tellegen, A. (1988). Development and validation of brief measures of positive and negative affect: The PANAS scales. *Journal of Personality and Social Psychology, 54*(6): 1063–1070.

Wechsler, D. (2009). *Wechsler individual achievement test – third edition (WIAT-III).* Minneapolis, MN: PsychCorp, Pearson Learning, Inc.

Wechsler, D. (2010). *Wechsler memory scale – fourth UK edition (WMS-IV UK)*. Oxford: Pearson Assessment.

Wechsler, D. (2012). *Wechsler preschool and primary scale of intelligence – fourth edition (WPPSI-IV)*. Minneapolis, MN: PsychCorp, Pearson Learning, Inc.

Wechsler, D. (2014). *Wechsler intelligence scale for children – fifth edition (WISC-V)*. Minneapolis, MN: PsychCorp, Pearson Learning, Inc.

Wentzel, K. R. (1998). Social relationships and motivation in middle school: The role of parents, teachers, and peers. *Journal of Educational Psychology, 90*: 202–209.

Wiederholt, J. L, & Bryant, B. R. (2011). *Gray oral reading test – fifth edition (GORT-5)*. Austin, TX: PRO-ED, Inc.

Wilkinson, G. S., & Robertson. G. J. (2006). *Wide-range achievement test – fourth edition (WRAT-4)*. Torrance, CA: WPS.

Williams, K. T. (2007). *Expressive vocabulary test, second edition (EVT-2)*. Minneapolis, MN: PsychCorp, Pearson Education, Inc.

Wilson, B. A., Greenfield, E., Clare, L., Baddeley, Cockburn, J. Watson, P., … Nannery, R. (2008). *Rivermead behavioural memory test – third edition (RBMT-3)*. Minneapolis, MN: PsychCorp, Pearson Learning, Inc.

Wilson, C. C., & Netting, E. (2012). The status of instrument development in the human-animal interaction field. *Anthrozoös, 25* supplement: S11–S55.

CHAPTER 13

Selecting Animals for Education Environments

Maureen MacNamara and Evan MacLean

Introduction

Selecting appropriate and effective animal participants is central to the design and implementation of any animal-assisted education (AAE) program. In this chapter, we examine ways in which the specific purpose of AAE informs animal selection criteria, and ensures a good fit for human and animal participants alike. We provide a model for conceptualizing the interface between classroom and student goals with the design of student-animal interactions and the selection of appropriate species and individual animals, and illustrate how it can aid educators in considering potential barriers (e.g., student medical, emotional, and cultural concerns). We conclude with a discussion of how increased knowledge regarding specific mechanisms in human-animal interaction will further enhance animal selection criteria, ultimately leading to more effective AAE programs.

Despite great potential for enhancing education environments, AAE activities can also present potentially stressful experiences for animals. For example, these activities may require animals to allow and even welcome unfamiliar humans to pet, or direct (training, riding) them for prolonged periods. It is unrealistic and incongruent with current knowledge of animal behavior to assume that any arbitrarily selected animal should be comfortable or capable of working effectively under these conditions (Gee, Fine, & Schuck, 2015).

A Four-Step Model

Previous chapters have explicated the variety of AAE populations and settings, each presenting a unique set of challenges. Thus, it is vital that methods for selecting, preparing, and integrating animals in pedagogy contain clearly defined expectations of how students will benefit from including animals in the learning process. Specifically, animals employed in AAE should be selected based on how well their natural and trained skills, and capabilities, fit what they are expected to *do* with, and for, the students with whom they interact. Our four-step model outlines this process, to assist educators and researchers in constructing AAE interventions, emphasizing (1) the goal(s) of the lesson or activity; (2) delivery method; (3) animal qualifications; and (4) considerations for selecting individual animals.

Clarify Goals

Previous chapters point to evidence-based applications of AAE for general and special student populations. Further, Gee, Fine, and Schuck (2015) discuss a variety of benefits accrued in AAE, including increased motivation to learn, improved concentration, cognitive function, and socio-emotional development. Development of a framework to categorize educational goals is useful in constructing an AAE strategy, as it can help educators consider the process and approach to lesson development. This important first step is often omitted from planning, but it is key for educators and researchers to first assess whether the educational goals could be attained through an alternative strategy (MacNamara & Moga, 2014). As with any other pedagogical tool, a clear conceptualization of how an animal will enhance students' educational experience and, yet, not present a barrier or distraction from learning is key.

The specific goals of AAE may limit the species that are appropriate (see below), but different species also may have various positive and negative affordances depending on the student population. For example, children may have allergies to certain animals, histories of traumatic experiences, or cultural prohibitions regarding certain species (Serpell, 2004). Furthermore, although often viewed as ideal "classroom pets," small animals (e.g., rodents, reptiles, amphibians) may pose health risks for students (e.g., students with compromised immune systems may be susceptible to bacterial flora common to reptiles). Therefore, when assessing AAE goals, educators must also consider both positive and negative effects of particular species on a population-specific basis.

Delivery Approach

We informally categorize delivery approaches as *implicit, explicit,* or *instrumental* (MacNamara, Moga, & Pachel, 2015), to provide parameters from which to consider the qualities and skills an animal brings to educational settings. A greater degree of animal-student contact demands more detailed definitions of "optimal animal characteristics."

In *implicit* interventions, animal inclusion enhances the educational milieu, and direct interaction tends to be limited; animals play a passive (and often indirect) role. For implicit AAE, the need for skills evaluation of individual animals is limited because the animal's physical qualities (e.g., color or size) or innate behavioral profile (e.g., singing or swimming) may be of greater consequence. For example, the classroom may contain an aquarium that students gaze at to calm difficult feelings. While it is important to select appropriate animals for implicit interventions, evaluating each animal for specific behaviors is less important than selecting a species that matches AAE goals.

A more focused assessment of animal skills and capacities is required for *explicit* AAE, as these interactions involve basic animal contact, most often to redirect attention and facilitate sensory/cognitive processing. Explicit intervention goals demand specificity of particular animal qualities and behaviors. For instance, an AAE program for children with attention disorders may employ a well-socialized rabbit to direct attention and encourage group exchange, particularly if the educator asks the children to identify and describe behaviors that are calming or nonthreatening.

Instrumental interventions represent the highest degree of contact between animals and students. In these, animals play a direct role in sculpting educational outcomes by providing novel opportunities for interaction and tactile stimulation. When targeted learning is the primary student goal, instrumental interventions offer a chance to test new responses and rehearse the most successful behaviors in increasingly challenging contexts. Instrumental AAE can also pose the highest risk for students, animals, and educators, therefore requiring the greatest specificity regarding the animal's capacities, skillset, and resilience. Consequently, they are best implemented with domesticated species – which have been artificially selected for tameness – and from which the most appropriate individuals can be identified through assessment of individual behavioral characteristics.

By combining specific AAE goals with intended delivery approach, we obtain a more complete picture of how an animal will interface with the education setting. Completion of these first two steps may reveal that a single animal may not have the capacity to fulfill the goals and delivery approach, that the goals require multiple delivery approaches or perhaps multiple animals to meet all educational aims.

Animal Qualifications – Developing Animal Job Descriptions

Just as job descriptions are useful in identifying the skills, education, and attitudes necessary for human vocations, so too animal job descriptions can detail the capabilities necessary for goal-specific AAE. In other words, by delineating the expected interactions between the animal, students, and education environment, educators can determine the constellation of animal traits necessary to actualize the specific learning goals and delivery approach. For example, contrast the expectations of a dog working in a classroom with children with autism and an explosives detection dog working alongside a military handler. The former must be able to rest quietly for long durations in public environments, be highly attuned to children's behavior, and have a friendly disposition when meeting new individuals. In contrast, the latter should be independent and energetic, capable of enduring long bouts of exercise in challenging physical environments, and wary of new and unfamiliar individuals while working. While dogs are an appropriate species for either role, the specific temperament and behavior requirements vary dramatically. Similarly, diverse AAE programs may pose very different requirements for animal participants, and clear job descriptions are essential for both the initial selection and subsequent evaluation of the animals that fill these roles. Accordingly, an ideal job description should address key points relevant to (1) the goal of including an animal; (2) session logistics (e.g., duration and type of contact between students and animals); and (3) optimal animal characteristics (both physical and behavioral).

185

The following provides an example of a job description for an explicit AAE program with the goal of improving peer interaction between students with intellectual disabilities:

A small animal capable of maintaining a calm disposition around 4–5 children (ages 7–8) for sessions of 15–20 minutes, 3–5 times per day. During lesson animal will be in a contained space (table top or on the floor with children sitting in a circle). Children will talk about, pet, and offer animal treats. Animal must accept occasional verbal outbursts and clumsy petting. Animal must accept treats gently. No other skills or coat texture or color required.

The job description describes basic animal traits and abilities necessary for working safely in specific AAE environments, and that relate to natural responses to stimuli, coping capacities, and skill in responding to human behaviors. Note that this description does not specify species or breed. While the majority of programs are developed around the animal(s) available, this practice has the potential to limit the benefits of AAE to those students most comfortable with traditional pets and often leaves out students with aforementioned challenges.

Animal Screening and Selection

The key objective of animal selection is to intentionally harness species-specific behaviors that optimally support the achievement of AAE goals. While a number of therapy animal organizations offer screening or selection "tests" to qualify for registry with the organization, these tools do not screen animals in terms of specific requirements for each setting (MacNamara & Butler, 2010).

The MacNamara Animal Capability Assessment Model (MACAM) (MacNamara et al., 2015) is designed to operationalize the job description as a profile for the ideal animal for that "job." The MACAM provides a systematic process for educators to develop a comprehensive animal profile based on four important categories: response to student stimuli; interaction with the environment; trained behaviors and equipment tolerance; and physical attributes. (Each item is described in detail in MacNamara et al., 2015.) Table 13.1 presents the MACAM for use in screening animals for AAE programs. This functional assessment model is adaptable to individual students or student populations.

Table 13.1 MacNamara Animal Capability Assessment Model

Response gradient – speed with which the animal transitions from one state to another as well as the presence or absence of transitional behaviors

A. **Reactivity** – Degree of reactivity; high or low (high degree of reactivity means the animal ramps up quickly within a certain behavior)

B. **Flexibility** – Degree to which the animal is flexible or stereotypic (responding to all stimuli with the same behaviors); regulation of response

C. **Behavioral cues** – Animal displays overt or subtle cues

Capacity – Degree to which the animal interacts with the environment

D. **Recovery** – Degree to which the animal copes with and recuperates from stimulation (tactile, olfactory, auditory, and visual)

E. **Affiliation** – Degree to which the animal spontaneously seeks interaction with strangers

F. **Behavioral repertoire** – Diversity of behaviors used by the animal to respond to stimuli

G. **Explicit communication** – degree to which the animal displays behaviors that the student population recognize as communication

Skills – Trained behaviors relevant to intervention aims

H. **Verbal response** – Response to verbal commands

I. **Gestural response** – Response to gestural commands

J. **Novelty response** – Response to new environments, activities or tasks

K. **Equipment acceptance** – Degree to which the animal manages variety of training or performance equipment

L. **Cue interpretation** – Degree to which the animal understands stranger's attempts of familiar cues/commands

M. **Attentional response** – Degree to which the animal uses observable behavioral cues such as eye contact and eye, head, and body orientation to respond to students

(continued)

Table 13.1 MacNamara Animal Capability Assessment Model
(continued)

Attributes – Physical characteristics contributing to delivery approach

N. **Species/breed-type** – Degree to which the animal may be associated with cultural, ethnic, or racial experiences

O. **Appearance** – Coat color, texture, markings, etc. (plumage/scale color)

P. **Size** – In relation to students and student experience

Q. **Vocalizations** – Loudness, tone, frequency, predictability

Adapted from MacNamara et al., 2015, with permission of the publisher.

The four MACAM categories provide a method for educators to describe their expectations of animal functioning during AAE. Consideration of all categories allows educators to reflect on how student experiences with animals may differ from their own. Further, the model enables users to customize the assessment to the particular AAE setting by providing an in-depth assessment of animals related to the work the animal will actually *do* when in contact with students.

To use the MACAM, one first creates an ideal animal profile based on the job description. For example, from the job description above the educator may develop an ideal profile for the first section, response gradient, as low reactivity, moderate flexibility, and few overt behavioral cues. This corresponds to the job description by requiring low reactivity to clumsy petting, a "relaxed" temperament, and expression of behavioral cues to guide the students. The second section, capacity, could define an ideal profile of moderate recovery, affiliation, minimal behavioral repertoire, and moderate engagement. The profile coincides with the job description that indicates low-key, short-term interactions with students not requiring prolonged interaction with any one student. The skills section has an ideal profile indicating that no specialized skills are necessary as the job description only states that the animal must be resilient to verbal outbursts and petting, possess a calm demeanor and willingness to take treats carefully. In the attributes section the ideal profile clearly delineates size, as the job description requires a small animal that can work in a confined space.

Once the ideal profile is created, one can evaluate and compare animals being considered against this profile. In an explicit intervention such as this, the species of choice should be one that all children are comfortable with and that is appropriate for their cultural backgrounds. For example, if a number of the children are fearful of dogs, species other than dogs should be considered. Unless the intervention is intended to treat dog phobia (which would involve a method called "prolonged exposure therapy" (Foa, Chrestman, & Gilboa-Schechtman, 2008)), educators should refrain from using animals that incite fear. To do so, with little regard to the speed, duration, and type of exposure, would be considered flooding – which is counterproductive for any fearful child, and will likely interfere with learning objectives (Cohen, Mannarino, Kliethermes, & Murray, 2012).

Consider how a well-socialized guinea pig could meet the requirements of this job description. The animal has relatively low reactivity, with interesting vocalizations; a capacity for recovery, affiliation, and engagement with a limited behavioral repertoire; few explicitly trained skills but trainable for simple tasks like "sit up"; and is small, portable, and may exhibit any of a variety of colors and coat textures – a good candidate for this particular type of AAE (e.g., O'Haire, McKenzie, Beck, & Slaughter, 2013).

Realistic Expectations of Animal Participants

The MACAM outlines a process through which educators can identify animals with appropriate traits for a wide range of education environments. However, despite the importance of animal selection criteria, it is the responsibility of the educator to assure that students do not jeopardize the animal's welfare or their own safety, and it is unrealistic to expect even the most tolerant animal to willingly accept all of the advances that students will be tempted to make. For example, it is common that students often wish to hug animals, not understanding that this form of affection will not be appreciated by the animal, and instead may provoke a fearful or aggressive response. Thus, even with careful selection criteria, educators play a key role in explaining and enforcing appropriate forms of interaction.

Case Study

The following example illustrates use of the MACAM for an instrumental program containing specific behavioral and skill expectations. A special education teacher's goal is developing social interaction skills between five 6–8-year-old children with autism. The children have been reluctant to engage with one another, avoid eye contact, speak infrequently, and have difficulty concentrating on group activities. The teacher thinks an animal might help to (1) capture their attention; (2) provide a focal point for group activity and communication; and (3) provide an opportunity for directly practicing social skills with a novel participant.

Recognizing that introducing an animal to this environment would provide challenges both for the students and the animal, the teacher first assesses whether the educational goals could be attained through an alternative strategy. S/he considers other types of games and activities that might foster attention and engagement with this population, but ultimately decides none of these alternatives would stimulate the students' interest, or create the same opportunities for feedback to the same extent as an animal. Because one of her/his goals for including an animal is to stimulate interest and conversation, s/he first considers an implicit approach – an aquarium with colorful fish would provide an excellent topic for conversation. Despite these advantages and meeting two goals, fish provide few opportunities for students to practice skills such as eye contact and interpretation of behavioral responses; s/he therefore considers more instrumental possibilities.

190

The teacher writes out an animal job description including the key capacities that will foster the educational goals and accommodate the unique qualities of her/his students. Several students have sensory sensitivities (do not like to be touched) and become anxious with loud or sudden noises. S/he needs an animal that is interested in people but allows people to approach, rather than first approaching them; is calm, minimally reactive; makes occasional eye contact with people; is capable of remaining in place for periods of 15–20 minutes; and accepts gentle petting. There are no other requirements for the animal's training.

The job description is used to create an ideal animal profile. In this example, the teacher is looking for an animal with low *reactivity* and high *flexibility* in the response gradient category. S/he uses the *capacity* category items to describe in detail her/his expectations for how the animal will respond to students and classroom activity. The skills profile will require a specific description of how the animal is expected to respond to cues from students, such that students see immediate responses to their attempts to communicate. The profile should also indicate that the animal should not vocalize loudly or unexpectedly as children in this class often experience sensory overload.

With this ideal profile, the teacher screens a number of possible candidates. S/he has a friend with a dog named Sunny who enjoys the company of children – a cheery golden retriever, bursting with energy, who loves to greet new people – often by licking the faces of his new friends. He typically barks with excitement. Although clearly a great dog, Sunny's profile does not match the response gradient ideal or the vocalizations attribute. In short, Sunny's natural behaviors are at odds with the special sensory requirements of these students.

Another candidate is a large spaniel called Jake, whose owner volunteers with the school. Jake shows interest in children, but allows them to approach him at their own pace, rather than rushing to greet them. When petted, he calmly gazes into the person's eyes; he responds to being talked to by slowly wagging his tail, and follows a number of basic commands even when these are spoken softly. Jake's presence is both captivating and relaxing, exactly the characteristics the teacher is looking for.

Interplay of Factors

AAE requires evaluation of all factors potentially contributing to, or jeopardizing, successful interventions. Accounting for the influence of the delivery approach, type of student-animal interaction, and the animal's capability for work in educational programs and classroom settings, represents educator due diligence. Working through all factors provides educators with purposeful guidelines for including animals in a variety of interventions.

Although a number of national, regional, and local organizations provide volunteers and their animals (primarily dogs) for work in a variety of settings, screening varies significantly between organizations, and many use one screening process to evaluate all animals, potentially missing factors critical to the success of a specific AAE program. The dominant AAE perspective is heavily human-centered – "what can animals do for students," with limited consideration of what interventions may do for, or to, the animals (Shapiro, 2008). Few studies have focused on the possible ill effects on the animals themselves (Serpell, Coppinger, Fine, & Peralta, 2010) and this remains an important priority for future research (e.g., Ng et al., 2014). Even with careful, considered efforts in animal selection, the potential for animal stress must be constantly considered.

Future Directions

The framework described integrates current theory and data regarding ways in which animals can have a positive impact in education settings, and how specific selection guidelines can ensure a good match between animal and human participants. However, most effectively implementing these guidelines will depend on advances in numerous areas of research. We highlight two areas where future work could have a profound impact on the processes by which animals are individually matched with, and evaluated for, each AAE program.

Mechanisms of Action

First, despite abundant evidence that animals can have positive impacts in many interventional contexts, the specific mechanisms through which human-animal interaction confers these benefits is a nascent although rapidly growing field of study. We anticipate that emerging data on specific psychobiological mechanisms will lead to continued refinements in our animal job descriptions in order to maximize program efficacy. For example, we briefly review some recent advances in understanding dog-human interactions that highlight how naturally occurring individual differences in dog behavior may have meaningful consequences on human responses, and how knowledge of these pathways creates further opportunities to optimize animal training, and selection criteria.

Relative to other animals, dogs are unusual in their sensitivity to human communication and behavior, making them a unique species for integration into education settings (MacLean & Hare, 2015). Dogs may create powerful opportunities for complex social interactions with humans, fostering social skills ranging from gestural communication to eye contact. Several studies have explored the biological correlates of these types of affiliative dog-human interactions, focusing on the neuropeptide oxytocin (Handlin et al., 2011; Miller et al., 2009; Nagasawa, Kikusui, Onaka, & Ohta, 2009; Odendaal & Meintjes, 2003). Oxytocin (OT) is a phylogenetically ancient peptide conserved across mammals, which has wide-ranging effects on social behavior, cognition, and stress responses (Donaldson & Young, 2008). Studies with humans and other animals reveal that OT release can facilitate the formation of social bonds, exert anxiolytic effects that promote calm emotional states and social engagement, and that affiliative social interactions can be a powerful trigger for the release of OT (Carter, 1998). Therefore, several researchers have proposed that the well-documented behavioral and physiological effects of HAI are consistent with an oxytocin-mediated response (Beetz, Uvnäs-Moberg, Julius, & Kotrschal, 2012).

To date, several studies support the hypothesis that OT may play an important role in HAI, as evidenced by OT release in both humans and dogs engaged in affiliative interactions (Beetz et al., 2012). However, some studies also suggest that human responses in this context vary largely as a function of dog behavior. Nagasawa et al. (2009) observed that dog-human dyads could be divided into two clusters (dyads in which dogs gazed at the human's face for short or long periods of time); the change in OT observed in humans varied as a function of the length of mutual gaze, and only humans receiving long bouts of gaze from a dog exhibited detectable increases in oxytocin. Therefore, oxytocin release appears *not* be a general consequence of human-dog interaction, but instead depends on key social behaviors which vary among individual dogs.

At present, we know little about the role of OT in HAI, or how OT-related effects may shape AAE. However, a substantial body of evidence suggests that OT could have important effects in education contexts, influencing processes ranging from empathy, to learning, and memory (Bartz et al., 2010). Given the current state of the evidence, it is premature to base animal selection on the potential to elicit OT-related responses. However, this is one example in which knowledge of underlying mechanisms could have important implications for selecting or training animals that could maximize these effects. Therefore, we expect that future research elucidating the specific mechanisms through which animals can enhance AAE will play an essential role in parallel refinements to animal training and selection criteria.

Animal Assessment Tools

Second, current models for animal selection delineate the range of factors that must be considered when matching species or individuals to AAE aims. However, there are few objective tools designed to assess relevant behavioral, cognitive, or temperamental traits in candidate animals. Many animal assessments are largely subjective, and depend on the working knowledge and intuitions of the practitioner. Several validated behavioral instruments have been designed for the screening and selection of dogs for other working roles (Duffy & Serpell, 2012; Svartberg, 2002), but there are currently no assessments tailored specifically for AAE programs. As with the earlier example, the development of comparable assessment tools for AAE will depend on future work measuring animal behavior in the context of AAE to identify specific animal characteristics associated with variance in student outcomes. These data will set the stage for evidence-based advances in selection criteria, ultimately transforming the selection process from art to science.

Conclusion

It is clear that there is much to learn about the selection, training, implementation, and care of animals involved in animal-assisted interventions (AAI). Expectations for animals involved in this work have changed dramatically since the first formal AAI programs were introduced. So, too, should the methods of selecting, preparing, and integrating animals in work where there are clearly defined expectations that students will benefit from their involvement in the learning process.

Animals employed in AAE should be selected on the basis of how well their skills and capabilities fit what they are expected to do with, and for, the students with whom they will interact. To ensure quality AAIs, it is critical that animals be treated as valued partners in a mutually respectful relationship. Animals' needs must always be considered, accommodated, and balanced with the needs of students. We must repeatedly ask, "What is this animal's experience?" and consider both what an animal can contribute to AAE, and how AAE will affect the animal.

To fully understand the role of animals in AAE also requires more than personal experience with one's own pets. Formal training in the many ways animals inhabit social, emotional, and physical worlds is necessary for educators to differentiate between the practices developed for volunteers visiting facilities with their companion animals and the practices necessary for the incorporation of animals in diverse AAE environments.

194

References

Bartz, J. A., Zaki, J., Bolger, N., Hollander, E., Ludwig, N. N., Kolevzon, A., & Ochsner, K. N. (2010). Oxytocin selectively improves empathic accuracy. *Psychological Science*, 21(10): 1426–1428.

Beetz, A., Uvnäs-Moberg, K., Julius, H., & Kotrschal, K. (2012). Psychosocial and psychophysiological effects of human-animal interactions: The possible role of oxytocin. *Frontiers in Psychology*, 3: 234. doi: 10.3389/fpsyg.2012.00234

Carter, C. S. (1998). Neuroendocrine perspectives on social attachment and love. *Psychoneuroendocrinology, 23*(8): 779–818.

Cohen, J. A., Mannarino, A. P., Kliethermes, M., & Murray, L. A. (2012). Trauma-focused CBT for youth with complex trauma. *Child abuse & neglect, 36*(6): 528–541.

Donaldson, Z. R., & Young, L. J. (2008). Oxytocin, vasopressin, and the neurogenetics of sociality. *Science, 322*(5903): 900–904.

Duffy, D. L., & Serpell, J. A. (2012). Predictive validity of a method for evaluating temperament in young guide and service dogs. *Applied Animal Behaviour Science, 138*(1–2): 99–109.

Foa, E. B., Chrestman, K. R., & Gilboa-Schechtman, E. (2008). *Prolonged exposure therapy for adolescents with PTSD emotional processing of traumatic experiences: Therapist guide.* New York: Oxford University Press.

Gee, N. R., Fine, A. H., & Schuck, S. (2015). Animals in educational settings: Research and practice. In A. H. Fine (Ed.), *Handbook on animal-assisted therapy. Theoretical foundations and guidelines for practice* (4th edn, pp. 195–210). San Diego, CA: Academic Press.

Handlin, L., Hydbring-Sandberg, E., Nilsson, A., Ejdeback, M., Jansson, A., & Uvnas-Moberg, K. (2011). Short-term interaction between dogs and their owners: Effects on oxytocin, cortisol, insulin and heart rate. An exploratory study. *Anthrozoös, 24*(3): 301–315.

MacLean, E. L., & Hare, B. (2015). Dogs hijack the human bonding pathway. *Science, 348*(6232): 280–281.

MacNamara, M. A., & Butler, K. A., (2010). Methods, standards, guidelines, and considerations in selecting animals for animal-assisted therapy. In A. H. Fine (Ed.), *Handbook on animal-assisted therapy. Theoretical foundations and guidelines for practice* (2nd edn, pp. 111–134). San Diego, CA: Academic Press.

MacNamara, M. A., & Moga, J. (2014). The place and consequence of animals in contemporary social work. In T. Ryan (Ed.), *Animals in social work: Why and how they matter* (pp. 151–166). London: Palgrave Macmillan.

MacNamara, M. A., Moga, J., & Pachel, C. (2015). What's love got to do with it? Selecting animals for animal-assisted mental health interventions. In A. H. Fine (Ed.), *Handbook on animal-assisted therapy. Theoretical foundations and guidelines for practice* (4th edn, pp. 91–101). San Diego, CA: Academic Press.

Miller, S. C., Kennedy, C., DeVoe, D., Hickey, M., Nelson, T., & Kogan, L. (2009). An examination of changes in oxytocin levels in men and women before and after interaction with a bonded dog. *Anthrozoös,* *22*(1): 31–42.

Nagasawa, M., Kikusui, T., Onaka, T., & Ohta, M. (2009). Dog's gaze at its owner increases owner's urinary oxytocin during social interaction. *Hormones and Behavior, 55*(3): 434–441.

Ng, Z. Y., Pierce, B. J., Otto, C. M., Buechner-Maxwell, V. A., Siracusa, C., & Werre, S. R. (2014). The effect of dog–human interaction on cortisol and behavior in registered animal-assisted activity dogs. *Applied Animal Behaviour Science, 159*: 69–81.

Odendaal, J., & Meintjes, R. (2003). Neurophysiological correlates of affiliative behaviour between humans and dogs. *The Veterinary Journal, 165*(3): 296–301.

O'Haire, M. E., McKenzie, S. J., Beck, A. M., & Slaughter, V. (2013). Social behaviors increase in children with autism in the presence of animals compared to toys. *PloS one, 8*(2): e57010.

Serpell, J. A. (2004). Factors influencing human attitudes to animals and their welfare. *Animal Welfare, 13*: 145–151.

Serpell, J. A., Coppinger, R., Fine, A. H., & Peralta, J. M. (2010). Welfare considerations in therapy and assistance animals. In A. Fine (Ed.), *Handbook on animal-assisted therapy: Theoretical foundations and guidelines for practice* (3rd edn, pp. 481–503). San Diego, CA: Associated Press.

Shapiro, K. (2008). *Human-animal studies: Growing the field, applying the field.* Ann Arbor, MI: Animals and Society Institute.

Svartberg, K. (2002). Shyness–boldness predicts performance in working dogs. *Applied Animal Behaviour Science, 79*(2): 157–174.

CHAPTER 14

Caring for Classroom Pets

Nancy R. Gee, John M. Rawlings,
Marguerite E. O'Haire,
Pauleen C. Bennett, Donna Snellgrove,
and Jose M. Peralta

197

Introduction

Previous chapters in this volume have indicated that bringing animals into classrooms is a popular way to teach students responsibility and empathy, engage and motivate them, and help them excel academically by providing a non-judgmental, supportive, and relaxing learning environment. Published activities and research findings almost exclusively focus on the real or perceived benefits to humans associated with such practices (Gee, Hurley, & Rawlings, 2016). Historically, few investigations have focused on the benefits or potential risks to the animals involved, despite real animal welfare concerns associated with maintaining an animal in a classroom full time.

We have grouped these welfare concerns into three general categories: 1) Living environment: size and type of enclosure, group versus individual housing, lighting, climate control, and location; 2) Care: food type, amount, and feeding frequency; water, bedding, or filters; environmental enrichment and care over weekends and school holidays; and 3) Interaction: species-specific behaviors and needs; appropriate type and length of interactions with humans (handling versus watching); and implementing an appropriate balance of human contact with quiet time to avoid stress or isolation.

We provide recommendations within these categories for animals commonly kept full time in classrooms. Further, we focus our discussion on "standard" classroom settings as opposed to more unique learning environments like residential care facilities, where someone is likely to be available to provide care and oversight around the clock.

Why Does Animal Welfare Matter?

Children may be exposed from infancy to the concept of animals in the form of a cuddly toy, often resembling a bear. As the child grows, the number of characters multiplies and further exposure through on-screen cartoon characters turns these inanimate comfort objects into fun animated characters portraying human characteristics and behaviors. However, these characters are not facsimiles of animals, and if our only exposure to animals were through such channels we would have a much distorted view of the animal world.

Some children are fortunate to live in a home where traditional companion animals share their space, and so have early exposure to real animals. Through parental guidance, children learn how to interact with these pets, empathize with them, and develop a sense of responsibility towards them. Too often though we hear stories of city children who have never seen a cow, rabbit, guinea pig, fish, or stick insect in its natural setting. How can these children be expected to empathize, understand, or respect creatures that are more conceptual than real?

Why are the principles of animal welfare important in this context? First, animals have needs that must be provided for if they are to live a life free from pain, suffering, and distress, irrespective of whether they live in the wild, on a farm, in a home, or in a school setting. Meeting the recommendations listed in this chapter for individual species should ensure that animals in classroom settings are treated well and live healthy lives. Second, children need to understand that classroom guinea pigs cannot be squeezed like a cuddly toy, that rabbits don't naturally eat burgers, and that clown fish require specific water and temperature conditions if they are to survive in captivity.

Definitions of animal welfare have evolved over time and we have begun to accept our duty of care towards them. Perhaps the most widely accepted view of good animal welfare is that of the Five

Freedoms: freedom from hunger and thirst; discomfort; pain, injury and disease; fear and distress; and freedom to behave normally. But what does this mean in practice? The needs of animals are typically discussed in the context of animal welfare legislation, which necessitates that animal welfare as practiced can be measured, assessed, and therefore complied with. These needs are similar to the Five Freedoms: a responsible person must, to the extent required by good practice, provide an animal with the resources to meet the need for a suitable environment and diet; the freedom to exhibit normal behavior patterns; housing with, or apart from, other animals, dependent upon the circumstances; and protection from pain, suffering, injury, and disease.

The question then is what constitutes good practice? In the following sections we describe what is generally considered good practice for species often kept in classrooms.

"Pocket Pets"

A popular choice for many classrooms is the "pocket pet," which refers to small domesticated rodents, such as guinea pigs, rats, mice, gerbils, and hamsters. They are often sought out by teachers due to their small size, presumed ease of care, and containment via a cage or similar enclosure to a controlled section of the classroom. Only diurnal pocket pets should be selected for classrooms, because disrupting the natural rhythms of nocturnal animals through classroom activities may lead to impaired immunological functioning, stress, and overall reduced welfare. This section therefore focuses on diurnal, domesticated pocket pets only, including guinea pigs and rats, excluding primarily nocturnal pocket pets such as mice, hamsters, and gerbils.

Living Environment

Guinea pigs and rats are social animals that should be housed with a same-sex, same-species mate, in a secure enclosure of at least 1 square yard for two animals. The top should be wire or a material that allows free air flow, the flooring solid (rather than wire, to prevent tangled paws or broken limbs), the bedding a natural, paper-based product that does not contain strong oils or create dust, which can be ingested and cause health problems. Bedding texture should allow for digging, nesting, and play. Hiding spaces such as igloos must be provided. Guinea pigs and rats are most comfortable in an environment of 65–75°F.; they can self-regulate their temperature environment to a degree if nesting materials are provided to burrow in for warmth (e.g., Gaskill et al., 2013).

Care

A free-feeding schedule can be used with a high-quality, species-specific pellet diet, with fresh fruits and vegetables provided as enrichment and to supplement vitamin levels. Fresh water should be available at all times via a non-clog, side-mounted dispenser. Water bowls can be easily knocked over or contaminated, thus are not recommended. Enclosures should be cleaned at least weekly, with spot cleaning as needed. Enrichment items should always be provided. They can be created from recycled materials provided by students, such as cardboard boxes or toilet paper rolls as tunnels or food toys. A running wheel is recommended for rats but not for guinea pigs, which tend to get their feet caught.

A consistent light/dark cycle is critical during every 24-hour period. For weekends and school holidays, the animals should be taken home for care by the teacher or a responsible family, with temperature-controlled vehicle transportation. The animals should always be monitored for signs of illness, such as loss of appetite, lethargy, or defecation abnormalities. A care schedule, user-friendly species-specific care manual, and signed agreement of responsibilities should be provided and adhered to by weekend and holiday caretakers.

Interaction

One of the most under-appreciated classroom activities is quietly observing natural animal behavior, and should be used prior to physical contact and handling. Non-contact interaction can also include creating enrichment toys, taking pictures, recording physical characteristics, or writing stories about the animals. For children younger than 5 years, the only form of physical contact recommended is gentle petting or touching while an adult holds the animal. Younger children often lack the physical dexterity and co-ordination to handle small pocket pets safely. Older children should handle the animals only under direct adult supervision. Diligent monitoring and education are critical to successful hands-on interactions with pocket pets.

There are two recommended ways to handle guinea pigs and rats. First, the animal can sit comfortably on a towel on the lap of a student seated on the ground, to prevent falls. This technique is most suitable to feeding and grooming activities. The animals will only eat if they feel safe and comfortable, so providing food is an excellent way to monitor their well-being, while simultaneously providing an interactive activity for students. Second, the student can hold the animal close to his or her chest. One hand or arm should be a support for the animal's body and legs, while the other is a protective guard against falling. This technique is most suitable for transporting the animal from the enclosure for feeding. Students should be provided with a visual demonstration, picture-based instructions sheet, and given verbal commands that focus on being gentle.

Based on clinical experience, we recommend that handling sessions last no more than 20 minutes, with 10-minute breaks in between. The animals should be monitored for signs of discomfort or fear, indicating that handling sessions should be terminated earlier or modified. One key predictor of comfort with human handling is early handling. Guinea pigs and rats that are not handled within the first few weeks of life may not be amenable to human interactions. Thoughtful and positive socialization is one of the best ways to increase the welfare of pocket pets in the classroom.

For rats, there is one final form of interaction worthy of note. Many rats enjoy playful handling, also known as "tickling" (e.g., Burgdorf & Panksepp, 2001). When socialized to be tickled, rats will follow a human hand around the cage and emit high-frequency vocalizations that indicate "laughter." It mimics their rough-and-tumble play with one another, and can be a fun and mutually enjoyable way to bond and interact with rats.

Fish

Although fish are the most popular classroom animal, given their reliance on their living environment and the associated equipment, only fish with relatively simple needs should be incorporated into a classroom. This will ensure a healthy environment can be maintained that meets the welfare needs of fish.

Living Environment

The first consideration is aquarium size: fish bowls and small aquariums are more difficult to care for than larger ones, as it is difficult to maintain good water quality and stable temperature. Minimum tank volume is 2.5 gallons; to keep several fish of different species, a tank of at least 13 gallons is necessary. Acrylic tanks are safer than glass, although they are more easily scratched. The aquarium should be positioned on a flat surface, with no direct vibrations, at a distance from any continual loud noises or sources of heat and out of direct sunlight to minimize algal growth. A stand can be used if it can hold the weight of the tank when filled with water. Freshwater aquariums can be used to keep either coldwater or tropical species of fish. Goldfish, a coldwater fish, can be kept at room temperature (as long as it is constant) but tropical species (e.g., guppies, bettas, and tetras) will require a water heater. A variety of ancillary equipment is also required, including a filter, gravel substrate, a gravel cleaner, thermometer, net, water conditioner, air pump, lighting, a secure lid, ornaments, plants (real or plastic), and a water testing kit. Aim to provide a natural set-up with decor that will provide shy fish places to hide.

Care

A new aquarium needs to be "matured" by growing a population of nitrifying bacteria in the filter media before introducing fish. The process can be speeded up using a "quick start" product. Monitor water quality regularly while the tank is maturing, then add fish gradually. Stocking a tank is not an exact science; it will vary in relation to the type of fish. Local aquatics stores offer guidance on stocking densities of specific fish. Good practice includes checking the tank water quality and making a partial water change of approximately 20% weekly. Ammonia, nitrite, and nitrate, as well as temperature, pH, and water hardness should all be checked using test strips. Although test kits are more accurate, it is recommended that they are only used by adults because they employ chemicals. Filters need to be checked for clogging, and will need regular cleaning. Never wash filter media in clean tap water, as this removes the beneficial bacteria; instead, use water siphoned from the tank during a water change. When topping up a tank, a dechlorinating product must be added to tap water to remove the toxic chlorine. Wash hands, rinsing off all soap, before putting them in the tank, and wash again afterwards as bacteria live in fish tanks.

Fish should be fed all they can eat in 1–2 minutes once or twice daily, and any uneaten food should be netted out. Most freshwater aquarium fish will accept ornamental fish foods such as flakes and small pellets, as well as frozen foods. Holiday feeder blocks can be used over weekends, although most fish will be fine left unfed for two days. For longer periods automatic feeders can be deployed,

202

although fish should be checked daily. For even longer periods, such as summer holidays, the tank will need to be moved to a location where the fish can be suitably cared for. Be observant of the fish: reduced feeding, erratic behavior, clamped fins, or gasping at the surface are all signs of problems. Water quality is often to blame, so immediately test the water, conduct a water change, and seek advice from a local aquatic store.

Interaction

A classroom aquarium functions on multiple levels. Learning about the tank and the need for maintenance routines to keep the fish healthy promote student engagement and responsibility. Feeding is a positive interactive experience. As they watch the fish get "excited" at feeding time, students learn the importance of a healthy diet. Lessons can be built around observing fish behaviors that differ among species, such as activity locations within the tank. Fish such as guppies may also breed in the tank; observing courtship behaviors and the birth of baby fish can be exciting. Tapping on the glass is stressful to fish, so controlling this practice is an opportunity to teach respect for animals. Similarly, students should be taught the importance of looking after the fish for their entire lives.

Amphibians

Frogs or toads are arguably poor choices for a classroom. However, hatching frog spawn and raising the larval tadpoles to metamorphosis can be a fascinating educational experience. Begin with netting a small clutch of eggs of a non-protected species from a local pond into a plastic container, and transporting them, along with extra pond water, to a prepared classroom aquarium (a valid fishing/small game license may be required). Aquarium water should be held at the same temperature as the pond from which they were collected, and should be gently aerated using an air pump. Tadpoles will eat algae and organic detritus, but it is easier to use crushed fish food flakes fed sparingly (little and often) to avoid fouling the water. As the tadpoles develop hind legs and become froglets, the aquarium will need landscaping to allow them to crawl out of the water. Froglets will eat small insects, such as aphids and micro worms. Once feeding becomes difficult it is time to release them back to the pond.

Turtles, Snakes, and other Reptiles

Since reptiles range from large turtles to tiny colorful geckos, there is a reptile to suit every setting. This variety makes it difficult to summarize their requirements.

Living Environment

Reptiles regulate their body temperature through behavior rather than internal mechanisms, so their environment must be set up to make effective regulation possible at all times. Reptiles should be kept in enclosures called terrariums, in which climatic variables like heat and humidity are monitored and adjusted automatically.

A terrarium must be child-proof, escape-proof, dust-proof, well ventilated, and provide a suitable habitat, which will vary depending on the species. Turtles and water snakes might need an aquatic terrarium containing fresh water deep enough for swimming, while many lizards, tortoises, and snakes require a dryer environment. Some reptiles need very little space but others might need space for a fairly large tree branch or hollow log. Flooring substrates must be chosen carefully, with reference to the species being kept. Natural or artificial features should be used to make the enclosure attractive to look at and comfortable for the animal.

Reptile enclosures should contain zones, at least one with a heat source so that the animal can warm up when necessary and one where it can cool down. For some species the heat source should be a special lamp, directed towards a flat rock, floating object, or tree branch. For others it might be a submersible heater. Special lighting is often necessary for the animal to synthesize important vitamins. Access to full sunlight can provide this, but reptiles also need to be able to avoid direct sunlight, and appreciate having access to a secure, dark space where they feel safe.

Almost all reptiles are solitary; some will injure or kill any other animal placed in their environment, even those of the same species. Even when injuries are not observed, housing reptiles together can create a stressful environment. If you must keep reptiles together, choose the species carefully, avoid keeping more than one male, try to match sizes, and ensure the environment allows private, safe spaces for individual animals.

Care

The terrarium should be checked daily and waste removed. Fresh water and food should be provided daily for most species, although some reptiles require feeding only every few days. Most reptiles are naturally clean, but terrariums and their contents should be washed and disinfected regularly, using reptile-friendly products.

Some reptiles are carnivorous and require crickets, worms, grubs or flies. Larger carnivores might require mice, rats, or small birds. Food animals can be purchased frozen and should be defrosted before being served. Other reptiles are herbivorous and need constant access to leafy greens and fruits. Fresh foods are important, but commercially prepared food is available for many species. Nearly all reptiles should receive a vitamin and mineral supplement to ensure their dietary needs are met.

An important part of caring for a reptile is understanding and monitoring its behavior. Any animal acting strangely should be checked by a specialist veterinarian but, with reptiles, strange behavior is sometimes perfectly normal! Some reptiles will stop eating and become inactive when the weather cools down; this "brumation" is similar to hibernation, and lasts 2–4 months. Special care is required to ensure that bromating reptiles maintain adequate hydration and body condition. Many reptiles shed their skin. With lizards this normally occurs in small sections that may not be particularly noticeable, but snakes can virtually appear to turn inside out. At this time provide a warm bath and a rough object, such as a branch or rock, against which the animal can rub itself to help dislodge the old skin.

Interaction

Reptiles can be fascinating to watch. Interacting with humans can be stressful for them, but many do not appear to mind being handled if accustomed to this from a young age and allowed plenty of rest. Adult supervision should be constant, and species choice is critical. Venomous reptiles are obviously a poor choice for classroom pets. Many lizards, skinks, and geckos have a defensive strategy if threatened, in which they discard their tail. While it eventually grows back, this may distress the animal as well as students who witness the event.

Birds

Living Environment

Many bird species originating from tropical or sub-tropical climates are kept in captivity and have adapted to temperate climates. They range in size from zebra finches (approximately 4 inches) or budgerigars (approximately 7 inches) to parrots (3–39 inches in length). Defining an ideal generic environment for birds is difficult but there are certain basic criteria that should be considered to meet their physical and behavioral needs.

The location of bird housing, inside or outside, affects the living environment. Caged birds should have the opportunity for free flight, which should not be hindered or prevented by, e.g., enrichment devices like perches, decorations, and toys. To encourage flight, a cage should ideally be longer than it is wide, typically at a ratio of 4:1 and wide enough for a bird to spread its wings. Cages and enrichment devices should be made of non-toxic materials, easily cleaned, sited away from drafts but with sufficient ventilation (typically provided by at least one side being wire mesh), and not placed directly in front of windows (to avoid overheating and exposure to stress). Perches should allow space for all birds to rest at the same time and be of an appropriate diameter for gripping. Lighting is important and can influence bird behavior significantly; they should have natural daylight, as indoor lighting often does not provide the right brightness or color spectrum and birds are sensitive to day length.

206

Care

The overall diet must be suitable for the species and nutritionally balanced. Commercially manufactured diets designed to meet individual nutritional requirements are available for many species. While a varied diet is sometimes recommended, some birds are known to avoid new food types unless these are introduced at an early age as there is a risk that birds will lose weight rapidly and die unexpectedly. Enough feed and water stations must be provided to allow all birds access without competition. Clean water for drinking must be provided, and both food and water containers should not be sited where they can easily be soiled by feces. Some birds need to bathe; a shallow water bath may be recommended. Provided with sufficient water, food, and natural lighting, birds can be left for short periods (e.g., a weekend), although it is better that they are checked daily.

Interaction

Birds tend to be sociable, seeking the company of their own kind to demonstrate their natural behaviors, but it is important to only mix compatible individuals to prevent aggression. Birds are easily start-led, so children need to learn that loud noises and banging the cage will harm them. Many birds become stressed when handled unless habituated to it; it is advisable not to catch the birds unless for veterinary reasons.

Insects

Living Environment

Living accommodation needs for insects vary widely. The shape (long insects often require taller enclosures), activity level (crickets that jump need a mesh lid on their container), temperature needs (insects from tropical climates may benefit from a heat mat beneath their housing), requirements for humidity (insects frequently need consistently moist but not wet ground cover), and need for light or darkness (some do best with natural light) all bear on appropriate housing. Ant farms should not be moved, as this will cause tunnels to collapse.

Care

Some insects are carnivores or omnivores, and will become canniba-listic if adequate suitable food is unavailable. Most are herbivores whose dietary needs can be met by commercially available foods, overripe fruits or vegetables, or plants freely available in the school-yard (once washed to avoid exposing the insects to pesticides). Some insects require calcium, through commercial supplements or a cuttlebone in the cage.

Interaction

As a rule insects are best observed, not handled, in classrooms. Many are fragile; for some any handling can be life-threatening.

Recommendations from a Veterinarian

Before bringing animals into a classroom, consider several ques-tions. Is it necessary to have a live animal in the classroom, or can the learning objectives be met in another way? Can you provide a healthy life for that animal, physiologically as well as psycho-logically, including over weekends and holidays? Investigate the care needs for the chosen species. Start with the basics in this chapter (see Table 14.1), then use other reputable sources; if in doubt,

Table 14.1 Select online resources

Topic	Resource
Animals	
Species selection	http://carefresh.com/petcare
Fostering	http://giveshelter.org/classroom-animals-in-schools.html
Animal welfare	
Five Freedoms	http://webarchive.nationalarchives.gov.uk/20121007104210/http:/www.fawc.org.uk/freedoms.htm
Needs of animals	http://legislation.gov.uk/ukpga/2006/45/contents
Laboratory animal welfare	https://grants.nih.gov/grants/olaw/Guide-for-the-Care-and-use-of-laboratory-animals.pdf
"Pocket pets"	
Guinea pigs	http://guinealynx.info https://www.guineapigcages.com
Rats	http://ratbehavior.org/
Rat tickling	http://vet.purdue.edu/discovery/gaskill/resources.php
Birds	
Bird housing	http://agriculture.vic.gov.au/pets/other-pets/birds/code-of-practice-for-the-housing-of-caged-birds
Fish	
Fishkeeping	http://practicalfishkeeping.co.uk/content.php?sid=5399
Aquarium sizes	http://ornamentalfish.org/wp-content/uploads/MINIMUM-AQUARIUM-SIZE.pdf
Turtles, snakes and other reptiles	
General classroom animals	http://animal-world.com/

Topic	Resource
General advice on reptiles	http://reptileexpert.co.uk/
Reptile selection	http://pets.petsmart.com/content/reptile/choosing-your-reptile.shtml
Teacher resource for reptiles	http://lrrpublic.cli.det.nsw.edu.au/lrrSecure/Sites/Web/14103/index.htm
Keeping reptiles in the classroom	Monlezun (2012)
Insects	
General insect care	http://amentsoc.org/insects/caresheets/ http://earthlife.net/insects/carelist.html http://petbugs.com/caresheets/
Ant farm tips	http://ant-farm-stores-review.toptenreviews.com/ant-farms-for-beginners-tips-for-good-ant-care.html
Veterinary recommendations	
Emergency planning	https://awic.nal.usda.gov/companion-animals/emergencies-and-disaster-planning
Poison control	http://petpoisonhelpline.com/ https://www.aspca.org/pet-care/animal-poison-control
Zoonotic diseases	http://cfsph.iastate.edu/Zoonoses/ http://cdc.gov/about/facts/cdcfastfacts/zoonotic.html

consult a veterinarian for good sources of information. Incorporate the animal into emergency plans for your classroom, including e.g., being snowed in and unable to get to the classroom, or what to do in an earthquake.

Prepare students for the animal's arrival. Start with a basic understanding of its needs, habits and behaviors, and the importance of respecting these at all times. Become familiar with the animal's typical behaviors and learn to interpret them to quickly recognize signs of stress and to modify the conditions or remove the animal. It may be appropriate to consider replacing the live animal with another resource, such as a video feed. Such circumstances could represent an opportunity to introduce students to the 3-Rs of animal research (replacement, reduction, and refinement; Russell & Burch, 1959) or the Five Freedoms.

Insure that the classroom is safe for the animal. Potentially harmful objects and toxic materials should be kept at a distance from the animal's living environment. Certain things that are safe for human consumption, such as chocolate or grapes, can be toxic to some animals even in small amounts. Consider the possibility for disease transmission. Precautions should be taken to minimize risk of zoonotic diseases (transmissible between animals and humans, e.g., salmonella from terrapins and frogs; psittacosis from birds).

Finally, establish a relationship with a local veterinarian or veterinary technician familiar with the species. Discuss the benefits of neutering (where practical) to prevent unplanned breeding and minimize unwanted behaviors. Have the veterinarian come to the classroom to discuss the animals and their needs. Their advice can prove invaluable and result in an improved experience for students and, perhaps more importantly, for the animals.

Conclusion

Including animals in classrooms can be fun and rewarding for students and teachers, and classrooms can provide comfortable homes for some animals while meeting their physiological, psychological, and social needs. The key to successfully including animals in classrooms is to do so responsibly. Study the species intensively before acquiring it. Think carefully about the logistics of housing, provision of daily care, and individual animal needs to live a good life. Be empathetic to each animal's situation, and discuss and demonstrate this to the students. Help students acquire depth of knowledge about the species and ask them to use their imaginations to see the world from the animal's perspective.

References

Burgdorf, J., & Panksepp, J. (2001). Tickling induces reward in adolescent rats. *Physiology & Behavior, 72*(1): 167–173.

Gaskill, B. N., Gordon, C. J., Pajor, E. A., Lucas, J. R., Davis, J. K., & Garner, J. P. (2013). Impact of nesting material on mouse body temperature and physiology. *Physiology & Behavior, 110*: 87–95.

Gee, N. R., Hurley, K. J., & Rawlings, J. M. (2016). From the animal's perspective – Welfare implications of HAI research and practice. In L. Freund, S. McCune, L. Esposito, N. R. Gee, & P. McCardle (Eds.), *The social neuroscience of human-animal interaction* (pp. 217–236). Washington, DC: American Psychological Association.

Monlezun, M. (2012). *Keeping reptiles and amphibians in the classroom.* Jacksonville, FL: 5th Corner Publishing, LLC.

Russell W. M. S., & Burch, R. L. (1959). *The principles of humane experimental technique.* Baltimore, MD: Global clearinghouse for information on alternatives to animal testing, Johns Hopkins University. Retrieved from http://altweb.jhsph.edu/pubs/books/humane_exp/het-toc _

211

CHAPTER 15

Creating an Atmosphere of Acceptance for HAI in Education – Future Directions

Nancy R. Gee, Aubrey H. Fine, Layla Esposito, and Sandra McCune

Introduction

This volume began with a brief discussion of how overwhelmingly popular animals are in educational environments and curricula. The chapters herein describe an emerging field in which evidence is accumulating on the topic of the efficacy of including and involving animals in classrooms. Although there has been progress in this emerging field, it is evident there is a need for more high-quality research investigating the psycho-educational impact of animals upon people and the impact of those interactions on the animals involved. These findings are critical to drive evidence-based practice that can be used to inform policy decisions. We believe that these changes will pave the way for acceptance of HAI in education settings.

The intersection of HAI and education prompts a number of fundamental and intriguing questions, the broadest of which is the overarching question of whether animals have an educationally relevant impact in classroom settings. It is imperative for educators and researchers to agree on the key pedagogies, curricula, and approaches that should be systematically investigated and ultimately translated into applied educational practices. The creation of a translational science pipeline to support practitioners in applying evidence-based HAI pedagogy is challenging but can be done.

While calls for increasing translational research exist in most disciplines, there is an especially great need in the field of HAI, where researchers and practitioners have often worked in silos. Indeed, too much of the practice of HAI has been based upon anecdotal experiences of positive benefits; treating practices as already known to be beneficial simply increases the challenge of those studying HAI who work to design research well-suited to informing real-life implementation and interventions. Two important strategies are required. First, match-making between scientists and practitioners at the formative stages of research is key, so that the studies conducted address questions that can best guide practice in education settings. Second, better efforts are needed in the dissemination of scientific findings so that practitioners and educators have a variety of sources (other than specialized journals) from which to gain access to the latest evidence.

213

It falls to researchers and practitioners to approach this broad issue of applying HAI in various school settings by choosing testable questions that can both examine the efficacy of specific practices and, if they are found to be efficacious, to ultimately investigate why that might be so – that is, the mechanisms that underlie those effects. It is apparent from the chapters in this volume that clever researchers and practitioners have already posed interesting questions, blazing trails of exploration into this exciting new area. It is our hope that a theory-driven approach to research will provide a scientific evidence base as well as real-life solutions to practical difficulties.

Educationally relevant theory-based questions need to be refined into testable hypotheses, from which researchers must develop and implement suitable research designs (as discussed in Chapter 11, by Connor and Herzog). Given a good design, the practical implementation of that design must be done in an ecologically valid way. We encourage researchers to think like teachers and journal reviewers at the design stage, that is, to question and critique the design practically and objectively, to read published critiques of HAI research (e.g., Kazdin, 2011), and to seek input from other researchers and educators before beginning data collection. There are no statistical analyses that can save a poorly designed study.

We urge researchers to seriously consider methodological rigor, wherein the goal is to implement a study that will produce results meeting standards for reliable evidence (Reyna, Benbow, Boykin, Whitehurst, & Flawn, n.d.). This is simply "the extent to which all aspects of a study's design and conduct can be shown to protect against systematic bias, nonsystematic bias, and inferential error" (Lorh & Carey, 1999, p. 472). In other words, the quality of the design and its practical implementation are such that the researcher will be in the best possible position to make evidence-based claims with confidence and ultimately recommend a specific practice protocol to educators and administrators. Attention will then need to be given to evaluating the efficacy of the practices as applied on a wider scale.

Future research must be well-planned and implemented, must investigate when, where, why, and how (conditions and mechanisms) animals may impact a variety of dimensions of pedagogy, such as cognition (e.g., executive function, learning, memory, language use and development), stress and anxiety reduction, or buffering in academic settings, and physical activity and play. An understanding of these dimensions is needed across a variety of populations, such as typically developing students, those with special needs (e.g., learning disabilities, attention deficit, autism spectrum disorder), and across various age groups (developmental aspects).

Applying What We've Learned

A recent Google search on the phrase "how to incorporate animals into classrooms" returned 18 million results ranging from specific examples, books, chapters, and journal articles to blogs on the topic. The chapters in this volume have revealed that what is missing from the available material is a solid evidence base to support these practices. For that reason, we have focused on discussing and evaluating the evidence to date with the aim of pointing the way for future research. However, we are also mindful that for the equation to be complete, we must provide evidence-based solutions that are relevant and useable for practitioners. Although at the present time there are limited resources for training and supporting educators in HAI, there are some existing centers throughout North America and

Europe where teachers can get training in animal-assisted intervention theory and practice. This training will also include a better understanding of animal behavior and welfare, key elements that must be considered to safely integrate animals in the classroom.

In the chapters throughout this volume is an emerging evidence base supporting the efficacy of HAI in classrooms. For example, Chapter 1 (Fine and Gee) notes that there are many early childhood and special needs classes that incorporate animals in their curricula. There is some indication that students in both of these environments may benefit from this type of alternative education. The animals may foster a more conducive learning environment and act as social catalysts for more positive interactions. The chapters by O'Haire and Gabriels (Chapter 7), as well as Schuck and Fine (Chapter 6), describe research evidence supporting this practice and include suggestions on how educators may practically incorporate animals into classrooms with students with autism and ADHD. Their research and suggestions for implementation provide a springboard from which future research may launch as well as a direction guiding explorations into other settings or populations. In Chapter 9, in their discussion of reading-to-dogs programs, Beetz and McCardle point out that a dog can support prerequisites of learning, but suggest that such practices should not replace reading instruction. They summarize findings that indicate that dogs are very helpful when combined with direct reading instruction, speculate that motivation and stress reduction may be potential mechanisms, but urge caution until more peer-reviewed research is available. More recently, a systematic review of the existing peer-reviewed literature on the subject indicates that reading to a dog may have a beneficial effect on a number of processes which contribute to improved reading performance, even in the absence of direct instruction or feedback (Hall, Gee, & Mills, 2016). It is important to point out that to achieve an acceptable level of literacy, reading instruction and feedback are critical, and practice feedback may be more important at specific points in a child's acquisition of reading skills, but this literature review also highlights the role that reading-to-dogs programs may play in reading practice and the resulting gains in reading achievement related to the simple act of practicing a nascent skill. Clearly, there is a need to better understand how and why animals may have an impact in education settings, and under what conditions, so that specific recommendations may be made for applied settings. The rationale for integrating animals into school-based curricula still lacks clarity. It is for that reason that we must continue to develop a clear translation of research to practice such that HAI can be more appropriately, reliably, and effectively conducted in classrooms.

It is critical that we begin to integrate animals more strategically in schools and with populations where the potential exists to understand, and to demonstrate, the efficacy of these interventions. Once effectiveness, safety, reliability, and usefulness have been demonstrated, the circle of new opportunities can be expanded. We suggest that practitioners start small and then expand their range of options. Applying the metaphor "taking a bite of the apple not eating the entire fruit" seems to be apropos here, for both research and practice (see e.g., Kazdin, in press, for his recommendation that researchers begin with "small theories" to move toward a more unified, overarching theory to undergird their work). It may benefit the professional community interested in expanding services of HAI in educational settings to start modestly. In this manner, they may establish a practice agenda that has realistic expectations. Unfortunately, there are still many sceptics with reservations about why one would incorporate animals into classrooms. We must explore, understand, and evaluate the merit of those reservations if we are to move the field forward.

Public Policy

An obvious starting point in this exploration is to examine public policy. To ensure that schools remain receptive to integrating animals into education settings, attention will need to be given to supporting public policy changes. These changes must occur to ensure that animals will be safely integrated into this environment. Strong research and legal reform are essential to underpin solid policy change if interaction of animals and children in this context can be shown to be safe and efficacious. Wider reform for our relationship with companion animals and our responsibilities is happening slowly (Council for Science & Society, 1988; Rowan & Rosen, 2005) but legislation and policies are fragmented and need to be standardized at local, state, and national levels. Policy guidelines need to be developed for educators, and educational institutions and authorities on how to implement and evaluate such programs.

As has been noted throughout this volume, numerous questions must be answered prior to establishing a wider acceptance of animal-assisted education in mainstream educational settings. The research should lead us to take more seriously the need to develop policies and practices that address those questions and answers that maximize the benefits and minimize the risks.

Advocacy that addresses legitimate reservations that many may have – such as legal liability, nurture and care for animals and students, parental qualms regarding interactions of animals with their children, and impact on teachers and the classroom milieu – are needed to educate the change makers, so they become more cognizant of the value of animals in this environment and how to minimize potential risks. Education leaders need to recognize that the catalyst of these efforts is not trivial and that there is a growing body of knowledge indicating that animals can make significant contributions to the education and well-being of students. These gatekeepers need to be educated and engaged. In Chapter 2, Meints, Brelsford, Gee and Fine highlight some of the legal issues that cannot be ignored, and in Chapter 3, Huss and Fine further discuss legal and policy issues. For public policy to be reformed, attention must be given to legislation and risk management concerns that may negatively impact positive future changes. To influence public policy, we need to consider some of the questions that leaders of school districts may have. Fine (2015) posed several of the questions at the 2015 workshop that was the initial catalyst for this book. They are the following:

A.   Cost: What are the attendant costs to provide the services and to initiate the research?

B.   Liability: What potential legal liabilities and foreseeable accompanying risks are inherent in implementation of said programs in our schools?

C.   Benefits: What are the best practices and methodologies that schools must implement to achieve success and to assuage administrators' concerns regarding the program?

D.   Public relations: Political dynamics, no doubt, must also be of concern. In order for change to occur, how can we engage potential allies – even hesitant proponents – to help promote implementation of the program in the schools? Administrators at the district and school sites, counselors, parent groups, student bodies, and local media are all important groups and avenues to promote the program.

Welfare of All Parties

Educators, students, and animals must all be safe in interacting with each other (Gee, Hurley, & Rawlings, 2016). Gee and Schulenburg (Chapter 12) discuss clearly all of the variables that must be considered to safely integrate animals in schools. These considerations must include the importance of well-informed educators who understand animal behavior, husbandry, and species-specific needs. We recommend that teachers provide clear and safe procedures for student-animal interactions in classrooms. Guidelines also need to be established to ensure that children safely interact with these animals and to ensure that animal welfare is safeguarded. Adherence to these guidelines in the long run will make policy and practices easier to modify.

Safety concerns for all involved (humans and animals), of course, must remain paramount. Nonetheless, the goal is to optimize interaction among all "beings." Additionally, teachers must be cognizant of all student physical and psychological health (e.g., phobic or allergic) reactions related to animal interactions and plan ahead for such possible consequences. Engagement and fruitful interaction among all participants are the objectives.

Final Thoughts

The beauty of writing the final chapter is that we have the privilege of having the last word. The major objective of this volume has been to provide a discussion of the existing evidence, examples of practical applications, and suggestions for appropriate incorporation of animals in school settings. We believe that animals are so commonly present in classrooms because parents, teachers, and students appreciate that there is something special and unique about our human connection with animals. It is due to this sentiment that we have witnessed the popularity of animals in various school settings. Although this is an exciting phenomenon, we believe that this form of HAI can be done more safely, effectively, and reliably by translating quality research into effective pedagogy.

Upon reflection, the intersection of HAI and education has had an exhilarating inauguration. Evidence has been presented indicating that HAI is effective, relevant, and valuable to the mission of educating students. Our own personal experiences have shown us that teachers, students, and parents can be deeply moved by these kinds of interactions. It is our hope that having animals in classrooms will now be understood and respected as being more than cute, touching, and warm and fuzzy. It is real, it is important, and it can be a valuable learning tool.

In closing, we would like to return to our opening paragraph in this volume, reiterating that these are exciting times for researchers and practitioners interested in the intersection of HAI and education. This volume was intended to provide a roadmap of the many and varied roles of HAI in education. The insightful authors of the various chapters have provided a compass to guide future exploration in this area. We don't pretend to have all the answers, but we certainly look forward to the journey ahead.

References

Council for Science and Society. (1988). *Companion animals in society*. Oxford: Oxford University Press.

Fine, A. H. (2015). Research and practice: Needs going forward. Research on human-animal interaction in education settings, May 27, 2015. Washington, DC: Workshop presentation.

Gee, N. R., Hurley, K. J., & Rawlings, J. M. (2016). From the dog's perspective: Welfare implications of HAI research and practice. In L. S. Freund, S. McCune, L. Esposito, N. R. Gee, & P. McCardle (Eds.), *The social neuroscience of human-animal interaction* (pp. 214–236). Washington, DC: American Psychological Association.

Hall, S. S., Gee, N. R., & Mills, D. S. (2016). Children reading with dogs: A systematic review of the literature. *PLoS one, 11*(2): e0149759.

Kazdin, A. E. (2011). Establishing the effectiveness of animal-assisted therapies: Methodological standards, issues, and strategies. In P. McCardle, S. McCune, J. A. Griffin, & V. Maholmes (Eds.), *How animals affect us: Examining the influence of human-animal interaction on child development and human health* (pp. 35–52). Washington, DC: American Psychological Association.

Kazdin, A. (in press). Strategies to improve the evidence base of animal-assisted interventions. *Applied Developmental Science* (accepted, June 2016).

Lohr, K. N., & Carey, T. S. (1999). Assessing "best evidence": Issues in grading the quality of studies for systematic reviews. *Joint Commission Journal on Quality Improvement, 25*(9): 470–479.

Reyna, V., Benbow, C. P., Boykin, A. W., Whitehurst, G. J., & Flawn, T. (n.d.). Report of the subcommittee on standards of evidence. In *Reports of the Task Groups and Subcommittees, National Mathematics Advisory Panel*.

Retrieved from http://2.ed.gov/about/bdscomm/list/mathpanel/report/ standards-of-evidence.pdf

Rowan, A. N., & Rosen, B. (2005). Progress in animal legislation: Measuring and assessment. In D. J. Salem & A. N. Rowan (Eds), *The state of the animals III: 2005* (pp. 79–94). Washington, DC: Humane Society Press.

220

Index

The numbers indicated in **bold** refer to figures and tables.

bettas 202

biological: basis of HAI 70; challenges 99; correlates 60–62, 192; measures x–xi, 99; regulation 47; science x (*see also* biopsychosocial model; psychobiological mechanisms)

biophilia 118

biopsychosocial model 99, **99**, 101

birds 34, 205–207, **208**, 210

bite 14, 16, 19–21, 29; dog 13–14; "one bite rule" 29; prevention 19 (*see also* Blue Dog program)

blood pressure 62, 100

Blue Dog program 15, 19–21

body language 44; dog 15, 17, 19, 21

bond(s) 43, 76, 192, 201

bonding: child-animal 76; measures of 173; school 44

breeds 186, **188**; commonly owned 13

brumation 205

budgerigars 206

bullying **175**

canine 48, 50; -assisted interventions (CAIs) 42, 71; -child bonding 76; -enhanced social skills training 49; visitation programs 50 (*see also* human-canine interaction)

cannibalistic 207

care: of animals 4, 31–32, 64, 75–76, **77**, **91–92**, 129, 145, 194, 197–198, 200–202, 204–207, **208–209**, 210, 217; health care settings 104; levels of 64; pet 6, 126; residential care facilities 198; standard of 102

caregivers/caregiving 118

carnivores 205, 207

categorization viii, 56–58, 127

causal claims 142–144

Centers for Disease Control and Prevention (CDC) 33–34

characteristics: animal 42, 184–185, 194; behavioral 185; of dog owners 103; equine 45; human 198; impairments of autism 84; interaction effects 153; learning 85; physical **187**, 200

chickens 34

childhood: disorders of 69 (*see also* early childhood education/learning); early 4–5, 128, 215

chronic: arousal 101; disease 99, 101; stress 98, 100–101, 129

classroom: AAI in 64, 94, 205; aggression 129; animals in ix–x, 4–8, 12–13, 15, 22, 28, 30, 33–34, 56, 64, **77**, 84, 86–87, 90, **91**, 92, 107, 126, 130–131, 158, 173, 197–198, 201, 207, **208–209**, 210, 212, 214–216, 218; -based counseling 46; challenges 84; dogs as members 49; dogs in 48–49, 59–60, 73, 143, 152, 185; disruption 144–145, 153; early learning 125; guinea pigs in 173, 198; HAI in ix, 50, 61, 126, 215–216; hygiene 91; observation xi; pet 64, 129, 183; practice xii; preschool 125; programs in 8; research x, 142; studies 105; teachers ix

clinical trials 147 (*see also* randomized controlled trial [RCT])

cognition 4, 45, 56–57, 61–62, 64–65, 129, 158, 163, **164**, **166**, 192, 214; social 88

cognitive: ability 161; arousal 71–73, 78; assessment tools 168; behavioral therapy 107; development 12, 63, 129, 183; engagement 129–130; flexibility 129; inflexibility 85; measures 56, **164**; mechanisms 63; performance 56, 61, 73; processes 57, 60, 62–64, 184; skills **77**, 127, 163; tempo 71–72, 78; traits in animals 173

college students 50, 62, 102–103

companion animals 4, 88, 98–99, 104–105, 126, 194, 198, **209**, 216

consent 15, 105

control: animal control authorities 30; of animals 29, 31; of attention 128; climate 197; of dog(s) 28, 35; executive 72; impulse **91**, 119; inhibitory 106, 129, 163; mental 106; poison **209**; self-control 60; of stress reactions 7

correlation 144

correlational 46, 142

cortisol 62, 71, 89, 100–102; levels of 47–48, 62, 103, 114–115, 119; production of 48 (*see also* salivary)

cost: dog bite 13–14; of animal inclusion in education settings 158, 173; for appropriate care 88; of tests/ measures **159–160**, **162**, **164**, **166**, **169–70**, **172**, **174**, **176**

223

228